Christotainment

CHRISTOTAINMENT

SELLING JESUS THROUGH POPULAR CULTURE

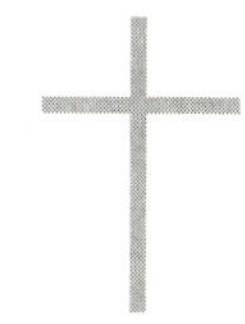

EDITED BY

SHIRLEY R. STEINBERG
McGill University

JOE L. KINCHELOE
McGill University

A Member of the Perseus Books Group

Published by Westview Press,
A Member of the Perseus Books Group

Find us on the World Wide Web at www.westviewpress.com.

Westview Press books are available at special discounts for bulk purchases in the United States by corporations, institutions, and other organizations. For more information, please contact the Special Markets Department at the Perseus Books Group, 2300 Chestnut Street, Suite 200, Philadelphia, PA 19103, or call (800) 810-4145, ext. 5000, or e-mail special.markets@perseusbooks.com.

Designed by Timm Bryson

Library of Congress Cataloging-in-Publication Data
Christotainment : selling Jesus through popular culture /
edited by Shirley R. Steinberg, Joe L. Kincheloe.
p. cm.
Includes bibliographical references and index.
ISBN 978-0-8133-4405-8 (pbk. : alk. paper) 1. Popular culture—Religious aspects—Christianity—History—20th century. 2. Fundamentalism—United States—History—20th century. 3. Popular culture—United States—History—20th century. 4. United States—Church history—20th century. 5. Popular culture—Religious aspects—Christianity—History—21st century. 6. Fundamentalism—United States—History—21st century. 7. Popular culture—United States—History—21st century. 8. United States—Church history—21st century. I. Steinberg, Shirley R., 1952– II. Kincheloe, Joe L.
BR526.C468 2009
261.0973—dc22
2008039362
10 9 8 7 6 5 4 3 2 1

CONTENTS

DEDICATION TO THOSE WHO HAVE
FANNED THE FLAMES OF CHRISTOTAINMENT:

James "Focus on the Family" Dobson, Rod "God's Soldier" Parsley, Roger "Fox" Ailes, John "sits on a blue throne" Hagee, Mel "Braveheart DUI" Gibson, Franklin "Billy's boy" Graham, Tim "never Left Behind" LaHaye, Kurt "Growing Pains" Cameron, "W," and heaven's newest resident, Jerry "moral majority" Falwell.

PREFACE

JOINING *TEAM CHRIST*: ON THE PATH TO CHRISTOTAINMENT

SHIRLEY R. STEINBERG

In the early part of 2008, CBS's *Big Brother* featured sixteen players who competed in an isolated house for $500,000. Players lived in a sequestered house for up to three months, attempting to be the last player and thereby secure the money. Players were not allowed to read, write, or have outside stimulation. They were, however, given the Bible, which was the only book in the house. After half of the contestants had been eliminated, one player discovered that reading the Bible was a way to avoid boredom. Eventually, three players began nightly readings, which included discussions of text.

Natalie, a self-proclaimed Christian, led the Bible group. The group members realized that their game was somewhat charmed as they were avoiding eviction, and Natalie informed them that Jesus Christ was steering the game. Indeed, *Team Christ* (TC) was blessed, and Jesus would not let them lose. The members of TC announced their Christianity and their belief that Jesus was their pilot. The game did not change: the participants played every dirty trick they could to have others evicted, sexual favors were given, and profanity was rampant, but TC's members knew they were invulnerable to the other players. Incanting that the *evildoers* could not win, TC was smug. During the final weeks of the game, every competition won by TC was attributed to Jesus. The only difference in the affect and demeanor of the members of TC was indeed that they were on Team Christ; their treatment of other players did not change, behind-the-back machinations continued, and slander and anger abounded. However, when the final houseguest standing was a Team Christ veteran, members were convinced that Jesus had blessed their union and controlled the game.

Probably the most incredible aspect of literal fundamentalist Christianity is the assumption that God, Jesus, or the Holy Spirit (or any combination thereof) actually watches mortals interact, interrupts life, and steers the course of believing beings. In situations with as much gravitas as *Big Brother,* a heavenly eye is on each eviction, even each power of veto. Not only is the Supreme Being all knowing and all powerful, but "he" is all over.

It is this literal reading of the New Testament that drives the twenty-first-century promoters and consumers of Christotainment. Like the commercial tie-ins one finds with a Disney movie and Burger King, fundamentalist Christian movements are creating tie-ins between products and Jesus Christ. Using sophisticated marketing techniques, churches, special interest groups, and self-anointed religious organizations are changing prophets into profits. When Joe Kincheloe and I first visited The Holy Land Experience in Orlando, Florida, we knew that the bar of Christianity had been raised to an entirely new level. With the increased popularity of groups such as Creed and the Jonas Brothers, we are hearing the musical blend of Christianity and popular culture: with gifts of one2believe plastic toys, children are encouraged to use biblical action figures to reenact scenarios; the purchase of the latest tchotchkies of What Would Jesus Do (WWJD) fridge magnets at airport stores is commonplace; and when we listen to the news, we hear the leaders of first world countries using the apocalyptic language of *good versus evil* and *fear versus salvation.* Jesus appears on T-shirts, bumper stickers, tattoos, jewelry, and television, as well as in the minds of consumers. Belief in Jesus Christ has become a multi-billion-dollar industry, and the ideological scribes of media and advertising continue to create text. Our participation in Christotainment ensures our place on Team Christ.

It is the capital, political, and personal power of Christotainment that has encouraged us to gather scholars to contribute to *Christotainment: Selling Jesus through Popular Culture.* Far beyond the power of kitsch, producers and consumers of Christotainment take popular culture seriously as a conduit through which to reach the potentially and already converted. Our purpose is to examine this remarkable phenomenon and to understand the political and ideological underpinnings of Christotainment.

Joe Kincheloe situates Christotainment as particular to the times in which we live. Setting the political and cultural stage, he sees Christotainment as an American phenomenon, intricately tied to Christian religious fundamentalism. Tracing the development of evangelicalism, he draws the connections between American evangelicals and political influence. Recalling the religious backlash against Darwin, he argues that the popularization of Jesus Christ was ushered in quickly in order to prepare masses for the upcoming Rapture. His introductory chapter introduces readers to the early practices and proselytizing nature of fundamental Christianity, Dominionism, and the holy marriage of politics and religion.

Kincheloe's second chapter historicizes the development of Christotainment, including the colonial and potentially fascist notions of right-wing Christian fundamentalism. It becomes clear that an integral part of understanding fundamentalism is the notion that if one is not saved, and one is not a believer, she or he will not make it to eternal life or even through the Apocalypse. To believe is not particularly sophisticated, a basic requirement being what Kincheloe refers to as a naïve realism and an unwillingness to query or challenge doctrine, mandates, or their interpretation. By examining different types of Christotainment, he maintains that scholarly examination of Christian fundamentalism and popular culture presents a troubling contemporary view of the power of political fundamentalist ideology.

Josh Newman and Michael Giardina discuss cultural politics vis-à-vis the alliance of NASCAR and Christianity. Noting the increase of "out" Christians in American sports, they compare these athletes with fundamentalist right-wing spokes*men*. Noting that "every top driver on the NASCAR circuit" is a member of a nonprofit Christian organization, they historicize the rise of Christotainment-inspired motor sports. As Christianity is woven into the logo and visuals of NASCAR, it is apparent that the sport is in tune with Christ.

Rhonda Hammer and Doug Kellner examine Mel Gibson's *The Passion of The Christ* through both a lens of cultural critique and an analysis of the news and hype surrounding the film. Discussing the multigenre aspect of the film, they see it as a "highly problematic version" of the final days of Christ's life. They also examine stereotypical patriarchal and anti-Semitic depictions, as well as Gibson's political and ideological attempts to "overwhelm [his] audience." Citing Gibson's propensity for historical revisionism, they make an excellent comparison between the filmmaker/actor and the G. W. Bush administration.

Two decades ago, it would perhaps have been a ridiculous stretch of the imagination to consider that vegetables might play the roles of missionary and religious teacher to millions of preschool children. However, as Michael Hoechsmann points out, *VeggieTales* are a well-established arm of Christotainment. Laden with nuance and a conservative Christian agenda, the children's cartoons proselytize to tots through moralistic stories and singing celery, carrots, and asparagus. Hoechsmann looks at the mediated franchise that has taken over DVDs, books, toys, and television programming.

A short analysis of the last twenty-five years of television drama leads me to conclude that, while tacit, the agenda of the writers and producers of what I call "born-again TV" is distinctly Christonormative in nature. In my chapter, I look at both small and silver screen dramas that are not marketed as religious, but are insidious in their attempts to hegemonically cultivate sympathetic viewers. Using content analysis and a phenomenological lens, I present repeating themes that support the overarching intent of fundamentalist Christianity to moralize, convert, and condemn.

Christine Quail examines Christogimmicks readily available for purchase anywhere in North America. She discusses their ideology, including protection, salvation, identity, conversion, and witnessing. Quail talks about the aims of marketing and the importance of creating a consumer culture that can sell identity. Looking at demographics and psychology, advertisers are able to identify a niche market and appropriately gear products and even belief to the targeted consumers.

Nurturing the "inner spiritual identity of a child" is an important task of fundamentalist Christians, according to Lisa Trimble. In order to attend to this parenting goal, marketers provide children with Christian alternatives to secular toys. Through different avenues, Christotainment targets children through militaristic programming, toys, camps, and ministries. Through the creation of 24/7 camps and endurance boot camps, Christotained children can be filled with the spirit and doctrine in hermetically sealed environments controlled by skilled merchants of Christ.

The final three chapters in this volume address the Christification of music. Drummer *cum* scholar Phil Anderson traces the natural rock 'n' roll roots of many Christian gospel singers and musicians. Apart from its entertainment factor, Anderson notes, a basic tenet of the music is indeed to convert and commit. Discussing the Christian lifestyle movement, he looks at the marketing and goals of seemingly benign lyrics and rhythms.

Silvia Giagnoni looks at crossover Christian rock and its place within the music industry. She notes that the genre of Christian rock is growing and that musical groups make a conscious decision when crossing over into mainstream music. That decision determines the capital gains of the group and can contribute to enormous success. Marketing for mainstream culture demands an understanding of contemporary youth culture and tastes by these groups.

Citing the culture war between "conservatives and progressive to radical artists in the underground punk rock music scene," Curry Malott looks at the various types of what he calls "counterhegemonic Christotainment" in punk rock. He examines songs and groups that are both Christian and anti-Christian and discusses the popular and political cultural readings in lyrics. Malott reminds us of the pioneering musical fascism proclaimed by Jerry Falwell and echoed by Tipper Gore, as well as of Christianity's profound influence on contemporary music.

Cultural scholar Henry A. Giroux completes the collection with a clarion call for readers to be aware of the serious crisis of religious fundamentalism and its affect on attempts at democracy. Frightening words remind us of the dangers of absolute moralism and its dangerous partnering with politics. Giroux calls for critique and political awareness in avoiding an increasingly Christotained world.

Putting this book together has been a collegial and provocative effort on the part of all of its contributors. As radical scholars, we all place ourselves within a web of reality that demands critique and political investigation. As we delved into the worlds of Christotainment, we were intrigued and engaged with the cultures we encountered. We hope this book will create dialogue and discomfort—for it is through discomfort that we are able to articulate those issues that threaten equity, freedom, and social justice. It is our goal to question traditional assumptions about Christianity and to construct new questions that involve the political and cultural ramifications of Christotainment.

We appreciate those who have discussed their experiences with us and our students, families, and friends who have assisted us with suggestions and comments. Special thanks to Victor Goebel, our graduate assistant, who is indeed a spectacular human being.

I

Selling a New and Improved Jesus

Christotainment and the Power of Political Fundamentalism

JOE L. KINCHELOE

Christotainment could only have materialized in this particular historical moment with its particular social and political characteristics. How long this moment will last, I don't know—I'm afraid it's not going away very soon. Popular culture has been a site of great consternation for evangelical fundamentalists. Understanding possibly on a subconscious level that they couldn't beat it, conservative Christians decided to counter it—and in the end appropriate it. This book tells the story of that appropriation and its expanding effects. Indeed, this appropriation has marked a new era in theological and, as we will see, social and political history. In this Christotainment-saturated context, what I am calling "political fundamentalism" is growing. Very importantly, its social and political influence is strengthening. Near the end of the first decade of the twenty-first century,

- over seventy million Americans call themselves evangelicals, while millions of others share beliefs with this group.
- four out of ten view the Bible as the literal word of God.
- 84 percent believe that Jesus is the Son of God.
- eight out of ten believe they will stand before God on Judgment Day and face consequences based on the Creator's decision.
- one-half believe that angels exist.

- over 66 percent openly say they have pledged allegiance to Jesus.
- 59 percent believe in the literal truth of the book of Revelation's description of the Rapture (McAlister 2003; Prothero 2003; Hedges 2006; Sheler 2006).

When these statistics are compared to those for Europeans, for example, stark differences emerge. Christianity in general is not as important to Europeans as it is to Americans. But the real difference emerges around fundamentalism, especially in its Americanized, politicized phase, which now exerts more influence than ever before on U.S. theology, society, and politics. While political fundamentalists can be found in Europe, they remain for the most part on the far fringe of everyday sociopolitical and theological life. The U.S. case is unique, although with fundamentalist missionary efforts, growth is occurring in diverse corners of the planet.

DEFINING EVANGELICALISM AND FUNDAMENTALISM

It would be remiss to deal with these issues without attempting to define the terms *evangelicalism* and *fundamentalism*. When I first wrote about these topics thirty-five years ago, this was a relatively easy exercise. The last three and a half decades, however, have brought numerous challenges to traditional definitions from the scholarly community as well as from fundamentalists and evangelicals themselves. Fundamentalists often feel that those who are establishing the definitions are individuals who despise their beliefs. There is some truth to this, as fundamentalists correctly argue that the "definers" use the term in a consistently negative way. Nevertheless, for those of us who are not fundamentalists, our observations of fundamentalist beliefs and actions may, by necessity, strike us as harmful and threatening. With these concerns in mind and in an effort to be as fair as possible, the following is as generic a definition of *evangelicalism* and *fundamentalism* as I deem possible.

Evangelicalism is characterized by a belief in the infallibility of scriptures, the sovereignty of God, the depravity of human beings, and the centrality of the conversion experience. Evangelicals have long accepted that salvation can be achieved only through the grace of God, the value of preaching, the death of Jesus for the sins of human beings, the supremacy of faith in the attainment of salvation, and the ethical content of Christian living as presented in the New Testament. Never a separate denomination, evangelicalism does not have a single moment of birth; rather, it represents the convergence of numerous theological and sectarian movements that slowly came together in America in the eighteenth and nineteenth centuries. Within evangelicalism, there is great diversity, theologically, socially, and ideologically. Any effort to generalize about the history of evangelicalism and its present status is virtually impossible.

Many evangelicals in the late nineteenth century embraced the social gospel movement; many contemporary evangelicals act bravely against prevailing beliefs about the poor and the racially and sexually marginalized. Obviously, the evangelical African American church would be a prime example of this diversity. While over 78 percent of its members describe themselves as politically conservative, there is evidence that this is changing. In 2004, for example, over seven million voted for John Kerry, and over nineteen million did not vote. In the contemporary era, wedge issues such as abortion and homosexual marriage keep many evangelicals voting Republican, even though they disagree with many of the party's domestic and foreign policies. Thus, it would be unfair to evangelicals to lump them all together as a monolithic right-wing group with the same view of Jesus, the demands of faith, and other doctrinal issues (Moore 1994; Sheler 2006; Goldberg 2007). In *Christotainment*, the editors and contributors will make every effort to avoid such distortion.

Now, carefully turning to fundamentalism, we can historically trace from the early nineteenth century a persistent radical strain of the evangelical movement. While maintaining the basic doctrinal tenets of evangelicalism, this radical contingent has often embraced an even more emotion-based, revival-oriented theology suspicious of clergy-mandated rituals. A key dimension of this dissenting tradition has been its consistent anti-intellectualism and distrust of rationality. Again, while there is diversity among fundamentalists—from Missouri Synod Lutherans and Pentecostals, for example—there is a *degree* of consistency among contemporary fundamentalists in their exclusionary perspectives toward God's truth and those who they consider nonbelievers. I won't go into detail about fundamentalist history here—that has been covered elsewhere on numerous occasions—but in the second and third decades of the twentieth century, the group that would come to be known as fundamentalists laid down the gauntlet against evangelicals and other Christians seen to be "modernizing" the faith with theological scholarship. In 1909, they produced a twelve-volume set of books entitled *The Fundamentals* to proclaim doctrinal truth to the world.

It took a decade, but by around 1919, conservative Christian panic over liberal influences in Christendom and the moral decay of American culture induced evangelical radicals to build new networks of like-minded believers. The soon-to-be-labeled fundamentalists came together to discuss what they could do to bring Christians back from their encounter with modernity, especially with regard to anti-Christian Darwinism. In their meetings they expressed their dire concerns about evolution and the changing role of women. The independence of the women of the twenties, they believed, was undermining the social fabric and the God-ordained dominance of men. From the fundamentalist perspective, scientific Darwinism and the ostensible breakdown of patriarchy and the social chaos surrounding evidenced the coming of the end of days. Believing tribulation and the Rapture were eminent, the word of Jesus had to be spread as quickly as possible. Thus, fundamentalists embraced radio with a proselytizing vengeance (Thomas 2005; Frykholm 2005; Sheler 2006). This fervor to engage the world through popular media has never abated. Twentieth-century Christotainment had taken a great leap forward.

AN AMERICAN JESUS: SELLING THE SAVIOR ACROSS THE DECADES

In the evangelicalism of the nineteenth century, we see the emergence of another theological phenomenon that would reach its zenith in the last half of the twentieth and the first decade of the twenty-first centuries: the Americanization of Jesus, especially in forms of Christotainment. Especially by the time of the flowering of post–World War II anticommunism and nationalism, Jesus virtually had to be an American so as not to disrupt the conflation of Christianity with Americanism. In post-1960s conservative efforts to "recover" what, it was perceived, had been "lost" by white Americans, men, and heterosexuals to the various liberation movements of the era, Jesus had to be *sold* as a true-blue American disgusted by the decadence and anti-Western undercurrents of the anti–Vietnam War, civil rights, sexual, feminist, Native American liberation, Latino pride, and gay rights movements. Indeed, Jesus had emigrated from Palestine and had secured his new American persona.

With the Son of Man's identity secure, the evangelicals could use their American marketing skills to plug him. Numerous examinations of "public opinion about Jesus" indicate that Jesus marketing has been a great success. Americans of all religious persuasions look at Jesus in a positive manner now that he is omnipresent in the domain of American pop culture. At the end of the first decade of the twenty-first century, you can't turn on the radio or TV, go to the movie theater, listen to contemporary music, or attend on- and off-Broadway musicals without encountering Jesus. This book wants to understand this merging of popular culture and Christian fundamentalism. In this context, we use a bricolage of methods to understand religious marketing, what such theotainment looks like, and its theological, cultural, social, and political effects. Our assertion is that such dynamics are changing the world in a dangerous and frightening manner (Neiwert 2003; Prothero 2003; Mahan 2005).

Of course, there's nothing new about evangelicalism, marketing, and entertainment in the United States. From the time of eighteenth-century revivalist George Whitefield, the dramatic was fused with the religious in such an entertaining way that tens of thousands of people would come to his services. So finely tuned was Whitefield's voice to the nuance of the theatrical that, contemporary observers reported, he could bring thousands to tears by him merely uttering the word "Mesopotamia." The sermons of the great evangelists of the First Great Awakening (1730s and 1740s) and Second Great Awakening (first three decades of the nineteenth century), including Jonathan Edwards, Charles Finney, and Lorenzo Dow, successfully merged drama and theology. The post–Civil War revivals of former shoe salesman Dwight Moody and his song leader, Ira B. Sankey, brought thousands from all around the nation to be entertained. Paul Rader, Aimee Semple McPherson, and many other early radio preachers of the 1920s exhibited great showmanship and maintained thousands and thousands of listeners around the country.

One of the most uniquely American dimensions of Christotainment—and one of the earliest and most successful—was the camp meetings of the Second Great Awakening. One of the most famous contemporary descriptions of these meetings holds that more souls were begot than saved. The meetings were like nineteenth-century Woodstocks, replete with outrageous preaching, wild displays of religious enthusiasm, prostitutes, moonshiners, gamblers, and other characters. I have long been fascinated by these "wild displays of religious enthusiasm." Once the Holy Spirit had descended on the assemblages, men and women filled with the spirit would engage in what were called the "exercises." These included such activities as barking, running in a straight line (there were always reports of broken noses from runners hitting trees), laughing (the holy laugh), jerking, marrying (a woman would be directed by the Lord to marry a particular man in the congregation), and whirling, among many others. Some of these meetings, held throughout the nation but predominantly on the Tennessee and Kentucky frontier, would attract over two hundred thousand people.

Over a century and a half later, Jim and Tammy Faye Bakker of Praise the Lord (PTL) Club fame and infamy would carry the tradition of the camp meeting into the late-1970s and 1980s hyperreality. As we'll discuss later, *hyperreality* is a term used to describe the contemporary cultural landscape marked by the saturating presence of electronic information and high-tech communication. In such a landscape, individuals begin to lose touch with the traditional notions of time, community, self, and history. In this circumstance, those phenomena displayed on electronic media assume a "realness" greater than they have when directly observed. Thus, in their heyday, Jim and Tammy—and many other media personalities—seemed to have a stronger presence in viewers' lives than everyday, real-life relationships. Thus, in this new cultural atmosphere, the Bakkers merged Disneyland with the orgasmic delights of the camp meeting. With the sexual and financial scandals that beset the couple, their version of Heritage USA fell apart. Evangelicals knew they had a good marketing idea, and numerous efforts to reconstitute the fundamentalist theme park continue into the twenty-first century. Suffice it to say that the Jesus marketed at Heritage USA was an American patriot (Moore 1994; Romanowski 2005).

THE IMPACT OF CHRISTOTAINMENT

In any cultural study, it is always difficult to assess the effects of the phenomenon in question. While visiting Christotainment centers, the Holy Land Experience in Orlando, for example, Shirley and I could easily see that many of those in attendance were visibly moved and took the entire experience very seriously. Others, it seemed, were curious cultural voyeurs who were astounded and clearly not emotionally and ideologically engaged by the events taking place in front of them. Individuals are active readers of Christotainment and other cultural forms; that is, they don't passively sit back and let the producers of popular culture impose particular belief structures on them. In the same context, both the popularity of Christotainment in its diverse forms and the ideological movement of the American toward more and more conservative politics seem to indicate that something is happening. Such forms of interaction at the most engage people in particular theological and ideological ways of seeing, while at the least they reaffirm the predispositions individuals bring to the rendezvous. We are particularly interested in the producers of Christotainment in this book, for we have reached the conclusion that there are dangerous agendas transcending merely the profit motive circulating among many creators of these phenomena.

DOMINIONISM AND THE RADICAL POLITICIZATION OF FAITH

The central group we are pondering in this context is the fundamentalist Christian group sometimes referred to as Dominionists. Most Americans are not as yet familiar with this term, which refers to the biblical interpretation that God gave *man* dominion over all things earthly. In the contemporary use of the term, this notion of dominion has been expanded to include control over the United States and, in turn, a fundamentalist Christian dominion over the world. These are not abstract ideas, as Dominionists now operate in all aspects of American life. In fact, during the second Bush administration, Dominionists were brought into most executive departments and the courts. This special brand of fundamentalism has successfully tapped into the fear, loneliness, and lack of connection Americans harbor in the twenty-first century. Many times, they gain support from fundamentalist Christians who don't know about or fully understand the group's ideological and geopolitical ambitions. Numerous Christians have been attracted to the Dominionists by their promise of a better day, a righteous, fundamentalist America that subdues all enemies and runs the world American style.

Employing the American Jesus and Christotainment, Dominionists do not numerically dominate fundamentalism; historically, however, smaller radical groups have been able to guide larger movements. This has already happened to some degree with this group. Dominionists have carefully engaged in their surreptitious political activities—sometimes successfully, sometimes not—in the process putting together mass communications complexes. Indeed, at the end of this decade, they own six TV networks and two thousand Christian radio stations, and they control the leadership of the Southern Baptist Convention, the largest Protestant denomination in the United States. This gives them access to most people in the country with their new language of democracy and freedom. Even long-standing definitions of such terms, not to mention progressive updates of the concepts, fade away in the fundamentalist "newspeak" of the Dominionists. Using the language of Christian love, empathy, and equality, Dominionists act on an entirely different set of values. In this way, they have set out to reshape the nation and the world.

The Dominionists' more malignant aspirations have already evoked and will continue to generate backlash from diverse groups, even from many who fall within the evangelical orbit. When a group openly speaks of the suppression of nonbelievers—"America is a Christian nation"—increased use of the death penalty, the end to all abortion no matter what the circumstances, and the closing of "government schools" (read public education), some people are going to react negatively. In an age of depoliticization and cynicism, far too many Americans are ignorant of the Dominionists' goals, don't believe "it could ever happen here," agree with many of their points, or are too cynical to think they can do anything about the damage such groups are exacting on the cultural fabric in general and on social and political institutions in particular.

In addition, Dominionists strategically use a stealth language to push forward some of their ideological issues. In the domain of same-sex marriage, for example, Glenn Stanton, a senior official of Dominionist-oriented Focus on the Family, confides that with this and other issues, you want to make God's case in secular language. This is the best way to win a Dominionist argument, for those who are political fundamentalists will already support the "correct" position. Stanton maintains that he and his fellow fundamentalists appeal to universal norms—by this he is referring to Western standards. Thus, using these tactics, Stanton maintains that he can speak about politics to his own community without alienating people who don't really know the relationship between his theological and political positions. These careful maneuverings have worked better than almost anyone expected, as Dominionists and their fundamentalist brothers and sisters in Jesus make a new path for America.

A central, if not *the* central, figure in Dominionist Christotainment is Tim LaHaye. I have been writing about LaHaye, who was recently named the most influential evangelical of our time, for almost thirty years. In the late 1970s and early 1980s, LaHaye and his wife, Beverly, were writing about the successful historical effort of the "secular humanists" to take over America and destroy all of the traditions Christian Americans held dear. Arguing that institutions such as the public schools were secular humanist plots to wipe out Christianity, LaHaye ended up in Ronald Reagan's White House telling the president about the Dominionist interpretation of American history. In recent years—as Doug Kellner and Rhonda Hammer explore in chapter 4 of this book—LaHaye has become the most successful writer of a series of books in publishing history.

LaHaye's *Left Behind* series, coauthored with Jerry Jenkins, has sold over seventy million copies. In book, children's book, movie, and video game formats, *Left Behind* has become a blueprint for the Dominionist future. In this context, Dominionist Christotainment works its magic. Take LaHaye on the war in Iraq. Using his many outlets for disseminating data, the world's most important evangelical promotes the view that the book of Revelation foretold the war. Following the logic that made LaHaye famous, his audiences learn that before the Rapture comes, Babylon (Iraq) must be rebuilt as the home of Satan (Saddam Hussein). This, LaHaye contends, is what Hussein was doing before George W. Bush decided to invade in 2003. Continuing, LaHaye warns that Hussein was not a Muslim but a Satanist and had plans to build a temple to Satan in Iraq.

Thus, for the millions of true believers who read LaHaye's nonfiction and fiction and watch his movies—he and Jenkins write about the world government of the Antichrist in one of their *Left Behind* novels, *New Babylon*—the Iraq War had an extra theological justification. Whether President Bush exploited these beliefs is subject to debate. From a discursive perspective, Bush peppered his speeches about the war with biblical phrases and language that reflected portions of the book of Revelation. The nation is riddled with debates over whether or not Bush purposefully employed this Revelations discourse to garner support for his policies. Honestly, I see no evidence to conclude whether he did or not. It is safe to say, however, that the president benefited from the connections made by many of the fundamentalist faithful (Mahan 2005; Thomas 2005; Hedges 2006; Pfohl 2006; Klemp 2007).

As previously mentioned, it is very difficult to determine the effects of any body of information, including popular culture, propaganda, advertising, or Christotainment, on the belief structures of groups and individuals. We do know, however, that producers of Christotainment like LaHaye continue to turn out their products, believing they have a religious and ideological effect, and that America, clearly for a plethora of reasons, has become more fundamentalist theologically and more right-wing politically (Kincheloe and Steinberg 2004; Hedges 2006). Just because someone reads a few of the *Left Behind* books or plays the *Left Behind: Eternal Forces* video game, he or she doesn't necessarily buy into a Dominionist theopolitical model.

Some readers and players view these books and games as they would any artifact from a science fiction or horror genre. Indeed, *Left Behind* has been reviewed and talked about on sci-fi and horror websites by fans who also love *Star Wars* and *Star Trek*. Like such pop-cultural icons, *Left Behind* also markets CDs, coffee cups, T-shirts, fan fiction, mouse pads, screen savers, and so on, ad infinitum. The Apocalypse and the Rapture now reside at the center of Christotainment—the end of the world is just so damned exciting. Books, publishing houses such as Warner and Bertelsmann, movies, videos, radio, interactive games, and local and national fun events push a Rapture politics and theology embedded in the everyday concerns of evangelical Christians.

Such commonplace concerns involve everything from tax preparation to child rearing, missionary activity, weight loss, and marital problems. The purveyors of Dominionism know that every time they speak or write to someone about their physical fitness, an opportunity will present itself to further their theological and ideological agenda. Fundamentalist leaders have found that appropriating popular culture via Christotainment works far better than simply denouncing it—the failed strategy of the past. Dominionists and other fundamentalists/evangelicals are busily working to produce a Christianized, multidimensional popular culture to create an alternate universe of amusement and leisure activities. What has emerged is Christotainment, a religiously and politically inscribed consumer's earthly paradise in which boredom can be quashed, practical advice can be given, and hearts, minds, and souls can be won for a new and improved Jesus and the baggage he has been burdened with in the twenty-first century (McAlister 2003).

DOMINIONIST POWER

I would not be honest if I didn't admit that the Dominionist success in promoting a shadowy view of an exclusionary, theocratic, antirational United States still amazes me after growing up in a Tennessee mountain culture saturated with Protestant fundamentalism. I am amazed but not surprised. Understanding the power and potential theopolitical influence of fundamentalism, I knew I had to understand everything about it. With this in mind, I wrote a master's thesis in history on the effect of evangelicalism on American political institutions and a doctoral dissertation on the tradition's capacity to shape educational organizations. Some of the first articles I published in the late 1970s and first years of the 1980s involved the emerging power of fundamentalism in American political life and social institutions. From my Tennessean vantage point, I could clearly see the storm that was brewing around the role of religion in U.S. political life. As I write and edit this book at the end of the first decade of the twenty-first century, my worst nightmares have materialized as this minority, albeit comprising millions of people, gains more and more control over governmental, social, and religious institutions.

One of the central strategies of the Dominionists involves their readiness to take advantage of the fear engendered by a military, social, cultural, or ideological emergency to promote seemingly simple solutions to the confusion that ensues; for example, "turn your lives over to Jesus," "trust in the Lord," "make America follow the dictates of the Bible," or "let us establish dominion over those who don't accept the word of God." September 11, 2001, was one of these moments of crisis. With a president and a Congress *sensitive* to their support, the Dominionists became the vanguard for demonizing the Muslim enemy (Kincheloe and Steinberg 2004), for suspending constitutional guarantees to those under suspicion of terrorism, and for preemptive wars in the Middle East to conquer the enemy and hasten the Rapture and the Apocalypse. Already strong in some political positions, the Dominionists gained power after September 11, which allowed them to move officially from the margins of the political order into the legislative, judicial, and executive branches of government.

Now a dominant force in the Republican Party, Dominionists often control or maintain a powerful presence in state GOP operations. Fronted by numerous organizations, such as the Family Resource Council, Dominionist senators and representatives promote creationism in public schools, capital punishment for doctors who perform abortions, stricter sodomy laws, more preemptive wars, bans on single mothers teaching in "government schools," a Bible-based legal system, and many more right-wing issues. While many dedicated organizations are devoted to publicizing these Dominionist activities—there's no need to expose them as they are mainly in open public view—the American public still seems unmindful of the implications of such political fundamentalist pursuits. In part, this is a manifestation of the American public's political naïveté and of the politics of knowledge that dominates American media in general and news coverage and education in particular.

One of the important ways in which such radical political fundamentalist ideas move from the fringe to the mainstream involves the Dominionists' media empire, which broadcasts fundamentalist preachers who take positions emanating from extremist circles and legitimizes them on TV and radio. Such ideas find their way into various dimensions of Christotainment that work to reinforce the ideas promoted by the ministers in a more palatable "politics of pleasure." Political positions that only a few years ago were thought to be the viewpoint of irrational zealots continue to move into the Republican Party and mainstream American sociopolitical life.

The idea of installing a "Christian" government whose legal system is grounded in a particular and highly problematic interpretation of the scriptures, not the Constitution, has now moved into the mainstream of American political life. Numerous conservative officeholders, as well as organizations such as the prominent Council for National Policy, now endorse such a position. My, how the American political landscape has changed; less than a decade ago, the label "conservative" described an individual who argued that the Constitution was the legal foundation of American government and should be followed in a strict and literal manner. Although this position is problematic in its dismissal of changing conditions and contextual data, it is a reasonable, moderate perspective in light of the Dominionists' Bible-based political and legal standpoint.

Consider for a moment the implications of such a scriptural political and legal framework. Those who would object to such a system are dismissed as heathens, atheists, outsiders, or secular humanists. Liberal concepts such as universal human rights crumble as the focus of the system involves the security of the "saved," who are the keepers of the truth. Here, entire sectors of the U.S. population are deleted from legal protection and political participation. The fact that a particular and highly problematic interpretation of the Bible is used as the grounding for a scripture-based system is profoundly significant in this context. Not only would non-Christians be excluded from legal protection and civil rights in the Dominionist system, but so would many devout

Christians whose interpretations of the Bible were deemed "incorrect." Depending on one's theological hermeneutics (the way she makes sense of scriptures), a Bible-based schema could be, and has been, used to justify everything from slavery and gender violence to acts of cruelty against "outsiders" in general (Neiwert 2003; Blumenthal 2005; Hedges 2006).

CHRISTOTAINMENT, LIBIDINAL INVESTMENT, AND NAVY SEALS FOR JESUS

In the Christotainment domain, we see various groups working to spread these militant, aggressive, and threatening perspectives into diverse groups, focusing on young people in particular. In recent years, an array of entertainment-based and proselytizing groups and organizations has emerged to immerse youth in macho, patriarchal, and militaristic modes of political fundamentalist belief systems, lifestyles, and activities. Take, for example, the work of Ryan Dobson, son of the powerful founder of the Dominionist Focus on the Family and media personality. In three recent books, *Be Intolerant: Because Some Things Are Just Stupid*, *2Die4*, and *2Live4*, Dobson the younger has grounded his brassy work with young people around the notion that kids need to get ready to die in the pursuit of a Dominionist revolution in America. In a manner not too different from that used to recruit mujahideen suicide bombers, Dobson, with the apparent blessing of his father and other fundamentalist leaders, shepherds his flock toward martyrdom for Dominionism (Hedges 2006).

Ron Luce's BattleCry, a fundamentalist Christian youth movement, proclaims to its followers that we are engaged in a war against the secular forces in the nation. He and his staff put together Christian rock concerts that have drawn twenty-five thousand attendees in numerous cities across the country, at which Luce tells his wildly enthusiastic and cheering fans that only the violent will gain hold of "the Kingdom." To accentuate the point, he combines his rock concerts with elaborate light shows that spotlight military equipment, posters with young people modeling military weapons, Navy Seals giving testimony to their fundamentalist beliefs and battle plans for the coming Dominionist revolution, endorsements of the war in Iraq, and letters from President George W. Bush validating the patriotic activities taking place at the events (Hubert 2006; Hedges 2006). Here is a description of the BattleCry spectacle from a reporter who attended a concert in Philadelphia in 2006:

> After Franklin "Islam is a Wicked Religion" Graham [Dominionist evangelist son of Billy Graham] came out to thunder against the evils of homosexuality and the Iraqi people (whom he considers to be exactly the same people as the ancient Babylonians who enslaved the tribes of Israel and deserving, one would assume, the exact same fate), we heard an explosion. Flames shot out on stage and a team of Navy Seals was shown on the big TV monitors in full camouflage creeping forward down the hallway from the locker room with their M16s. They were hunting us, the future Christian leaders of America. Two teenage girls next to me burst into tears and even I, a jaded middle-aged male, almost jumped out of my skin. I imagined for that moment what it must have felt like to have been a teacher at Columbine high school. 10 seconds later they rushed out onstage and pointed their guns in our direction firing blanks spitting flames. About 1000 shots and bang, we were all dead. (World Can't Wait 2006)

Delirious is a Christian rock band that sometimes plays at BattleCry events singing words like, "We're an army of God and we're ready to die. . . . Let's paint this big ol' town red. . . . We see nothing but the blood of Jesus" (Hedges 2006, 30). As the band blasted out its Christian heavy metal at the concert in Philadelphia, its lyrics were simultaneously projected on giant rock concert screens to make sure the young crowd didn't miss the Dominionist message being delivered. They didn't, as seventeen thousand young believers chanted in response to the band, "We are warriors." This, of course, is only one dimension of the Christian music scene, as Philip Anderson and Curry Mallot will illustrate in their chapters in this book. Growing numbers of Christian bands are performing in a wide variety of musical genres and within the theological and ideological diversity of evangelicalism/fundamentalism. Christian music festivals, such as Creation, take place every summer in the hills of south central Pennsylvania, drawing almost one hundred thousand young people.

These bands and concert promoters are keenly aware of the registers of affect such music and events traverse. Dominionist Focus on the Family understands the absurdities of the old fundamentalists' idea that if a listener plays a record backwards, satanic messages can be heard or that rock is a form of "jungle music" (read African American–inspired and not to be tolerated). Focus music promoters know that pop music is a key theater in the "war" for youth libidinal investment, desire. In the spirit of what Anderson writes in chapter 9, rock and other forms of beat-based music, no matter what the lyrics, engage a bodily relationship with the listener. Secular observers of Christian music concerts regularly discern a libidinal frenzy among stimulated concert crowds that points to the visceral power of the beat. As was the case with the transcendent ecstasy produced by the camp meetings in the early nineteenth century—many husbands did not want their wives attending such meetings—many contemporary fundamentalists fear that if not authoritatively directed, such energy will be used in ways not conducive to the fundamentalist cause. Among the Dominionists, such ecstasy is central to manipulating young people into serving their militaristic 2die4 ambitions (Hendershot 1995; Hedges 2006; Sheler 2006).

SETTLING THE SCORE WITH NONBELIEVERS: DOMINIONISM AS A CHRISTOFASCIST MOVEMENT

The new and improved Jesus referenced in this chapter's title refers, as previously mentioned, to an Americanized Jesus, as well as to a macho, kick-the-heathens'-ass savior. One of the great American evangelical/fundamentalist theological innovations has been to remake Jesus as an epic *personality* whose "eye is on the sparrow" and with whom we develop a personal relationship. This notion seems so commonplace, so natural within contemporary evangelicalism/fundamentalism, that it is hard to believe that in Christian history it is a relatively recent invention of nineteenth-century American theologians. This epic personality has continued to evolve in recent years as fundamentalists groups—particularly Dominionists—have produced the badass savior, only employing in limited contexts the Prince of Peace persona. No wimpy, girly Jesus for me, Jerry Falwell wrote in the early 1980s, setting a trend of fundamentalist calls to represent Jesus to the world (in Falwell's words) as a "he-man."

Dominionist leaders and the producers of Christotainment heard these calls loud and clear. In the last volume of the *Left Behind* series, for example, *The Glorious Appearing*, the Jesus who returns to Earth would never be confused with the loving Lord who promoted selfless love and forgiveness. That guy long ago departed for calmer climes. The new Jesus has undergone an extreme makeover and is now the judge executioner of the Jews, Muslims, Hindus, Buddhists, atheists, agonistics, and even members of the United Church of Christ. This killer Jesus, as described by LaHaye and Jenkins, releases a metaphorical sword from his mouth that invisibly spins through the air, exacting God's judgment on the unbelieving swine. We Christians, the story goes, gave the unbelievers chance after chance to accept Jesus as their personal savior. The time finally came when we did what we had to do to establish our rule, his rule on Earth (Little 2006; Pfohl 2006).

Like George W. Bush and his good-versus-evil rhetoric in the War on Terror, the political fundamentalists allow no ambiguity in their war against the sinners and nonbelievers. Those who don't fit into the narrow definitions of Christianity offered are undoubtedly headed for the divine tortures that media commentators such as Pat Robertson or Rush Limbaugh seem to wish on those who would pursue social justice. In the *Left Behind* series, many of those who are slaughtered at the Battle of Armageddon are the leftists that describe good Christians as "right-wing, fanatic, fundamentalist faction" zealots. They are the American Jews descended from the barbarians responsible for the brutal whipping and crucifixion of Jesus in the gospel according to Mel Gibson in *The Passion of The Christ.* Gibson's portrayal of the violence of the crucifixion is so exaggerated that Jesus would have died many times before getting to Calvary. In the film, Jesus moves from macho he-man to dark graphic novel superhero. He even bursts out of the tomb looking gallant and fearless—and very marketable—rising from the dead to the sound track of military drums. Batman, Superman, Spiderman, and Gibson's Jesus are all consumable products ready for sequels (McAlister 2003; Smiga 2006; Little 2006; Marquez 2006).

Historical analyses consistently make the argument that fascism always takes years and years to emerge in its mature form—in the case of Hitler's Germany with its brownshirts, mass political gatherings, violence, tactical harassment, and genocide. Even in Nazi Germany, fascism emerged slowly as a dispersed rural phenomenon and slowly moved to Munich and the other cities around the country. In the United States, in a society marked by a lost sense of belongingness, community disintegration, and sociopolitical amnesia, rurally grounded hyperpatriotic/nationalist groups have come closer together with a rurally based political fundamentalism. In this emerging coalition, aided and abetted by Christotainment's fundamentalist talk shows and right-wing radio, a revolutionary movement is taking shape. A blueprint is being drawn for a theocratic utopian society that creates a political fundamentalist tyranny, a catalyst for a theofascist state.

Americans do not presently live in a fascist state. I want to make that perfectly clear. What I am grappling with here involves analyzing Dominionism and the Christotainment that accompanies it in relation to questions about an emerging fascism or fascist tendencies. These questions are asked with an open mind and no final pronouncement on the answers. Indeed, I may eventually find that examining Dominionism and other forms of political fundamentalism through this lens may not contribute to our understanding of the theopolitical phenomena in question. It is important to note that fascism has historically comprised dynamics that are culturally familiar and in and of themselves seem rather harmless, even noble. Moreover, such dynamics have to be viewed in this comfortable way for the fascistic process to emerge successfully. Thus, when social conditions reach a crisis status, the emerging movement is ready to take advantage of a new receptivity to its message.

In the cyberworld of the blogosphere, one of the great postulates that has surfaced in the collective wisdom of the cybercommunity is that she who first mentions fascism in a thread of debate loses the argument. According to this axiom, I just lost any argument I was making. In this political fundamentalist context, I am willing to take the chance because there do seem to be fascistic tendencies dancing around in the cultural ether. This articulated, I bristle at the inappropriate, indeed hyperbolic, usage of the term *fascism* by both the Right and the Left in the public conversation. Unfitting usage of the term so egregiously dishonors those millions of individuals who have lost their lives to real-life fascist movements around the world. Suffice it to say, I am careful with the term.

My point within the critical ideological context from which I emerge (see Kincheloe 2008a and 2008b) is that the American and other Western societies need to be intimately acquainted with political fundamentalism and the Christotainment it produces to win adherents via a politics/theology of pleasure. Not only is it the civic duty of all Americans to understand political fundamentalism and its fascist tendencies, but, in particular, I believe it is the ethical obligation of all individuals who call themselves Christian to know what is being done in the name of their faith. Many Christians who come from different theological and political orientations often say to me, "I am shocked by the new Jesus being sold by the Dominionists. What happened to the Jesus who counseled us to love our enemies?" As an educator, I would argue that not knowing the Bible and the religious texts of many other religions severely handicaps one in the effort to become a good citizen of the world, an educated person, a human being who understands history, philosophy, politics, literature, art, and so on, ad infinitum. This lack of knowledge pushes one into a precarious naïveté, a truncated outlook as restricted as that of those who proclaim with no rigorous investigation that any holy scripture is the literal, unfiltered word of the Creator. Such modes of ignorance undermine the civic and theological conversation and contribute to the destruction of democratic and positive theological spheres of human activity (Neiwert 2003; Leupp 2005; Hedges 2006).

In this uninformed state, individuals become highly vulnerable to the colonizing effects of this emerging Christofascism. Here the political fundamentalists steal peoples' individual stories only to replace them with narratives in which the uninformed are relegated to the lower rungs of the cryptofascist status hierarchy. In these low-level roles, they become characters in constructions that serve the needs of those in leadership positions. In this fascist cosmos, leaders place great emphasis on the iconographic and aesthetic dimensions of the meetings they plan, always focusing on the romantic and mystical dimensions of the belief structure. Such dynamics work to enhance the seductive aspects of the group, placing even more affective pressure on the uninformed to grant their consent. Christotainment picks up on these romantic and mystical elements of fascist aesthetics and takes them to new levels of sophistication.

BattleCry's rock concerts are excellent examples of the fascist spectacle that operates to manipulate and guide the affective investments of young people. BattleCry and countless other similar types of Christotainment elicit jouissance, love, desire, hate, and feelings of belonging. In numerous ways, participants feel empowered, endowed with a new sense of purpose in life. When religious news broadcasts from the Christian Broadcasting Network (CBN) and the public affairs programming are added to the libidinal experience of the gatherings, a new theological and political consciousness emerges. Such knowledge producers operate much like those data producers at Walt Disney World who provide narratives on American history to the park's visitors. These faux historians have provided narratives to connect a plethora of facts and pseudofacts in the process turning American history into a fairy tale of virtuous heroes who wanted only to do good in the world. Of course, in hyperreality these stories become more real than any other national narratives.

Political fundamentalist history books used by homeschoolers and Christian schools tell a similar story of the founding and early decades of American history. As the story progresses, we begin to see a litany of satanic enemies, from the founders of public schooling to government leaders who established social policies for the poor. Novelist and social theorist Umberto Eco (Neiwert 2003) contends that contemporary Dominionist and political fundamentalist discourse and knowledge politics are grounded in a fascist marinated Orwellian newspeak that unites the believers and degrades those who are in someway "different." Multiple sources, forms of knowledge employing a wide variety of media, create a discursive universe of newspeak that manipulates meanings for the larger good of the cause. In the process, Christotained political fundamentalism, with its fascist tendencies, induces millions to become God's soldiers against the multiple enemies of Jesus.

Mel Gibson's establishment of "validity" in *The Passion of The Christ* illustrates well the validation of such knowledge processes. Careful to produce tiny details of supposed historical accuracy, including the use of the Aramaic language, Gibson and his production team induce viewers to believe that if this depiction of the crucifixion is true, then the contemporary fundamentalist proclamation of Jesus's message must be literally true as well. He is simply more believable when portrayed in the dominant media of the day. Numerous individuals asserted after seeing the film, "Jesus is so human in the film. . . . Jesus is really one of us" (Smiga 2006). This is newspeak in hyperreality, as the "realer real" of Christotainment productions such as *The Passion* brings innumerable converts. When these factors are added to the vile and often gratuitous dimensions of the anti-Semitism of the film, the Christofascistic imprint is indelibly darkened.

The theologically bigoted and naïve Gibson and his political fundamentalist fellow travelers seem totally unaware that the phenomenon of blaming of the Jews for Jesus's death only emerged as a political strategy when the early Christians sought favor as they operated in the Roman Empire. It was much easier and most definitely politically expedient to exonerate the Romans and scapegoat the Jews in such a matrix of power. Gibson completely ignores these well-established historical dimensions of the early Christians' cynical blaming of the Jews in a fascistic effort to demonize and otherize the nonbelievers (see Gertrud Schiller's *The Iconography of Christian Art* for a seminal expansion of these themes). A close reading of the Aramaic screenplay reveals almost unbelievably anti-Semitic background dialogue that places the Jews at the time of the crucifixion in a most unfavorable light. We don't even need to bring in the diatribes of Gibson and his father against Judaism to clearly see the hatred of Jews embedded in the film (Mazur and Koda 2001; Miles 2006).

In the next chapter, we continue to examine these themes, especially the way Christotainment and political fundamentalism fit into larger sociopolitical movements. In this context, we examine the way Christotainment has helped "recover" forms of dominant power believed to have been severely subverted by anti-Christian elements in American society. In this context, Christotainment becomes a central force in contemporary American culture and politics.

References

Blumenthal, M. 2005. Air Jesus. *MediaTransparency*, http://mediatransparency.org (accessed August 29, 2008).

Frykholm, A. 2005. The gender dynamics of the *Left Behind* series. In *Religion and popular culture in America*, ed. B. Forbes and J. Mahan. 2nd ed. Berkeley: University of California Press.

Goldberg, M. 2007. The rise of Christian nationalism. *Humanist* 67, no. 5: 29–33.

Hedges, C. 2006. *American fascists: The Christian Right and the war on America.* New York: Free Press.

Hendershot, H. 1995. *Shaking the world for Jesus: Media and conservative evangelical culture.* Chicago: University of Chicago Press.

Hubert, D. 2006. G. I. Jesus? Denouncement of right-wing Christian BattleCry. BuzzFlash, www.buzzflash.com/contributors/06/05/con06203.html (accessed August 29, 2008).

Kincheloe, J. 2008a. *Critical pedagogy primer.* 2nd ed. New York: Peter Lang Publishing.

______. 2008b. Critical pedagogy and the knowledge wars of the twenty-first century. *International Journal of Critical Pedagogy* 1, no. 1: 1–22.

Kincheloe, J. and S. Steinberg. 2004. *The miseducation of the West: How schools and the media distort our understanding of the Islamic world.* Westport, CT: Praeger.

Klemp, N. 2007. Beyond God-talk: Understanding the Christian Right from the ground up. *Polity* 39: 522–544.

Leupp, G. 2005. Fighting for the work of the Lord: Everybody's talking about Christian fascism. *Counterpunch*, www.counterpunch.org/leupp01131005.htm (accessed August 29, 2008).

Little, W. 2006. Jesus's extreme makeover. In *Mel Gibson's Bible: Religion, popular culture, and* The Passion of the Christ, ed. T. Beal and T. Linafelt. Chicago: University of Chicago Press.

Mahan, J. 2005. Conclusion: Establishing a dialogue about religion and popular culture. In *Religion and popular culture in America,* ed. B. Forbes and J. Mahan. 2nd ed. Berkeley: University of California Press.

Marquez, J. 2006. Lights! Camera! Action! In *Mel Gibson's Bible: Religion, popular culture, and* The Passion of the Christ, ed. T. Beal and T. Linafelt. Chicago: University of Chicago Press.

Mazur, E., and T. Koda. 2001. Happiest place on Earth: Disney's America and the commodification of religion. In *God in the details: American religion in popular culture,* ed. E. Mazur and K. McCarthy. New York: Routledge.

McAlister, M. 2003. An empire of their own. *Nation,* September 4, www.thenation.com/doc/20030922/mcalister (accessed August 29, 2008).

Miles, J. 2006. The art of *The Passion.* In *Mel Gibson's Bible: Religion, popular culture, and* The Passion of the Christ, ed. T. Beal and T. Linafelt. Chicago: University of Chicago Press.

Moore, R. 1994. *Selling God: American religion in the marketplace of culture.* New York: Oxford University Press.

Neiwert, D. 2003. Rush, newspeak, and fascism: An exegesis. Orcinus, http://dneiwert.blogspot.com/rush%20newspeak%20%20fascism.pdf (accessed July 15, 2008).

Pfohl, S. 2006. *Left Behind:* Religion, technology, and the flight from the flesh. *ctheory.net,* www.ctheory.net/articles.aspx?id=557 (accessed August 29, 2008).

Prothero, S. 2003. *American Jesus: How the Son of God became a national icon.* New York: Farrar, Straus, and Giroux.

Romanowski, W. 2005. Evangelicals and popular music: The contemporary Christian music industry. In *Religion and popular culture in America,* ed. B. Forbes and J. Mahan. 2nd ed. Berkeley: University of California Press.

Sheler, J. 2006. *Believers: A journey into evangelical America.* New York: Penguin.

Smiga, G. 2006. The good news of Mel Gibson's *Passion.* In *Mel Gibson's Bible: Religion, popular culture, and* The Passion of the Christ, ed. T. Beal and T. Linafelt. Chicago: University of Chicago Press.

Thomas, P. 2005. Christian fundamentalism and the media. *Media Development,* www.wacc.org.uk/wacc/publications/media_development/2005_2christian_fundamentalism_and_themedia (accessed July 18, 2008).

World Can't Wait. 2006. A carnival of theocrats. *Daily Kos,* www.dailykos.com.story/2006/5/15/04817/0699 (accessed July 18, 2008).

11

Christian Soldier Jesus

The Intolerant Savior and the Political Fundamentalist Media Empire

JOE L. KINCHELOE

It is important to place Christotainment and political fundamentalism in a larger historical context to help explain why so many Americans have bought into such a potentially fascistic movement. Such a metahistorical consciousness helps construct an awareness of the contemporary appeal of regressive, oppressive, and undemocratic social, cultural, political, educational, and theological activities. In this domain we create a critical consciousness about these right-wing influences in light of one of the dominant sociopolitical, cultural, and philosophical dynamics of the last five hundred years of human history: European, and especially in the last hundred years, American colonialism.

Though it is rarely discussed in the public conversation about theology and its political dimensions, the ways of seeing constructed by the last five hundred years of Euro-American colonialism have a dramatic effect on what goes on in the everyday life of Western societies in general and American society in particular. After several centuries of violent exploitation, the early twentieth century began to witness a growing impatience of colonized peoples with their degraded sociopolitical, economic, and educational status. Five hundred years of colonial violence had convinced Africans, Asians, Latin Americans, and indigenous peoples around the world that enough was enough. Picking up steam after World War II, colonized peoples around the world threw off colonial governmental strictures and set out on a troubled journey toward independence. The European colonial powers, however, were not about to give up such lucrative socioeconomic relationships so easily. With the United States leading the way, Western societies developed a wide array of neocolonial strategies for maintaining the benefits of colonialism. This neocolonial effort continues unabated, and in many ways with a new intensity in an era of transnational corporations and the "War on Terror," in the twenty-first century.

Appreciating these historical power dynamics and their influence is central to our analysis of Christotainment and its political universe. Though in the twenty-first century most Americans are not aware of it, this anticolonial rebellion was a central factor in catalyzing the liberation movements of the 1960s and 1970s that shook the United States and other Western societies. The civil rights movement, the anti–Vietnam War movement, the women's movement, the American Indian Movement, and the gay rights movement all took their cues from the anticolonial struggles of individuals around the world. Martin Luther King Jr., for example, wrote his doctoral dissertation on the anticolonial rebellion against the British led by Mohandas Gandhi in India. King focused his scholarly attention on Gandhi's nonviolent colonial-resistance tactics, later drawing upon such strategies in the civil rights movement.

By the mid-1970s, especially in the United States, a conservative counterreaction to these liberation movements was taking shape with the goal of "recovering" what was perceived to be lost in these movements (Gresson 1995, 2004; Kincheloe et al. 1998; Rodriguez and Villaverde 2000). Thus, the politics, cultural wars, and educational and psychological debates, policies, and practices of the last three decades cannot be understood outside of the efforts of conservative forces to "recover" white supremacy, patriarchy, class privilege, colonialism, heterosexual "normality," Christian dominance, and the European intellectual canon.

These modes of dominant power are some of the most important defining macroconcerns of our time, as every social, political, and even theological issue is refracted through their lenses. Any view of the social domain conceived outside of this framework becomes a form of ideological mystification. This process of ideological mystification operates to maintain present dominant-subordinate power relations by promoting particular forms of meaning making and political action. In this colonial context, ideological mystification often involves making meanings that assert that non-European peoples are incapable of running their own political and economic affairs and that colonial activity *was* a way of taking care of these incapable peoples. In a theological context, these modes of meaning making tell fundamentalists that their religious way is the only way and that the rest of the world must be evangelized and made to accept their orthodoxy. If an individual is not saved, he or she will have to be put to death in the Apocalypse.

Employing the rhetoric of "loss," the right-wing advocates of recovery spoke of the loss of social order, discipline, civility, moral standards, educational excellence, proper English, and family values. Because of the pursuit of social justice and racial/cultural diversity, America itself was in decline. As a direct result of the women's and gay rights movements and other justice-based and inclusive notions, Christianity itself was perceived to be under attack. The secular humanist reformers, political fundamentalists asserted, wanted to destroy Christianity. In the rhetoric of recovery, the notion of loss and falling moral standards has always been accompanied by strategically placed critiques of affirmative action, racial preferences, feminism, homosexuality, and multiculturalism. Though the connection was obvious, plausible deniability was maintained, with the political fundamentalists claiming, "We are not racists or sexists," "We love the homosexuals, just not the sins they commit," and "We only want to protect our country from the destruction of its most treasured values."

By the 1970s, with the emergence of this ideology of recovery, the very concept of government with its "public" denotations began to represent the victory of minorities and leftist concerns about the inequities of race, class, gender, and colonialism. "Big government" became a code phrase for anti-white-male social action in the recovery discourse. Indeed, in this articulation, it was time to get it off "our" backs. Thus, privatization became more than a strategy for organizing social institutions. Privatization was the ostensibly deracialized term that could be deployed to signify the recovery of white, patriarchal supremacy. In the same way, the word "choice" could be used to connote the right to "opt out" of government-mandated "liberal" policies. Like good consumers, "we" (Americans with traditional values) choose life, privatized schools, the most qualified job applicants, and Christian values over the other "products."

Thus, in the grander sense, we choose the private space over the *diversity* of the public space. In rejecting the public space, the right wing and its fundamentalist allies rejected the *existing* political domain, a choice that resonated with many conservative white Christians throughout the nation. Indeed, any political action on our part, the advocates of recovery asserted, will be represented as antipolitical. We will work to make sure that traditional "political types" are defeated by anti-big-government agents who will work to undermine the public space with its social programs, infrastructures, schools, and secularist, anti-Christian policies. Indeed, politicians who are not born-again Christians working to dismantle the public space and academics who are not denouncing the secular humanist academy are not our types of people. In the recovery, the institutions of public government and education must go. Both institutions, the right-wing argument goes, display the tendency to undermine the best interests of fundamentalist white people, particularly "true" Christian white males (Kincheloe and Steinberg 1997; Kincheloe 2001).

With this larger macrohistorical sense of the right-wing recovery movement, we can now focus more specially on Dominionism's and Christotainment's relationship to the social impulse in the last years of the first decade of the twenty-first century. Political fundamentalism's textual literalism and black-and-white view of the world dovetail smoothly into the recovery context. Diversity—respect for the viewpoints of non-Western peoples, men and women oppressed by colonialism, individuals from differing social classes, genders, and sexualities, and so forth—demands that multiple perspectives be entertained and taken seriously. Such a situation requires complex comparative analysis, a sense of multiplicity, interpretative skills, and knowledge in diverse contexts and domains. Recovery-based political fundamentalism offers a way out of this complexity and ambiguity, as it promotes the simplicity of literalism. In this social and theological configuration, individuals no longer have to grapple with textual meanings, the historical and social contexts in which a text has been produced.

All the believer has to do is trust in God and accept things as they seem to be on the surface. Objects in the rearview mirror are exactly as they appear. Thus, within fundamentalism as well as other social dynamics, we can observe the recovery of a naïve realism that simply ignores the deeper questions of meaning that attend any form of social, cultural, political, educational, and theological activity. Indeed, the *realism,* the final truth of Mel Gibson's *The Passion of The Christ,* is a key aspect of its appeal. The torture and the blood are real—albeit it hyperreal in the context of a media saturated culture. This recovery of naïve realism is also illustrated in Christotainment by Precious Moments (PM) products. A brand of collectible porcelain bisque figurines based on illustrations by fundamentalist Christian artist Sam Butcher, Precious Moments provides widely recognizable teardrop-eyed children presenting sentimental, hypersincere missives of religious inspiration.

In the spirit of the spectacle of Christotainment, a Precious Moments theme park was built in Missouri in 1989 to provide a deeper immersion into the PM universe. A careful analysis of the company's figurines and other products reveals a recovery of innocence motif that takes an aesthetically grounded political stand against the complications of diversity in all its perspectival and cultural/race-based manifestations. The Precious Moments cosmos is sanctified and in its Christian purity shows us how wonderful the world could be if everyone surrendered to the authority of literalist fundamentalism. The birth of Precious Moments in 1977 parallels the emergence of a wide variety of sociopolitical and theological institutions and organizations dedicated to political fundamentalist recovery: an outbreak of fundamentalist-led school textbook and curriculum battles (1974–present), the Moral Majority (1979), the national syndication of the 700 Club (1974), Focus on the Family (1977), and so on (Rycenga 2001; Taylor 2006). The appearance of such sociotheological phenomena pointed to a sea change in American consciousness. This change would alter the social and political landscape for the next four decades.

From Precious Moments, to *The Passion of The Christ*, to the theopolitical talk shows on the 700 Club and many other political fundamentalist programs, one underlying assumption remains the same: we need to return to a better time in a glorified past. The social and political inscriptions on this notion are often quite obvious. The past longed for was a time when "minorities" knew their place, when homosexuality was a mental illness to be hidden, when women stayed home and out of the public sphere, when class hierarchies were respected. In these days of trial and pretribulation, it is important to recover some of the power lost by dominant groups in this context. This recovery motif is overt in Merle Haggard's 1982 country music hit, "Are the Good Times Really Over," in which he wishes that "Coke" was still "Coca-Cola" and remembers when a joint was a questionable place to hang out. In the discursive universe of recovery, where political fundamentalists dream of a return to the good ol' days—or if that's not possible, look forward to the "theological cleansing" of the Apocalypse—one observes over and over again the sense of persecution political fundamentalists sense in contemporary America.

At a recent convention of the National Religious Broadcasters (NRB), for example, the central theme of the meeting revolved around what to do about the persecution of Christians. Held at the Anaheim Convention Center in February 2005, speaker after speaker talked to enthusiastic audiences about the harassment true believers had to face. Given the political power the NRB had gained through media outreach and political connections, the cries of persecution came across more as an effort to rally the faithful than to provide a fair assessment of the status quo. Nevertheless, other political fundamentalist groups continue to focus on this theme.

In the recovery rhetoric, such proclamations of victimization are essential in order to garner support against the "outsiders" who now have the privilege: African Americans because of affirmative action, women because of the feminist movement, gays and lesbians because of the political success of the "homosexual agenda," and America's enemies because of so many liberal/leftist political figures who are more concerned with the needs of other nations (e.g., illegal immigrants) than with the concerns of Americans here at home. Here we are, speakers admonished those attending the gathering, facing Islam's effort to conquer Christian lands, and the secularists don't want the United States to take the Muslims on militarily. We have to fight for Jesus, as the book of Revelation tells us (Blumenthal 2005; Taylor 2006). This literalist simplicity permeates all dimensions of the Dominionists' and political fundamentalists' reading of the word and the world. This literalist dynamic becomes a central dimension of understanding Christotainment and the threats that it poses to democracy, justice, and even world peace.

CHRISTOTAINMENT AND RECOVERY: THE POWER OF ANTI-INTELLECTUALISM

Whenever any text is interpreted literally without the benefit of historical, social, and cultural contextualization and consideration of its relationship with other texts, much understanding and meaning is lost. When such a literal reading is placed in an entertainment and marketing format, even more of the original text's significance and consequence is removed. The study of these dynamics of interpretation and meaning making, so central to the issues discussed in this book, are simply not important in the collective consciousness of the political fundamentalists. Part of the explanation for this involves the vicious anti-intellectualism and even antirationality of many—certainly not all—

of the political fundamentalists in question. A mature theology examines the process by which canonized and noncanonized religious texts were written, the lives and times of the authors, the multiple contexts of which they were a part, linguistic and sociopolitical factors in the translation process, and so forth.

Rigorous scholars of Christianity, Judaism, Islam, Hinduism, Buddhism, and other religions understand that these are difficult and complex questions. The writers of the four Christian Gospels, for example, took, as all researchers do, a variety of written and oral sources and synthesized them into a narrative about the life of Jesus. And like researchers, the gospel writers employed creative processes to transform their data into a narrative form. They left some information out and emphasized data that fit into the narrative format they had chosen, most likely unconsciously, for their presentation. Which texts were included in the Bible and which ones were left out is another profoundly complex issue, as theological scholars study the arguments and politics surrounding how such choices for inclusion or exclusion were made by early church leaders.

As individuals come to understand more and more of these factors, the depth of their understanding of the meaning of a theological tradition and their own investments in it becomes more sophisticated. Such scholarly dynamics are not a part of the political fundamentalist universe and the Christotainment they produce to win new converts to the fold. Critical observers find this tendency to be highly problematic and even frightening in the kinds of blind faith and zealotry it can produce. In my own experience, while teaching about Western educational history, I found myself in unusual situations as I engaged graduate students in a study of early Christian education. As I discussed the history of the construction of the Bible and particular belief structures, I would look around the classroom to find that many of my students coming from fundamentalist backgrounds were sobbing. When I asked why they were so upset, the students told me that they didn't believe in looking at the Bible in a historical way. Several of the students had talked to their ministers, who instructed them to pray out loud while I covered these dimensions of early Christian history. Thus, as I taught my lessons on the topic, numerous students prayed aloud to make it through a class directed by a satanic force.

Thus, the very idea of dealing with the tough scholarly issues that always accompany theology is antithetical to the Dominionist and political fundamentalist outlook. The "scholarship" that does take place in the political fundamentalist domain often amounts to little more than an effort to find anything that could be taken as evidence for the literal truth of the Bible. At the Holy Land Experience, for example, individuals who call themselves professional biblical archeologists give authoritative presentations on the extensive research they've conducted to prove that what they have in the park is an exact replica of Jesus's tomb. A few moments of questioning the "experts" quickly reveals that the professional status of many of the authorities is based on little preparation outside a brief experience with a fundamentalist seminary. The presenters' qualifications as biblical anthropologists—or any other kind of anthropologist—is highly suspect.

This quest to prove the literal truth of the Bible is itself a highly selective literalism. The late theological scholar William Sloane Coffin (Hedges 2006) maintained that these selective literalists choose small parts of the Bible that conformed to their personal theology and ideology, ignoring, misrepresenting, or fabricating all the other parts. For example, many ask, if one accepts the word-by-word veracity of the Bible, why would one eat prohibited shellfish? Such literalist readings are inherently flawed: if the Bible is totally true, then all of its proclamations must be followed to the letter. Or, if one does not accept this set of literalist assumptions, then the scriptures must be studied and interpreted in a profoundly different way—one that studies the conditions of their production, as well as sociopolitical factors that shaped them, and examines why a particular text was included as the word of God and another was not. Theological literacy, regardless of one's beliefs or nonbeliefs, becomes more and more important in a society threatened by the extremism of Dominionism and political fundamentalism and their savvy marketing skills as displayed in Christotainment.

Thus, once again, forms of theological literacy become extremely important in the contemporary sociopolitical context. Moreover, in a globalized context marked by the rise of fundamentalism, the study of comparative religion becomes more and more important in this era if we are not to be misled by religious fear and hatemongers who attack other religious traditions in an effort to build up their own. Contrary to the charge of political fundamentalists with their distortion of court rulings about teaching religion in public schools over the last five decades, religion should be addressed in schools in ways that raise theological literacy. Such teaching should not promote a particular faith over others; the Lemon test coming out of the Supreme Court case *Lemon v. Kurtzman* in 1971 ruled that a theology course in public schools should not advance or inhibit religion. Such a goal becomes, of course, in the complexity of the twenty-first-century political and educational landscape extremely hard to accomplish, as political fundamentalists frame a fair analysis of different religious traditions as being intrinsically anti-Christian. Such fundamentalist advocates want nothing less than full religious indoctrination with their theology in public schools.

In the context of this overview of political fundamentalist and Dominionist anti-intellectualism, it is fascinating to examine the political fundamentalist Protestant reaction to Gibson's *The Passion*. A central tenet of such fundamentalist Protestantism has involved avoiding Catholic-type use of crosses with corpses in worship services. Gibson's *The Passion* is a movie-length expression of such corporal, blood-rite dimensions of pre–Vatican II Catholicism—a point seemingly missed by the enthusiastic Protestant viewers of the movie. My point here is not to validate the history of anti-Catholic attitudes among Protestants but simply to point to the theological inconsistency of the Protestant promoters of the film around the theology of the cross.

In this bizarre, anti-intellectual context, political fundamentalists and Dominionists work to insulate believers from the influences of the secular world. Such insulation creates circumstances where the faithful can live in a fundamentalist community, send their children to fundamentalist schools, go to a fundamentalist tax accountant, get fundamentalist marriage counseling, watch fundamentalist TV and movies, go to fundamentalist theme parks, and vacation at fundamentalist resorts. By carefully staying within such an environment, individuals can go for years without hearing, watching, or reading anything that would challenge their belief structures (Smiga 2006; Miles 2006; Taylor 2006; McKenna 2006; Chancey 2007). Thus, a vicious and harmful anti-intellectualism in the world of political fundamentalism is allowed to flourish. Without moderating contact with diverse viewpoints and insights, the vilification of those who don't accept political fundamentalist doctrine continues to intensify.

THE SUCCESS OF POLITICAL FUNDAMENTALISM AND CHRISTOTAINMENT

Political fundamentalist power and ideological influence is still growing in the United States and in other parts of the world. Christotainment has played a central role in this success. As the early 1980s witnessed the lucrative deployment of political fundamentalist's plan to use media in new and creative ways, the mainstream Christian denominations in the United States lost power over the ways they were represented by TV news and various other knowledge producers. The prevailing post–Scopes trial (involving the teaching of evolution in Tennessee in the 1920s) representation of Protestant fundamentalists as hicks and fools was supplanted with a view of mainline Protestants as aging, boring bleeding hearts. In the popular media, these mainline Protestants were losing the struggle for the hearts and minds of America, as declining membership and fiscal problems dominated news stories about them.

When such denominations pursued social action around issues of social justice for the marginalized, women's rights, or corporate misdeeds, diverse forms of media increasingly ignored them. Over the last decade, fundamentalists have been interviewed over and over again on Sunday morning mainstream network talk shows, while Presbyterians, Methodists, Lutherans, United Church of Christ adherents, American Baptists, and African Methodist Episcopalians have been virtually banished from such programs. The work of religious groups such as the Methodist Church, the Interfaith Alliance, or the Progressive Jewish Alliance to address the failures of social policy, the justice system, efforts (or lack thereof) to address homelessness, health care management, and countless other humanitarian problems are buried by the contemporary media.

Such unsurprising activity doesn't make news in the same way that Pat Robertson's pronouncements on the causes of disasters like Hurricane Katrina in 2005. On the 700 Club, Robertson announced that Katrina was the second national disaster in a row that had struck America after the Academy of Television Arts and Sciences had selected "avowed lesbian" Ellen DeGeneres to host the Emmy Awards. After her first invitation, the September 11 attacks occurred, and after her second, Katrina hit her hometown of New Orleans, Robertson stated. "Is it any surprise that the Almighty chose to strike at Miss DeGeneres' hometown? . . . America is waiting for her to apologize for the death and destruction that her sexual deviance has brought onto this great nation" (Ontario Consultants on Religious Tolerance 2005). The fact that Robertson's pronouncements could be made to TV audiences measured in the millions and that comments such as his would constitute the religious news of the day points to the success of political fundamentalism and its media strategies. Indeed, reporters from Robertson's Christian Broadcasting Network (CBN) now appear regularly as guest commentators on other TV and radio networks. These appearances give a legitimacy to Robertson's work that reinforces the success of the Christotainment media empire.

As one political fundamentalist recently put it to a scientist, we (political fundamentalists in the United States) now constitute a world empire, and when we engage in any activity, we produce our own reality. Indeed, their political success and the power of their Christotainment have convinced American political fundamentalists that the Jews have relinquished the title "God's chosen people" to the "true Christians" of America. Continuing, the fundamentalist advocate asserted,

> While you're studying that reality—judiciously, as you will—we'll act again, creating other new realities, which you can study too, and that's how things will sort out. We're history's actors . . . and you, all of you, will be left to just study what we do. (Goldberg 2007, 29)

Such a position emerges from the success political fundamentalists enjoyed in the George W. Bush administration in relation to science policy (Prothero 2003; Winston 2007). Far too often, scientific research was trumped by the ideological concerns of right-wing fundamentalists—for example, stem-cell research, definitions of life, global climate change, environmental pollution, the Terry Schiavo case, and so forth. Such a rejection of reason forces numerous scholars and other individuals to retaliate by embracing universal forms of reason. Thus, in the name of protecting rationality from fundamentalist attack, such agents assert a new and often oppressive form of Western reason that is sensitive to innovation and advancement coming from new research and analysis as well as engagement with diverse peoples around the world. Such "intellectual protectionism" has had a negative impact on U.S. scholarship.

Radical fundamentalism and its Christotainment have exerted a profound influence on a number of social and cultural levels. The power of the political fundamentalists' and Dominionists' politics of knowledge to engage changes in consciousness has rearranged the structure of world politics. As the media-friendly talk show hosts of CBN peddle what to many of us seem literally crazy opinions about manifestations of present-day miracles and Jesus's direct intervention in the political events of the day, millions of people listen, believe, and send millions of dollars to support CBN's and Pat Robertson's work. This decade-after-decade ability to raise money provides some evidence of the success of political fundamentalism and its Christotainment. With CBN's "kingdom," as it is often labeled, hundreds of millions of dollars have been raised to support the network and countless projects that reach an estimated 1.6 billion people. The expressed purpose of CBN is to prepare the people of the earth for the Second Coming and the formation of Jesus's kingdom in this world. In this context, CBN uses its media network to teach young and old how to help establish God's kingdom and how to operate in it on a daily basis.

A frequent routine on the 700 Club, the flagship program of CBN, involves Pat Robertson and his cohosts announcing a limited-time telephone pledge campaign near the beginning of a particular day's program. Typically, five to ten minutes are dedicated for watchers to call the network and pledge a contribution. As the time counts down, Robertson tells viewers about the gifts that donors will receive—for example, videos/CDs and books featuring lessons and sermons about world affairs and the coming Apocalypse. Concurrently, video "packages" are shown as the time deadline comes and goes, always with extra time added, that portray individuals who, after giving to the 700 Club, experienced unexpected riches. Of course, this is a manipulative technique that attempts to squeeze as much money as possible out of people regardless of their families' economic needs. Ironically, it encourages a form of gambling where individuals in need wager that if they give to the 700 Club, God will provide them a profit on their original investment.

Key to CBN's success and to Christotainment in general is the subtle dynamic interplay between the apocalyptic and the optimistic, between fear and promise. In typical Rapture politics, Robertson and his staff broadcast that God will bring violent retribution at Armageddon; yet, despite this looming orgy of killing, there is happy talk about living a prosperous American life with an abiding belief in a seemingly happy savior—except when he decides that the mere existence of feminists and homosexuals demands that many people die in natural or human-made disasters. The juxtaposition of the dark and the happy Jesus is theologically tricky, for one is never sure what side of his personality the Son of Man is going to display. Despite the thorny representations of Jesus, the success of CBN and its plethora of projects is beyond dispute. The network, its Regent University in Virginia, and the Dominionist American Center for Law and Justice have been based on the notion that "Jesus is

Lord of all the world . . . of government, and the church, and business, and hopefully, one day, Lord of the Press" (MinistryWatch 2008). With the continuing success of Robertson and CBN, everyday seems to bring that theocratic dream closer to reality. How much success can CBN achieve?

THE VILIFICATION OF "OTHERS"

Recently, in a Fourth of July issue of *Precious Insights*, the magazine for Precious Moments collectibles, collector Judi Thomas wrote,

> While the majority of Americans still hold to a belief in the Judeo-Christian values on which this nation was founded, we find ourselves in a quagmire of lurid and disgusting art. . . . If America were a neighbor or friend, we would send "get well" cards and flowers . . . because America is sick. If America were a toddler, we would spank her and put her to bed for a nap . . . because she's stubbornly pushing the limits of reasonable authority. (Quoted in Rycenga 2001, 150)

The point here is clear: American is a Christian nation, but a wide group of others have stained it and moved it away from its initial holy calling. These others are the shared nemeses of the recovery movement discussed earlier: nonwhites, feminists, homosexuals, and immigrants. These are the ones who need to be punished because they continue to push "the limits of reasonable authority." As citizens of a Christian country, political fundamentalists and Dominionists find the idea of accommodating different types of diversity repugnant. In this context, the faithful can save America, the Christian nation, only by recovering its true heritage and restoring its government to its biblical foundations. The fact that the nation never used the Bible as the basis for its government is irrelevant in this context.

One can only imagine the impact such actions and such fundamentalist belief structures can have on relationships between differing religious groups. The actions of political fundamentalists in every faith, obviously in the twenty-first century, have had profound effects on every aspect of contemporary life. The concept of ecumenicalism cannot survive when one group holds no respect for the religious precepts of another. When political fundamentalism enters the conversation, there is a rise in interreligious hostility and a breakdown of cultural accord in local situations. In some parts of the world where fundamentalist Christian missionaries are particularly disrespectful of other cultures, there has been interfaith violence. In the black-and-white Manichaean fundamentalist view, any sense of complexity, contextual understanding, multiplicity, or paradox fades away quickly, like May snow in the Laurentians.

This fundamentalist disdain for nonbelievers unites seamlessly with the larger right-wing xenophobia of the recovery movement. With regressive forces including, but not limited, to the political fundamentalists, reality comes to be seen across a great gulf of distortion. Many media outlets produce distorted pictures of Africans, Muslims, South Americans, and indigenous peoples from around the world, portraits that represent them as irrational and barbaric peoples and that influence U.S. foreign, economic, and educational policies. The lead up to George W. Bush's war in Iraq and the war itself have been covered with little concern for the Iraqi people, who have been killed in numbers measurable only in the hundreds of thousands. The political fundamentalist and Dominionist view of Islam is so egregiously degrading that it often takes one's breath away.

Contemporary orientalism (the condescending historical Western view of the Arab and Islamic world, as well as parts of the Asian world, that positions these regions and their peoples as exotic, shadowy, alien, and incapable of rationality) is promoted by fundamentalist and particular dimensions of secular TV, film, CDs, and video games. Such a powerful politics of knowledge engages the consent of individuals to dominant forms of xenophobic political fundamentalist and imperial American power in the world. Any Christotainment is more powerful when it engages pleasure as it makes its theological and ideological thought. In spite of its new high-tech accoutrements, neo-orientalism still views Islam as a violent and derivative religion of sodomites (Thomas 2005; Miles 2006; Taylor 2006; Chancey 2007). Check out the comments of almost any political fundamentalist preacher—John Hagee, Rod Parsley, Franklin Graham, Pat Robertson to name a few—to get a feel for the viciousness of these Islamaphobic comments.

As just one of hundreds of examples, take Republican Party activist Rev. Rod Parsley from Ohio. Islam, he maintains, is an "Antichrist religion" based on lies and trickery. Muhammad "received revelations from demons and not from the true God. . . . Allah was a demon spirit." Making no distinction between Islamacist terrorists and everyday Muslims, Parsley states, "There are some, of course, who will say that the violence I cite is the exception and not the rule. I beg to differ. I will counter, respectfully, that what some call 'extremists' are instead mainstream believers who are drawing from the well at the very heart of Islam" (Corn 2008). Thus, God has given America a mission, Parsley claims: "The fact is that America was founded, in part, with the intention of seeing this false religion destroyed, and I believe September 11, 2001, was a generational call to arms that we can no longer ignore" (Corn 2008). Parsley is just another mainstream political fundamentalist TV minister calling for America to annihilate Islam.

Nonfundamentalist groups of Christians, as previously mentioned, are often "otherized" in ways similar to non-Christians. One of the most respected transdenominational Christian organizations in the world, the National Council of Churches (NCC), was founded in 1950 to promote Christian unity. Bringing together mainline Protestant churches with the historically African American denominations and Eastern Orthodox churches, the NCC was viciously attacked time and again for its alleged Communist sympathies. Political fundamentalist operatives planted stories in media such as *Reader's Digest* and even *60 Minutes*. This view of the other, no matter the nature of the difference, has induced political fundamentalists to see left-wing plots to destroy "true Christianity" around every theological, social, and cultural corner. In the last decade's War on Terror, we can see how political fundamentalists have molded a war against progressivism in all of its expressions. Indeed, such a war becomes a quasifascist form of bullying, all in the name of faith-based initiatives, traditional values, and a new, more spiritual America. Free speech in this context is framed as anti-Christian, anti-American activity, and high-level cognitive analysis is viewed as a dangerous pursuit (Neiwert 2003; Winston 2007).

CHRISTOTAINMENT AND THE POLITICAL FUNDAMENTALIST MEDIA EMPIRE: THE POWER OF POPULAR CULTURE

The media empire that political fundamentalists and Dominionists have constructed in less than three decades boggles the mind. In addition to the well-known Pat Robertsons, James Dobsons, and James Kennedys, countless other, lesser-known figures with religious-based political-action organizations make strategic use of the political fundamentalists' media empire to further specific agendas in the Dominionist orbit: Gary Bauer of American Values, Donald Wildmon of the American Family Association, and Tony Perkins of the Family Research Council. The electronic reach of these individuals and their groups is virtually unlimited. The success of the religious Right is intimately tied to this multifaceted media empire with its ability to market Jesus in creative new ways. At the time of this writing, political fundamentalist media outlets are not as big and widely dispersed as secular networks, but this relationship is changing. Christian radio is booming because of the success of contemporary Christian music. Between 2002 and 2005, the Christian radio audience grew 33 percent. Since 1998, the audience has grown 85 percent. Such growth in English-language media is unprecedented (Blake 2005; Thomas 2005; Sheler 2006).

The political fundamentalist media empire is, at the end of the first decade of the twenty-first century, an omnipresent feature of the American theological and political landscape. The power of the empire is testimony to the organizational abilities of the zealots and, in turn, to the threat they pose to the fragile precepts of American democracy. The informational enclave that they have created for the faithful is unprecedented in human history. Via the power of this knowledge vortex, millions and millions of people have been persuaded into joining amazingly well-regulated and forceful voting blocs. While they certainly do not all think and receive fundamentalist media messages the same way, a huge percentage of them vote the same way and engage in comparable forms of political action.

Through the use of media-created networks, political fundamentalist churches become local command centers for political fundamentalist, mainly Republican, candidates and organization centers for particular social/moral political issues. Many of the children who are reared in such environments either go to Christian schools or are homeschooled. In these situations they are rarely confronted with concepts or data that contest the biblical certainties and the interpretations of scriptures that become theological and political verities. In these places, children learn that God created the world in six days, evolution is a satanic theory, liberals and progressives are attempting to destroy God's sacred plan for America, public education is a secular humanist plot to wipe out Christianity, and so on. Those youth who grow up in the knowledge enclave and decide to attend college are channeled into fundamentalist colleges. These "institutions of higher learning" advance the central purpose of political fundamentalist education: obedience. Those who fail to break away from this indoctrination take their places as soldiers for Jesus, working to subvert an open, diverse democratic society.

Most Americans are unaware of how big a network the previously discussed CBN is. It employs one thousand people and has broadcasting centers in three U.S. cities and in Israel, India, Ukraine, and the Philippines. And, of course, CBN is merely one fish in the political fundamentalist sea of media—an empire that has come into being outside of mainstream attention. With more and more TV and radio stations coming on the air every month, the faithful can now subscribe to a Christian direct-broadcast satellite network that broadcasts more than forty evangelical radio and TV stations, including God TV, the Miracle Channel, and Smile of a Child TV. Recently added to the channels available on Sky Angel are the Military Channel and Fox News Channel. A typical feature on CBN might include a "magazine package" with a tour of Jerusalem and an interview with Mel Gibson. Along with Gibson, a CBN reporter visits many of the locations where *The Passion* was filmed.

Other reporters walk through the Garden of Gethsemane where Jesus prayed on the night he was arrested. The journalist meanders down the Via Dolarosa, the road on which Jesus carried the cross. Along the narrow Via Dolarosa, tourists are everywhere, and the reporter conducts interviews with individuals, many weeping, who tell him that their visit to Jerusalem means so much more after having viewed Gibson's *The Passion*. As a moment of crisis, September 11 catalyzed the political fundamentalist media empire, and the growth has not diminished since. Features grounded in theological justifications for the War on Terror and the battle against Islam look and technologically "feel" like *Dateline NBC*, ABC's *20/20*, or CNN's *The Situation Room* with Wolf Blitzer.

Sky Angel subscribers can get all of the Christian-based current affairs programs, talk shows, sermons, movies, dramas, sitcoms, reality shows, and children's cartoons they want and supplement them with the right-wing "advocacy journalism" of Fox News. As the years pass, political fundamentalists have become increasingly adept at cloaking a heavily biased and news-distorting viewpoint as fair and balanced. The "talking heads" that appear on political fundamentalist news are chosen from a limited consortium of theological leaders and Republican politicians. Even on the financial-management and marriage-counseling programs, ideological coaching is omnipresent. Most researchers posit that such media help steer issues from the fringe to the mainstream. For example, the effort of Terry Schiavo's parents to prolong her life had been covered in detail by CBN and other political fundamentalist media for years before the story moved into the mainstream and became an issue fervently debated in the U.S. Congress. The ability of the political fundamentalist empire to shape the discourse of American politics in the contemporary era is daunting (Blake 2005; Hedges 2006; Klemp 2007).

Obviously no media news can be objective given the constraints of context (time and place); however, the political fundamentalist media empire has become particularly skillful at covertly influencing audiences. Focus on the Family's children's radio show and cartoon series *Adventures in Odyssey,* which first aired in 1987, is an excellent example of how political fundamentalist/Dominionist Christotainment operates. The central objective of the long-running and widely heard and watched series is to inculcate Christian values and make sure child viewers begin to understand a larger political fundamentalist worldview. Focus on the Family founder, James Dobson, has grandiose expectations for *Odyssey,* as he has produced more covert versions of the show for public schools and distribution to nations around the world, such as China. Central to the purpose of *Odyssey* in all of its versions is the stealth promotion of political fundamentalist ideological and theological viewpoints among child viewers.

Odyssey's child protagonists have sometimes found themselves in circumstances marked by interreligious warfare. In two episodes, for example, Alice and Timmy are transported to a country called the Northern Territory of Merus, a land curiously similar to a nineteenth-century America where the followers of God are fighting the terrorist "pagans." The pagans are barbarians, and the followers of God, of course, are all moral, civilized, sympathetic, and honorable characters. As immigrant pagans are attempting to impose their religion on the righteous, God commands his followers to bomb the pagan temple. As God's army defeats the pagans, the faithful want to crown the commander, Fletcher, king, but he says that *man* must not rule over the kingdom; only God is entitled to establish a government (ReligiousTolerance 2002; Klemp 2007). The violent and theocratic Dominionist themes embedded in the show are evident. Many observers find remarkable the open delineation of such perspectives in what vociferous defenders label as an innocent kid's show promoting traditional values. It doesn't take an expert textual analyst to discern what is going on here.

Political fundamentalists and Dominionists didn't completely understand the power of their Christotainment until the 1999 release of the action-packed apocalyptic blockbuster *The Omega Code*. The typical Hollywood marketing tactics were not employed in this movie's launch. Promoters used no prerelease press viewings, solicited no reviews in the standard print and TV outlets, and spent virtually nothing on advertising. Matthew Crouch, son of Paul and Jan Crouch, owners of the largest Christian TV network, Trinity Broadcasting Network (TBN), exclusively used his parents' communication system to promote the film. As a result, *The Omega Code* became the tenth-largest money-making film on its opening weekend.

These statistics startled the media establishment, Hollywood moguls, and the owners and executives at TBN. Robert Higley, TBN's vice president of sales and affiliate relations, spoke for the network when he stated, "We had no idea we had that power in America" (Blake 2005). It did not take long for media entrepreneurs to notice the power of the political fundamentalist market. By 2006 media corporations were scrambling to tap into this huge market, as the world's largest media conglomerate, Rupert Murdoch's New Corporation (NewsCorp) created FoxFaith. This division of Murdoch's media empire was dedicated to Christotainment, promising to produce at least twelve Christian films per year (McKenna 2006).

In the commodified, globalized hyperreality of the twenty-first century, all dimensions of life can be bought and sold—the market helps shape all social functions. The salvation and ideology of the political fundamentalists are often promoted in a package—be born again, join our political movement, and gain free access to our real estate agents, financial counselors, twelve-step program for sex addicts, and child care. Call now; operators in our church are standing by. In the political fundamentalist media empire, the raison d'être of capitalism is not lost: growth and expansion at any cost. In pursuing this goal, "pastropreneurs" have come to understand that they must be superior marketers, talented salespeople, gifted fund-raisers, and professional money managers. Salvation here has been turned into a product, as religion, ideology, entertainment, and commercial dynamics blend into a church casserole of indistinguishable ingredients. As customers consume the casserole, they obtain not vitamins and minerals but conceptions of success, communities of friends (as business contacts), a shared mythology, and collective icons, rituals, and narratives around which to build their identities in a complex and ambiguous world.

Obviously, the power of consumption-based practices in a society grounded in popular culture is not lost on the political fundamentalists and Dominionists. Popular culture's power involves its ability to connect with us on a wide variety of levels. If popular culture and Christotainment only engaged us on a conscious and traditional rational level, then research into the domains would be rather simple and straightforward. We could employ commonly used statistical and ethnographic research methods to find out with some degree of precision what is going on in the production and reception dimensions of the process. But like the social world in general, such assumptions about popular culture/Christotainment operating only at the conscious/rational level of human endeavor is profoundly reductionistic and simplistic.

Traditional modes of research typically engage only this conscious/rational level. Interviews that take what is said at a literal level and survey instruments using graduated scales (strongly agree, agree, no opinion, disagree, and strongly disagree) fail to contextualize participant responses in larger social and cultural contexts, historical moments, and political processes. They also neglect levels of the social unconsciousness revealed in subtle (and, as we've seen, not so subtle) ways in the productions of popular culture and, of course, in the individual receiver's unconsciousness. In so many research projects in which I and countless others have been engaged, interviewees have a terribly difficult time articulating the diverse influences popular-cultural engagements have on them.

This is not an unusual finding in contemporary societies, for this is a topic that is rarely, if ever, discussed in public or private conversations. Many respondents simply have no experience considering such effects or even realizing that such influences exist. Many social structures and sociopolitical assumptions—for example, the naturalness of consumption in everyday human life—are so taken for granted that they are invisible to the average viewer. Many political fundamentalists (and, obviously, many others who believe violence, sex, and many other dimensions of popular media exert deleterious consequences) have thought about these dynamics in their own theological and ideological contexts. In the political fundamentalist milieu, observers focus on the satanic and secular humanist influences they believe to be embedded in many aspects of popular and youth culture. Nevertheless, there is a prevalent belief in Western societies that entertainment is, after all, simply entertainment. A significant portion of the population simply dismisses the idea that there are embedded and often imperceptible social, cultural, and political inscriptions in these media productions.

A short chat with many of the viewers of *Adventures in Odyssey*, as previously referenced, reveals that, at a conscious level, they will not admit that it is more than a "cute radio show and cartoon." Those who produce media for Christotainment know there's more to the story than what is being told to academic ethnographers in such interviews. These political fundamentalist media experts have become adept at framing their narratives in a way that makes sense in pop-cultural, entertainment-based settings. This works well around numerous categories of power. For example, around gender dynamics, time and again we can see particular forms of gender inscription that is central to the theology and ideology of political fundamentalism and the Christotainment stories produced.

In everything from Marabel Morgan's 1970's best seller *The Total Woman*, Laura Doyle's *The Surrendered Wife*, Henlen Andelin's *Fascinating Womanhood*, Sharon Jaynes's *Becoming the Woman of His Dreams*, and J. S. Salt's *How to Be the Almost Perfect Wife: By Husbands Who Know* to the *Left Behind* series, the images of the alpha manly man and the submissive Christian woman are omnipresent. The quantity and fervor of these portrayals fit to perfection the needs of the recovery of patriarchy perceived to have been fatally weakened by the "feminazi" movement. Millions of men and women have bought into these "recovered" gender roles in a way that helped make feminism a dirty word in numerous contexts. The political fundamentalist and Dominionist media empire is alive and well, growing and adjusting itself to meet the challenges of an ever-changing hyperreality and the ideological needs of the moment. Growth is the order of the day, and at the end of the first decade of the twenty-first century, there are few signs that Christotainment's momentum is slowing (Mazur and Koda 2001; Frykholm 2005).

Left Behind references pepper sermons around America as fundamentalist preachers use books' and movies' apocalyptic images to engage the attention of their listeners. Rev. Gary Frazier, for example, the founder of Discovery Ministries out of Texas, preaches to a tour group in Israel (the Holy Land) visiting where Armageddon will take place. As the tourists look at the vista from the top of the hill of Megiddo, Frazier explains what will take place during the final days. "How many of you have read the *Left Behind* prophecy novels?" asks Frazier, and most people in the group raise their hands. With his voice filled with emotion, the preacher tells the crowd, "The thing that you must know is that the next event on God's prophetic plan, we believe, is the catching away of the saints in the presence of the Lord. We call it 'the Rapture.'"

This kind of fiction-based theology "works" in a marketing sense because in America it exploits the Americanized and well-liked Jesus. In a nation that is divided along every conceivable axis of race, class, gender, sexuality, ideology, and religion, Jesus remains a popular and cross-cultural, albeit an unstudied and slightly mysterious, persona. Indeed, if there is one thing on which many Americans can agree, it is that Jesus is "good." This has become more and more the case with the evangelical effort to make him more of a personality over the last several decades. In this American incarnation, Jesus has become, and is of course sold as, the exemplary male, the action hero, the representation of human possibility.

The Savior in the twenty-first century is the commodified American "uniter, not divider" who can bring all theologies together. For the political fundamentalists, this he's-got-personality Jesus is problematic in that many nonbelievers and peoples of other faiths do not even view Jesus as Christian. In the same way, Thomas Jefferson argued almost two hundred years ago in his meticulously researched "Jefferson Bible" that people have to make a distinction between Jesus's religion and religion about Jesus. It will be fascinating to watch the effects on this ecumenical view of the Redeemer of the political fundamentalist marketing remake of Jesus into the kick-ass warrior. The action-based video depictions of an intolerant, macho savior could affect the current era of good feelings toward Jesus (Prothero 2003; Unger 2005; Smiga 2006).

Such concerns are not a part of the fundamentalist mind-set, as they continue to turn out a seemingly infinite amount of Christotainment. Every year, the true believers produce thousands of albums and movies; they generate a new Christian gothic novel every week, along with thousands of other Christian fiction genres, including Christian knockoffs of Harlequin romances; they publish fundamentalist guides to sex, magazines, leaflets, and brochures; they manufacture posters of Christian rock stars and other figures, greeting cards, games, T-shirts (one favorite with the caption "fast break" sports a picture of a Christian basketball team with half of its members flying off the court in the Rapture), coffee mugs ("drink ye, for the Lord is good"), jewelry with messages, and much more.

The best-selling Christian books do not directly address theological or ideological topics but are concerned more with family issues, life crises, dealing with dying parents, and marital problems. In the spirit of fundamentalist anti-intellectualism, students of Christian books note several trends, including an effort to make books look less like traditional books, with larger and larger print, more white space in the margins, and a steady decline in page length. While books are still profoundly important in Christian bookstores, the rise in Christotainment products has made fundamentalist books only one of many articles for sale in such venues. In 1978, for example, 68 percent of Christian bookstores sales were books; by the 1990s, print materials accounted for only 49 percent of sales, a figure that has held steady through the first decade of the twenty-first century (Moore 1994; McDannell 1995; Hoover 2005; The Church Bookstore 2008).

Interestingly, political and analytical theological books do not sell particularly well in Christian bookstores. Such a reality may provide compelling insight into the politics of fundamentalism in particular and of hyperreality in general. Unlike a previous time when particular forms of rational argumentation convinced individuals of the legitimacy of theological and ideological positions, in the contemporary electronic reality, such logical appeals are not nearly as effective in altering consciousness as culture-based forms of affective and pleasure-producing texts. This is, of course, the heart and soul of Christotainment with its power to persuade around a politics and theology of pleasure. The books, movies, merchandise, video games, cartoons, TV series, music, and so forth of Christotainment often work best as they construct a cosmos of sentiment and feeling.

A display in a Precious Moments gift shop reads, "Precious Moments are your passport to loving, caring, and sharing." In this caring cosmos, sentiment always trumps reason and analysis. An evocation of emotion is far more important than a cogent insight. In making such an argument, I am in no way devaluing the importance of affect and emotion in human affairs. The point is not that reason should take precedence over feeling but that political fundamentalists manipulate theological and ideological investment by deploying affective factors in crass and covert ways. Our careful study of Christotainment reveals the myriad ways that such sentiment is used to promote blind forms of theological belief, an unthinking patriotism, a retrenchment of patriarchy and white supremacy, and the demonization of the other.

Those individuals and families who trim their trees with "His truth is marching on," "Trust and obey," and "Onward Christian soldiers" Precious Moments ornaments are not simply celebrating Christmas but also reaffirming state and patriarchal power. The commodification of Christmas in this context is situated in a mythologized consumer universe of sentiment: the nostalgic idea and the affect it creates around returning to the ways our ancestors celebrated Christmas are simply not based on historical data. Contemporary notions of a traditional Christmas were created at the end of the nineteenth and beginning of the twentieth centuries. Someone who lived before 1840 in the United States would find these romantic notions of traditional celebrations of Christmas hard to fathom. So much of what political fundamentalists seek to "recover" from America's Christian past simply constitutes recently manufactured dimensions of affect-producing Christotainment. The rewriting of Christian history around these family-oriented, loving holidays and other rituals is a key practice in the construction of consciousness-changing affective investment (Rycenga 2001; Clarkson 2004). No one, however, can dispute its marketability and ideological power.

References

Answersingenesis. 2008. Creation scientists and teachers comment. *Answersingenesis*, www.answersingenesis.org/articles/2007/08/03/creation-scientists-teachers-comment (accessed August 29, 2008).

Belden, D. 2008. Backwards Christian soldiers. *Australian Rationalist*, www.rationalist.com.au/archive/79/p34-36_ar79.pdf (accessed July 15, 2008).

Blake, M. 2005. Stations of the cross. *Columbia Journalism Review*, May–June, http://cjarchieves.org/issues/2005/3/blake-evangelist.asp? (accessed July 15, 2008).

Blumenthal, M. 2005. Air Jesus. *MediaTransparency*, http://mediatransparency.org (accessed August 29, 2008).

Chancey, M. 2007. A textbook example of the Christian Right: The National Council on Bible Curriculum in public schools. *Journal of the American Academy of Religion* 75, no. 3: 554–581.

Church Bookstore, The. 2008. Website. The Church Bookstore, www.thechurchbookstore.com/a.php?articleid=12679 (accessed July 5, 2008).

Clarkson, F. 2004. Theocracy vs. democracy in America. *Daily Kos*, www.dailykos.com/story/2004/12/29/191619/98 (accessed August 29, 2008).

Corn, D. 2008. McCain's spiritual guide: Destroy Islam. *Mother Jones*, March 12, www.motherjones.com/washington_dispatch/2008/03/john-mccain-rod-parsley-spiritual-guide.html (accessed August 29, 2008).

Creation Museum. 2008. www.creationmuseum.org (accessed August 29, 2008).

Eco, U. 1995. Ur-fascism. *New York Review of Books*, June 22, www.pegc.us/archive/Articles/eco_ur-fascism.pdf (accessed August 29, 2008).

Economist. 2005. Jesus, CEO: Churches as businesses. *Economist*, December 20, http://findarticles.com/p/articles/mi_hb5037/is_200512/ai_n18254076 (accessed August 29, 2008).

Forbes, B. 2005. Introduction: Finding religion in unexpected places. In *Religion and popular culture in America*, ed. B. Forbes and J. Mahan. 2nd ed. Berkeley: University of California Press.

Fredrikson, P. 2006. No pain, no gain. In *Mel Gibson's Bible: Religion, popular culture, and* The Passion of the Christ, ed. T. Beal and T. Linafelt. Chicago: University of Chicago Press.

Frykholm, A. 2005. The gender dynamics of the *Left Behind* series. In *Religion and popular culture in America*, ed. B. Forbes and J. Mahan. 2nd ed. Berkeley: University of California Press.

Goldberg, M. 2007. The rise of Christian nationalism. *Humanist* 67, no. 5: 29–33.

Gresson, A. 1995. *The recovery of race in America*. Minneapolis: University of Minnesota Press.

_______. 2004. *America's atonement*. New York: Peter Lang Publishing.

HBO. 2008. Interview with Justin Fatica. HBO, www.hbo.com/docs/programs/hardasnails/subject_interview.html (accessed August 29, 2008).

Hedges, C. 2006. *American fascists: The Christian Right and the war on America*. New York: Free Press.

Hendershot, H. 1995. *Shaking the world for Jesus: Media and conservative evangelical culture*. Chicago: University of Chicago Press.

Hoover, S. 2005. The cross at Willow Creek: Seeker religion and the contemporary marketplace. In *Religion and popular culture in America*, ed. B. Forbes and J. Mahan. 2nd ed. Berkeley: University of California Press.

Hubert, D. 2006. G. I. Jesus? Denouncement of right-wing Christian BattleCry. BuzzFlash, www.buzzflash.com/contributors/06/05/con06203.html (accessed August 29, 2008).

Hutson, J. 2007. Pentagon adopts missionary position on homoerotic art. Talk2Action, www.talk2action.org/story/2007/8/8/182310/3445 (accessed August 29, 2008).

Information Clearing House. 2007. We're dealing with a Christian Taliban. Information Clearing House, September 7, www.informationclearninghouse.info/article18334.htm (accessed July 2, 2008).

Jones, L. 2007. Onward Christianist soldiers. World Can't Wait, December 2, www.worldcantwait.net/index.php?option=com-content&task (accessed August 29, 2008).

Kincheloe, J. 2001. *Getting beyond the facts: Teaching social studies/social sciences in the twenty-first century*. 2nd ed. New York: Peter Lang.

Kincheloe, J., and S. Steinberg. 1997. *Changing multiculturalism*. London: Open University Press.

Kincheloe, J., S. Steinberg, N. Rodriguez, and R. Chennault. 1998. *White reign: Deploying whiteness in America*. New York: St. Martin's Press.

Klemp, N. 2007. Beyond God-talk: Understanding the Christian Right from the ground up. *Polity* 39: 522–544.

LaHaye, T. 1980. *The battle for the mind*. Old Tappan, NJ: Fleming H. Revell.

Leupp, G. 2005. Fighting for the work of the Lord: Everybody's talking about Christian fascism. *Counterpunch*, www.counterpunch.org/leupp01131005.htm (accessed August 29, 2008).

Little, W. 2006. Jesus's extreme makeover. In *Mel Gibson's Bible: Religion, popular culture, and* The Passion of the Christ, ed. T. Beal and T. Linafelt. Chicago: University of Chicago Press.

Mahan, J. 2005. Conclusion: Establishing a dialogue about religion and popular culture. In *Religion and popular culture in America*, ed. B. Forbes and J. Mahan. 2nd ed. Berkeley: University of California Press.

Marquez, J. 2006. Lights! Camera! Action! In *Mel Gibson's Bible: Religion, popular culture, and* The Passion of the Christ, ed. T. Beal and T. Linafelt. Chicago: University of Chicago Press.

Mazur, E., and T. Koda. 2001. Happiest place on earth: Disney's America and the commodification of religion. In *God in the details: American religion in popular culture*, ed. E. Mazur and K. McCarthy. New York: Routledge.

Mazur, E., and K. McCarthy, eds. 2001. *God in the details: American religion in popular culture*. New York: Routledge.

McAlister, M. 2003. An empire of their own. *Nation*, September 4, www.thenation.com/doc/20030922/mcalister (accessed August 29, 2008).

McAuliffe, J. 2008. An interview with R. J. Rushdoony. The Forerunner, www.forerunner.com/revolution/rush.html (accessed August 29, 2008).

McDannell, C. 1995. *Material Christianity*. New Haven, CT: Yale University Press.

McKenna, B. 2006. The prophet motive: U.S. faithful form rich market. *Globe and Mail*, September 25, www.theglobeandmail.com/servelet/sotry/lac.20060925.rfaith25/tpstory/business (accessed August 29, 2008).

Meyer Sound. 2006. Fellowship Church worships with Meyer Sound's MILO. Meyer Sound, www.meyersound.com/news/2006/fellowship_church (accessed August 29, 2008).

Miles, J. 2006. The art of *The Passion*. In *Mel Gibson's Bible: Religion, popular culture, and* The Passion of the Christ, ed. T. Beal and T. Linafelt. Chicago: University of Chicago Press.

MinistryWatch. 2008. Christian Broadcasting Network/CBN/700 Club/Pat Robertson. MinistryWatch.com, www.ministrywatch.com/mw2.1/f_sumrpt.asp?ein=540678752 (accessed August 29, 2008).

Moore, R. 1994. *Selling God: American religion in the marketplace of culture*. New York: Oxford University Press.

NationMaster. 2008. Biography of Rushdoony. NationMaster.com, www.nationmaster.com/encyclopedia/Rousas-John-Rushdoony (accessed August 29, 2008).

Neiwert, D. 2003. Rush, newspeak, and fascism: An exegesis. Orcinus, http://dneiwert.blogspot.com/rush%20newspeak%20%20fascism.pdf (accessed July 2, 2008).

Ontario Consultants on Religious Tolerance. 2005. Why did Hurricane Katrina happen? Religious Tolerance. http://www.religioustolerance.org/tsunami04.htm (accessed July 3, 2008).

Peterson, G. 2005. The Internet and Christian and Muslim communities. In *Religion and popular culture in America*, ed. B. Forbes and J. Mahan. 2nd ed. Berkeley: University of California Press.

Pfohl, S. 2006. *Left Behind:* Religion, technology, and the flight from the flesh. *ctheory.net*, www.ctheory.net/articles.aspx?id=557 (accessed August 29, 2008).

Prothero, S. 2003. *American Jesus: How the Son of God became a national icon*. New York: Farrar, Straus, and Giroux.

ReligiousTolerance. 2002. Conservative Christian radio programs which target Wiccans and other neopagans. ReligiousTolerance.org, www.religioustolerance.org/chrw_rad.htm (accessed August 29, 2008).

Rodriguez, N., and L. Villaverde. 2000. *Dismantling white privilege*. New York: Peter Lang Publishing.

Romanowski, W. 2005. Evangelicals and popular music: The contemporary Christian music industry. In *Religion and popular culture in America*, ed. B. Forbes and J. Mahan. 2nd ed. Berkeley: University of California Press.

Rycenga, J. 2001. Dropping in for the holidays: Christmas as commercial ritual at the Precious Moments Chapel. In *God in the details: American religion in popular culture*, ed. E. Mazur and K. McCarthy. New York: Routledge.

Scalia, A. 2002. God's justice and ours. *First Things* 123: 17–21, www.firsthings.com/ftissues/ft0205/articles/scalia.html (accessed July 2, 2008).

Scalzi, J. 2007. Your Creation Museum report. Scalzi.com, http://scalzi.com/whatever/?p=121 (accessed August 29, 2008).

Sheler, J. 2006. *Believers: A journey into evangelical America*. New York: Penguin.

Smiga, G. 2006. The good news of Mel Gibson's *Passion*. In *Mel Gibson's Bible: Religion, popular culture, and* The Passion of the Christ, ed. T. Beal and T. Linafelt. Chicago: University of Chicago Press.

Taylor, M. 2006. The offense of flesh. In *Mel Gibson's Bible: Religion, popular culture, and* The Passion of the Christ, ed. T. Beal and T. Linafelt. Chicago: University of Chicago Press.

Thomas, P. 2005. Christian fundamentalism and the media. *Media Development*, www.wacc.org.uk/wacc/publications/media_development/2005_2christian_fun damentalism_and_themedia (accessed July 3, 2008).

Unger, C. 2005. American rapture. *Vanity Fair*, December, www.vanityfair.com/politics/features/2005/12/rapture200512 (accessed August 29, 2008).

Urban, H. 2007. Machiavelli meets the Religious Right: Michael Ledeen, the neoconservatives, and the political uses of fundamentalism. *Journal of Ecumenical Studies* 42, no. 1: 76–97.

Weitzel, R. 2008. U.S. military's Middle East crusade for Christ. Countercurrents.org, June 10, www.countercurrents.org/weitzel100608.htm (accessed July 3, 2008).

Wilson, B. 2007. What if God tells you your blender is evil? Talk2Action, www.talk2action.com (accessed July 2, 2008).

Winston, D. 2007. Back to the future: Religion, politics, and the media. *American Quarterly* 59, no. 3: 969–989.

World Can't Wait. 2006. A carnival of theocrats. *Daily Kos*, www.dailykos.com.story/2006/5/15/04817/0699 (accessed July 5, 2008).

Yurica, K. 2004. The despoiling of America. Information Clearing House, www.informationclearinghouse.info/article5646.htm (accessed August 29, 2008).

III

Onward Christian Drivers

Theocratic Nationalism and the Cultural Politics of "NASCAR Nation"

JOSHUA I. NEWMAN AND MICHAEL D. GIARDINA

Wherever we look in American society today, we see links between sports and religion and even the confusion of one with the other. . . . At some points in the past they have seemed at odds, but recently, and increasingly, they have served one another and become inseparable.

—Robert J. Higgs (1995, 1)

Our modern-day myth arc goes something like this: as the juggernaut of modernity dragooned the cultural and social fabric of a post-Tocquevillian America (Levy 2006), a market-based materialist praxis of competing bodies and competitive ideologies (competing for resources, jobs, food, shelter, the American dream, and so forth) refocused a population's attention *away* from asceticism, Puritanism, and the "moral imperatives" of civic engagement and *toward* discourses of individual success, "hard work," the disciplined body, and an eternally *un*achievable meritocracy. As a result, sport—the cultural form that perhaps best brings to life such an industrialized, hypercompetitive, modernized, marketized hegemony—began in many ways to metaphorically displace religion as the prevailing "opiate" of the American masses (Guttmann 1986; Higgs 1995). While religious pundits and critics alike may quiver at such a trifling dismissal of organized faith's hallucinogenic qualities, it is nonetheless hard to argue against the notions that, in contemporary America, (1) sport culture has ascended to the forefront of social, cultural, political, and economic relations,[1] and (2) as the epigraph to this chapter suggests, this contextually specific sporting boon has not necessarily come at the expense of organized religion's stronghold on the imaginaries of the American populace; rather, it has been abetted by industrialized America's underlying, yet resolute, devotion to new forms of "muscular" Christianity (Guttmann 1978; Putney 2003). Despite ostensible contradictions between modern sport's "win at all costs" pathos and the "love thy neighbor" ethos of Christianity (evangelical or otherwise), today's neo-Rooseveltian sporting ascetic squarely situates these amusements and pastimes as vital components of the character- and nation-building machinations acting upon, and performed by, a national populace living in the apocryphal (new) "American century."

In this chapter, we argue that corporate sport is now returning the favor. Despite a tendency among "serious" cultural scholars to trivialize sport through academic renditions of erudite watercooler talk in bookish jock speak (see the critiques offered by Andrews 2002; Donnelly 2000; T. Miller 2001), sport has emerged as a significant, if not powerful, technology of citizenship under the throws of America's "Great Moving Right Show" (see Hall 1984). And if the soul of the Christian Right movement has in recent decades galvanized that rightward shift through an offensive, if seemingly populist, public pedagogy emanating from the telegenic evangelism and linguistic stylings of the "moral majority," the body cultures of sport have equally given performative and corporeal credence to this mind-soul solidarity. The "Right bodies" of the contemporary sporting spectacular now, more than ever, articulate a normative mind-body-soul discursive triumvirate through a full panoply of sanctimonious declarations of celebrity athlete parishioners. For example, well-known sports figures, such as National Football League (NFL) quarterback Kurt Warner, professional golfer Zach Johnson, NFL head coach Tony Dungy, deceased former player Reggie White, boxer Evander Holyfield, and many outspoken members of the Colorado Rockies baseball team actively employ a complex regime of mediated evangelism imbricated in public expressions of their chosen religion (Leitch 2008), while a sizable majority of other amateur and professional athletes similarly engage in various religiously inflected signifying acts (e.g., emphatically pointing to the heavens after scoring a goal, publicly asking "the Lord" for success in an important match, or brandishing "WWJD" bracelets or cruciform necklaces in "postgame interviews"). Likewise, scores of journalists (e.g., Liz Peek, Thomas O'Toole, and Steve Hubbard) and sporting intermediaries (e.g., Fellowship of Christian Athletes and Athletes in Action) have ascended to prominence in the public sphere through their discursive musings and mediations on the celebration of American sport's seemingly ineluctable ability to foster "faith," "fellowship," and "the right sort of values" among both viewers and participants alike.

By way of this critical analysis, we argue that in a what might be described as a postpious sporting malaise ("sport as business" meets "playing for the love of the game")—whereby grand religiosport narratives have been constructed as theological/moralist alternatives to mainstream stories of steroid crises and superhuman body performance (e.g., Lance Armstrong, Barry Bonds, and Roger Clemens), cheating scandals (e.g., the much ballyhooed surveillance schemes of the NFL's most successful franchise, the New England Patriots), misogyny from high-profile athletes (e.g., Mike Tyson, Brett Myers, Rae Carruth, and various members of the Minnesota Vikings), and the demise of (faux) amateurism (e.g., various Olympic Games scandals and rampant recruiting violations within *almost every* NCAA member institution)—many prominent celebrity athletes and mass media elites have recentered the cultural pedagogies of the North American sporting popular around a hyper-Christian politicoreligious lingua franca in the tradition of a fundamentalist Right coalition ushered in by the likes of Pat Robertson, Jerry Falwell, James Dobson, Mike Huckabee, George Allen, and Rick Santorum (Scherer 2004).

To give focus to our analysis here, we dissect the most "righteous" bodies of the North American sporting popular: the brazenly "virtuous" corporealities made popular through the performative politics of the National Association for Stock Car Auto Racing (NASCAR) and its celebrity drivers. As we aim to illustrate, NASCAR's brand of auto-sport culture offers a contextually significant mélange of contemporary "Southern" (read regionalized, white, masculine) identities, regimes of crass capital accumulation, new idioms of theocratic nationalism(s), and politically important forms of proselytizing sporting piety.

As members of a collective configuration dominated by the identity politics languaged around discursive formations of "warriors for Christ" (Shaftel 2008b, D4) and "NASCAR dads" (Elder and Greene 2007; Vavrus 2007), this conglomeration of NASCAR's drivers, owners, vendors, media personalities, and fans have in recent years been remediated under the popular racin'- and God-loving sobriquet "NASCAR Nation," a double entendre that refers both to an imagined spectator community dominated by "rural, small-town, mostly white, Southern fans of America's fastest growing spectator sport" (Derbyshire 2003, 29) and to the broader configurations of conservative American nationalism under the George W. Bush presidency.[2] Although Christianity and race car culture have shared a mutually sacrosanct bond since the first green flag waved on the sandy beaches of Daytona, these articulations of Jesus Christ, politics, and stock cars have in recent years been made more important, if not imperative, by their dialectic interdependencies with a contextually specific "conjuncture" of corporate capitalist neoliberalism and faith-based, GOP-dominated neoconservatism.

It should come as no surprise, then, that as the broader NASCAR Nation has seen a resurgence of evangelical fundamentalist discourse during the "glorious" Ronald Reagan/George (H.) W. Bush/Mike Huckabee era, the sport that has most closely aligned itself with each striation of this theocratic and political neoconservatism has experienced tremendous growth in an otherwise stagnating North American sport marketplace.[3] And with specific regard to *Christotainment*'s central theme, no other North American sporting institution has been so morally commodified, theocratically entertainmentized, and openly evangelicized over the past few decades than has NASCAR. Indeed, from top to bottom, and when read through the politics of representation operative in the current sociopolitical context, the identity politics of the NASCAR Nation (popularly) imagined community have been repackaged as spectator-based sporting solidarity for a post–September 11 neoconservative "biblicalism" (Hedges 2007). And while this theocratization of stock car culture has partially (and perhaps organically) evolved out of the sport's Bible Belt genealogy and white, working-class regionality, it has in recent years been problematically inculcated and cross-fertilized by the trappings of fundamentalist ideologues, corporate capitalists, and right-wing political intermediaries.

In what follows, then, we illustrate how the cultural politics of NASCAR Nation have been co-opted by the conjunctural juggernaut of neoconservative polity and neoliberal capitalism and how stock car and political intermediaries have ordered the confluence of the *sign value of stock car iconicity* to the "*surplus value of rapture*" (Hedges 2007) to reproduce the iniquitous conditions of production (and consumption) within broader formations of NASCAR Nation and beyond. Moreover, we make the case that NASCAR has been a key ingredient in the sociopolitical adhesive that sutures neoliberal market regimes to neoconservative identities and ideologies within contemporary Americana (and vice versa). While neoliberalism and neoconservatism are two distinct "political rationalities" with few overlapping qualities, that conjuncture, to paraphrase Wendy Brown (2006), has been effective in hollowing out a democratic political culture and producing undemocratic forms of citizenship. It has produced a condition whereby *citizens of the conjuncture*, Brown writes, "love and want neither freedom nor equality . . . expect neither truth nor accountability in government and state actions . . . [are] not distressed by exorbitant concentrations of political and economic power, routine abrogations of the rule of law, or distinctly undemocratic formulations of national purpose at home or abroad" (2006, 692).

But how are these discursive formations of citizenship formulated, articulated, and regulated, and by whom? How are the auspices of "a rationality that is expressly amoral at the level of both ends and means (neoliberalism)" allowed to paradoxically intersect with a rationality "that is expressly moral and regulatory (neoconservatism)" (Brown 2006, 692)? More importantly, "how does support for governance modeled on the firm and normative social fabric of self-interest marry or jostle against support for governance modeled on church authority and a normative social fabric of self-sacrifice and long-term filial loyalty, the very fabric shredded by unbridled capitalism" (Brown 2006, 692)? In what follows, we sequentially respond to each of these questions by rethinking and illuminating the role sport culture, and particularly NASCAR, plays in normalizing the logics of citizenship within this contextually specific neoliberal/neoconservative conjuncture.

SHEPHERDS AND MISSIONARIES OF A POST–SEPTEMBER 11 *APOCALYPTO*

Anyone who has ever attended a NASCAR event, whether he or she came away with deep affinity or apathy for the sport, will likely agree that the most stultifying aspect of the live spectacle is stock car racing's *inimitable intensity*. A day at the races will leave spectators covered in rubber particles and brake dust, nearly deaf, and in awe of the death-defying proximity at which these drivers race at speeds nearing two hundred miles per hour. And as racing neophytes and well-versed racing aficionadas/os alike will concur, there is a palpable sense of *danger* shared by drivers and fans at these events. This omnipresent anxiety is abetted by the fact that since 2001, some of racing's most-beloved icons—such as Dale Earnhardt Sr. and Adam Petty (progeny of the Petty family racing legacy), as well as lesser-known drivers Kenny Irwin and Tony Roper—have suffered life-ending injuries while competing in the NASCAR circuit. When asked why deaths in auto racing were six times more common than deaths in football, former NASCAR CEO Bill France famously proclaimed, "Because we go six times faster!" (quoted in Zweig 2007, back cover). As most race fans are apt to prognosticate, a hard crash into Turn Four is "all that stands between these drivers and their maker."

And so, perhaps more so than in any other sport, the NASCAR story is underwritten by a subtext of mortality. NASCAR's celebrity athletes (the latter loosely defined as such) are given license (if not encouraged) to *bear witness* to the perilous balance between practicing their craft on earth and practicing for some otherworldly afterlife. As earthly beings who are in "constant dialogue with their own mortality," the vocal majority of NASCAR's cruciform-wielding driver celebrities often evoke the corporeal and narrativized pedagogies of, as race fans often put it, "those who stare death in the face, put the pedal to the metal, and leave the rest up to the good Lord." NASCAR drivers are indeed vocal, if not vigilant, in their appraisal of the Lord's work. As stock car racing's most penitent driver celebrity, Morgan Shepherd, lauded, drivers are free to make the Christian faith a matter of public knowledge: "I commend NASCAR and the sport I'm in. They're not afraid to stand up for what's right. They let us come in and worship. . . . We can pray before races. I know they've taken a lot of heat" (quoted in Newberry 2004, 1).

But this is not an isolated proclamation from a paladin driver-evangelist. Rather, the faithfulness of many of NASCAR's most visible personalities is actively *promoted* as part of NASCAR's "family-oriented" brand identity. In his recent autoethnographic treatise into the "soul" of the sport, L. D. Russell's *Godspeed: Racing Is My Religion* (2007) offers a compelling, if more than slightly doting, account of how NASCAR's tremendous "existential appeal" is a product of an assemblage of strategically orchestrated activities, celebrity discourses, and sanctimonious spaces emanating from, and appealing to, its fans' "value-based" sensibilities. Under such a religious sport order, racing icons such as Shepherd and popular team owner Joe Gibbs (former head coach of the NFL's Washington Redskins) frequently make appearances at revivals and community churches, spread the gospel at local political (always Republican) rallies, and offer witness at promotional events in conjunction with NASCAR races being held in the area (Gibbs and Abraham 2002). Drivers such as David Reutimann and Mark Martin often cite scriptures during postrace interviews (Warren 2007). Moreover, NASCAR's internal publicity department generates numerous Christian-heavy "stories of inspiration" each year, many of which make their way into marketing and promotional materials, major newspapers, television programs, and Internet websites (see Canfield et al. 2003; Smith 2001). The racing league also sanctions its own public relations specialists to develop prepackaged, faith-based media content meditating on the struggles of drivers, owners, and fans "finding their way" through Christ (Associated Press 2004a; Richardson and Darden 1997).

The governing body makes conspicuous the faithfulness of many of the sport's most visible personalities as a way to carve out NASCAR's niche in the crowded North American sport marketplace. Prior to the start of each race—and to the delight of a throng of 150,000 or so race fans in attendance—every driver, pit crew member, team owner, and available NASCAR official spectacularly congregates along pit road to take part in the traditional prerace invocation. In turn, fans stand at attention en masse to hear the Lord's Prayer, a discourse that is almost always evoked by "men of the Christian faith" (Russell 2007). It is important to note that this practice is unique in North America professional sport, as such a mandatory religious appraisal cannot be found in the spectacular machinations of major ballparks, football stadia, hockey rinks, or basketball arenas.

Joe Gibbs famously put the intensifying stock car–Christian nexus in perspective this way: "If you ask me personally, are we better performers for knowing we have a personal relationship with Christ, I think I am. I think God makes everything about everything. I think he has a hand in the outcome" (quoted in *Religion and Ethics Newsweekly* 2001). In the public discourse, this underlying confidence in *preordained success* and faith in "God's plan" seems to be of rudimentary concern for most NASCAR celebrities. As is the case in many other sports, these competitors engage in belief that strength of conviction, rather than human agency, is the overdetermining factor in deciding competitive success. A simple equation has dominated the American public sphere in recent years: Jesus rewards his most loyal servants with the victories and spoils that the Bible says they deserve. Success is a reflection of godliness, and failure awaits the nonbeliever (Domke 2004; Mansfield 2004).

Informed by this sanctimonious pedagogy, *every* top driver on the NASCAR circuit is a member of Motor Racing Outreach (MRO), a non-profit 501(c)(3) Christian organization founded in 1988. The traveling fellowship comprises evangelical chaplains who travel the NASCAR circuit ministering to high-profile drivers, their pit crew members, and their families about the gospel of Jesus Christ (*Religion and Ethics Newsweekly* 2001). Moreover, it facilitates a "traveling Sunday school" for children and conducts Bible study groups that are widely attended by drivers and crew members before each Sunday's race (MacGregor 2005). Sunday morning services are also provided for merchants, vendors, and members of the media. It is not uncommon for these services, and particularly those held for the drivers and their families, to attract 250 to 300 parishioners (Hua 2005; Jenkins 2001). Dale Beaver, former assistant director of the MRO, explained that these meetings teach NASCAR celebrities how to expand their roles in the public promotion of a belief in a Christian manifest destiny: "God is using these people in high profile positions whether they are the drivers or the ones that make it happen. God is using them to say 'I'm still here, I'm not silent, and I still care for you'" (quoted in Fotta 2004, 6).

When asked about their membership in the organization, most drivers recycle a recurring theme: in the life-endangering world of stock car racing, the MRO offers a means to salvation amid the eminent perils of such a high-risk sport (Shaftel 2008a). In an interview for a PBS special titled *NASCAR and Religion* that aired immediately after Dale Earnhardt's passing, "NASCAR wife" (see Lipsyte 2001) Stevie Waltrip, life partner of MRO chairman Darrell Waltrip, explained, "There's always the possibility your husband can be injured or killed. Because of MRO there is a reaching out and comforting to the wives and families" (quoted in *Religion and Ethics Newsweekly* 2001). In these MRO sessions, driver celebrities are counseled on how to spread the gospel by offering testimonials of God's work during pre- and postrace interviews, through Internet confessionals, and in "meet-and-greet sessions" with fans (Clarke 2001).

Take the case of the famous Petty racing family's public pronouncements in the months following the racing death of their son, Adam: Kyle Petty (himself a celebrated NASCAR driver and son of "The King," the legendary NASCAR driver Richard Petty) became a vocal public advocate of the Christian faith and the work of the MRO. In a well-publicized interview, one that reflects the general tenor of most drivers' public contemplations of the afterlife, Petty stated, "The only thing that sustained us was our faith in God. . . . We went straight back to the Bible and read the Bible, and found our comfort there" (quoted in Bochon 2008). The renowned racer, who these days proclaims that he races "for his late son and the Son of God," continued, "Every night before we go to bed we gather to say prayers. That's a big part of who we are and how we handled Adam's death" (quoted in Bochon 2008). Adam's grandfather Richard Petty evoked a similar faith-based public pedagogy: "If you know me, I'm not an emotional person outside, this is the way its supposed to be, now we've got to pick it up and go forward with it because somewhere down the line the Good Lord's got a PLAN and we're a part of that plan." Petty continued, "We've got to continue to go forward to try to make that plan work" (quoted in Bochon 2008). By way of his death on the racetrack and his father's paternal longings for absolution, Adam Petty was transformed into another of the "glorious works" of the Lord. As his father would later intimate, with the "help" of the MRO, Adam's death was a catalyst for reconcentrating his family's devotion and leveraging his celebrity as a way to "spread the gospel": "We've been able to use Adam as a platform to witness to other people. I think in any kind of tragedy, that's what you do. You don't just stop. It's what you do after the tragedy that counts" (quoted in Harris 2005).

In this way, the celebrity paradigms of NASCAR Nation integrate "Q rating" with missionary work. As evangelical Pastor Beaver explained to ABC's *World News Tonight,* for members of the MRO, the logic is clear: "Athletes are so worshipped by the fan base that I try to help these guys deflect that worship to one who is greater than they" (quoted in Harris 2005). To such an end, many of NASCAR's celebrity drivers indeed refer to themselves as "missionaries" (Rhee 2005, 1): "NASCAR is another community, another workplace . . . and any workplace is a mission field. If you want to call us missionaries, sure, but we're here amongst our friends. For us, it's an opportunity for us to help our friends," posited Billy Mauldin, president of Motor Racing Outreach (quoted in Rhee 2005, 1). The missionary work of these NASCAR celebrity drivers extends beyond counseling or dealing with tragedy and into the realm of conversion (Harris 2005).

Champion driver Jeff Gordon, who famously reads scripture during caution periods of each race (Caldwell 2001), offers his celebrity appeal in advertisements intended to stir membership interest in the Church of Jesus Christ. Popular drivers Mark Martin, Jeff Green, and Joe Nemecheck are only a few of the many drivers who offer "witness to Christ's glory" by way of extensive declarations on NASCAR and MRO-related promotional materials (MacGregor 2005; Menzer 2001; G. W. Miller 2002; Newberry 2004). In total, the MRO alone spends nearly $2 million a year to prepare drivers to spread the Gospel most effectively to spectators and fans (Rhee 2005).[4]

In many ways, the cultural and economic investments by the MRO are meant to mark off NASCAR Nation as a religious territory guided by *one* particular voice: that of "Jesus Christ, Our Lord and Savior." This particular gospel, it can be argued, is the leviathan of homogenizing faith revival, whereby an evangelical Christian hegemony holds "the spiritual mortgage on all things NASCAR" (Nethaway 2006, 5). The intensity of such a structured, "top-down" evangelism can be measured by the performances of sporting godliness as featured "in the pits" and on weekly telecasts of the NASCAR spectacular. On his popular website, RacewithFaith.com, Morgan Shepherd explains his calling at length:

> February 23rd, 1975 I accepted Jesus Christ as my Savior. I was at the lowest point in my life when the Lord let me know I had to change one way or the other. When I came back from the race in Daytona that year, my wife, at that time, had left me. So then I thought I would live it up. After a weekend of partying, I was feeling so bad in the morning after an evening of drinking. I began to think, that if all this is so great, why do I feel so bad in the mornings? The only time I felt good was when I was drinking. So, I had really hit bottom. I had always gone to church and knew about the Lord, but I guess, I had never really turned my life over to the Lord. He let me get to a desperate point in my life. On a Tuesday night, February the 23rd, in my home, I fell down on my knees and I began praying for God to change my life. I believe that if you turn things over to Jesus, things will change within your heart. Alcohol was a problem in my life. I did not drink that much, maybe once or twice a month, but whenever I drank it always seemed like I ended up in trouble. God took the desire for alcohol out of my life February 23rd, 1975. He made me hate everything that alcohol stands for. (Faith Motorsports 2000)

These types of online testimonials are commonplace in the cyberspatial realms of NASCAR Nation. Wildly popular driver Jeff Gordon often countenances the Lord's role in his continued racing success and encourages his fans to follow suit:

> I welcomed God into my life a few years ago. I regret that I did not do it sooner. Embracing His faith has made a tremendous difference in my life and my overall well-being. I pray regularly. I know that God can be a tremendous inspiration through good times and bad. When you are involved in a dangerous sport like auto racing, you rely on a higher power to keep you safe and overcome adversity. Whether I win or lose a race, I am content with the outcome knowing that I can always trust in God's goodness. We all have to experience our own spiritual journey. But if you embrace God's power, I believe you will live your life with a renewed joy and a heightened sense of fulfillment. Motor Racing Outreach has also been a part of my life. Their mission is to introduce the racing community and its fans to personal faith in Christ. MRO has helped me to develop and continue my relationship with God. Their staff is available to help you as well. (Gordon 2008)

Through various MRO promotional materials widely distributed at NASCAR events to the gathered congregation of spectators, fans are introduced to the *theological philosophies* of their favorite drivers, including Jeff Green, Dale Jarrett, David Green, Mark Martin, Lake Speed, and Darrell Waltrip. The lattermost contributor offers the following testimonial:

> I've been a Christian since 1983 but even then I was more interested in what Darrell Waltrip wanted than what God wanted. As I began to grow as a Christian I began to realize that there were more things in life more important than winning races and what I thought. I began to see that serving God needed to be first. God showed me just how blessed I was in having such a strong Christian wife and how children are a true blessing as well. The most important thing to do is to pray and study the Bible. God can take your need and bless you as well as others around you if you put Him first. (Waltrip 2005)

The uncontested hegemony of Waltrip's brand of Christianity, together with the lack of an alternative brand within racing circles, continues to normalize the problematic religious and cultural politics he and his film house are peddling. All this has not been lost on NASCAR's only Jewish driver (and only driver of a non-Christian denomination), Jon Denning. In a recent interview, Denning described his unique way of performing a conciliatory "Jewishness" in an otherwise Christian-dominated space: "I feel like every time I'm down here, I have to put on a little bit of an act. I have to remind myself of where I am" (quoted in Froymovich 2007, B8). Denning's "sense of ostracism" (Froymovich 2007, B8) in some ways confirms not only the spiritual uniformity within NASCAR Nation but the performative politics of driver celebrities in recapitulating such a heterogeneous state of faith.

Through a multilayered complex of public mediations, Shepherd, Gordon, Waltrip, Gibbs, and numerous other NASCAR celebrities offer a superfluous narrative and gesticulative synopsis of the moral climate of a sanctimonious NASCAR Nation. The subtext of these discursive formations, however, is perhaps more significant in that these symbolic representations of the religious Right authorize more incisive idioms of neoconservative, end-times fundamentalism. By "standing for" and "doing" what is "right," these driver apostles rearticulate a prevailing discourse within contemporary America: that of living with fear and preparing for the Rapture in a post–September 11 world (Denzin and Giardina 2007; Domke 2004; Kincheloe and Steinberg 2006; Wolf 2007). Much like their neoconservative fundamentalist contemporaries in other realms of the American mediascape, these mouthpieces of NASCAR Nation are creating a story: "It's a tale about a godly country," writes Michelle Goldberg, "blessed for its piety, that began to go wrong in the nineteenth century and sank into unimagined lows in the twentieth. Charles Darwin's theory of evolution eroded people's faith in man's dignity and God's supremacy" (2007, 7). As the story goes, suggests Goldberg, "Franklin Delano Roosevelt's New Deal brought socialism to America and began the process by which government, rather than churches, became the guarantors of social welfare" (2007, 7). And with this proselytizing imperative, of course, comes new forms of power: namely in the forms of the social spoils of *rapture spectacular* and the profitability of *market indoctrination*.

THE SPORTING AMUSEMENTS AT SIX FLAGS OVER JESUS

Just as this active "witnessing" from the majority faction of NASCAR celebrity drivers has popularized the hegemony of conservative socioreligious ideology (if not functioning as an instrument for the amalgamation of the two), the sound bite culture of the sporting hyperreal has been equally consequential in galvanizing NASCAR Nation's cultural politics to the *life-and-death* "political politics" (Morris 1989) of Bush-era neoconservatism. Members of NASCAR Nation are inundated with recurring themes orchestrated by a political regime attempting to scare the division of church and state out of the U.S. Constitution. Echoing fearmongering political, religious, and cultural intermediaries, as well as the "fear-based" doctrines of contemporary right-wing political ideologues, such as Tom Delay, Karl Rove, and Alberto Gonzales—those who openly declare that "the United States of America is a Christian nation, and the public acknowledgement of God is undeniable in our history" (quoted in Goldberg 2007, 27)—the iconic mouthpieces of contemporary NASCAR Nation inundate their spectator fans with rhetorical declarations of the *eternal return of rapture* and a spectacular discourse of inevitability.

A cursory review of political and religious narratives emanating from NASCAR Nation's most visible politicos and sporting icons in recent years offers an important, contextually specific "end-times" public pedagogy, one that tells us that we must have faith in God's plan for the war in Iraq, that leaders such as former president George W. Bush are the "right men" for the job of leading us toward the end times, that our collective paranoia of the interloping "Other" (immigrants, gays and lesbians, "welfare moms," dark-skinned "thugs," folks with names like Cho and Obama) is indeed a "gift" (De Becker 1998), and that "faith" and "hope" are the clearest (re)solutions for a failing domestic and global neoliberal capitalist order (Domke and Coe 2008).

With Bible in hand and a vast post–September 11 lexicon of "terror," "fear," and "moral" panic at their disposal, a cacophony of right-wing voices ranging from Ann Coulter to George W. Bush has bombarded a broader NASCAR Nation in recent years with the twin techniques of theological paranoia and backlash xenophobia. Narrated through a politically contrived "War on Terror" and condemnation of a global rise in "Islamofascism," the first decade of the twenty-first century has borne witness to a widespread neoconservative commercialization of religious fervor gripping the United States. Abetted by the "culture wars"[5] of the 1960s and forward, which are still fresh in our minds (e.g., debates concerning abortion rights, gay rights, affirmative action, and drug policy), religiously inflected popular entertainment (e.g., Tim LaHaye's best-selling, rapture-based *Left Behind* book series[6]), sports-arena-sized megachurches (e.g., Willow Creek in Illinois, Southeast Christian Church in Kentucky, and World

Harvest Church in Ohio), and right-wing talk radio of an "echoing press" (e.g., Rush Limbaugh, Michael Savage, Pat Buchanan, and Bill O'Reilly) (Domke 2004) have all become normalized mainstays in popular iterations of consumer culture. These manifestations have been employed with some degree of success by right-wing politicians (e.g., Allen, Brownback, Bush, Frist, Santorum, Palin) in order to galvanize support for their respective fundamentalist agendas (e.g., antichoice, antigay, anti-immigrant, antiwoman, and antiblack).

Correlative to our purposes here, neoconservative politicos such as those discussed above have furthermore made the physical spaces of NASCAR Nation (the tracks, the hypermediated consumer spatialities, and so forth) their peripatetic campaign headquarters. Presidents, senators, representatives, governors, mayors, and councilpersons have aggressively canvassed NASCAR Nation and integrated the stock car spectacular as a significant part of their "campaign strategies." It is important to note that there is historical precedence for this implicit articulation going back at least as far as 1961. In that year, and on the grounds of the Darlington Speedway in South Carolina prior to the start of the Southern 500 race, the late segregationist senator Strom Thurmond gave a major speech in which he stated in part, "In 1861 South Carolina was the first to secede from the Union. And if necessary, it will be the first to secede in 1961!" Brock Yates, writing for the ultraconservative magazine *American Spectator*, describes the affective response that followed Thurmond's oration thusly: "The crowd went mad. Guns were fired. The Stars and Bars waved everywhere. Rebel yells filled the grandstands and 'Dixie' was sung in drunken reverie" (2005, 14). Likewise, in 1984, Ronald Reagan, ever displaying the faux air of the common-man hero, reflected the vox populi when he, as Bush would twenty years later, similarly made a much-ballyhooed public appearance at a NASCAR event in Daytona Beach, Florida:

> It was a day that NASCAR fans will never forget. With the President in the press box and the immense tail of Air Force One visible from the airfield behind the Daytona International Speedway, Reagan watched Richard Petty—the sport's most popular driver—win his unprecedented 200th race during the running of the July 4, 1984, Firecracker 400. (Yates 2005, 15)

This explicit conjoining of (right-wing) politics to NASCAR continues unabated. To give but one example, during the 2006 midterm election season,

George Allen routinely brandished the microphone at races in his home state of Virginia and emphatically, persistently declared that NASCAR fans were "his people" to rave reviews in his (failed) race for a U.S. Senate seat.[7]

It is equally important to note that Democratic Party politicians have similarly tried to avail themselves of NASCAR Nation, albeit it to decidedly mixed results. One the one hand, and despite his best attempts, Bill Clinton was never able to curry favor with NASCAR Nation. In 1992, for example, while campaigning in South Carolina, then *governor* Clinton visited the Darlington Speedway, fans roundly booed him as he waved to the grandstands, and NASCAR officials had trouble persuading drivers even to pose for pictures with Clinton or show him around their cars, lest they look like they were supporting a Democrat (even one from the South). On the other hand, some Southern "centrists" (read neoliberalists with a "moderate" social agenda) have found modest success among the NASCAR faithful, as former Florida senator Bob Graham, U.S. Representative Heath Shuler, and former Virginia governor Mark Warner were each able to ingratiate themselves with the sport and its followers in the run-ups to their respective elections.[8]

None of these politicos turned racing enthusiasts, however, has been able to graft a sport-specific "mandate" to the extent that George W. Bush was able to achieve during the 2004 election. In the lead-up to that year's presidential contest, many political "pundits" (rightly) predicted that the members of NASCAR Nation would play a significant role in determining the outcome of that year's race (the political one). George W. Bush and his high-profile farrago of "babysitters" (Cheney, Rumsfeld, and so on) quickly became fixtures at the weekly racing series, bringing with them rhetorical declarations of a return to Christian "fundamentals," the abolition of affirmative action, increased autonomy for homeland security, a retrenchment of "gay rights," a recentering of middle-class American "family values," a "tougher approach" to stopping immigration in the wake of September 11, and the demise of "big government."

This automation of what William Connolly (2005) refers to as a Bush-era "evangelical-capitalist resonance machine" came into focus in the lead-up to the 2004 Daytona 500 as the president circled the track and effectively forged a powerful symbolic relationship between stock car/automobile culture and the cultural politics of neoconservatism:

> He emerged from the only SUV in the entourage to an incredible roar of approval. The crowd responded to the SUV as a symbol of disdain

> for womanly ecologists, safety advocates, supporters of fuel economy, weak-willed pluralists, and internationalists. Bush played upon the symbol and drew energy from the crowd's acclamation of it. Resentment against those who express an ethos of care for the world was never named: a message expressed without being articulated. (Connolly 2005, 879)

Through high visibility and promissory discursive stylings at this and numerous other races, the Republican Party seized NASCAR Nation (and its citizens) as a central territory in "red state America." This successful symmetry of sport and political ideology led one analyst to later proclaim, "Right now Republicans rule. They control the White House, both houses of Congress and most state governments. The basis of the Republicans' ruling majority: NASCAR Nation" (Schneider 2004).

The GOP, of course, did not stumble onto NASCAR Nation. As both Esther Kaplan in her muckraking exposé *With God on Their Side: George W. Bush and the Christian Right* (2005) and Michelle Goldberg in her equally pertinent book *Kingdom Coming: The Rise of Christian Nationalism* (2007) make abundantly clear, most social, scientific, civic, artistic, and political organizations across the nation have been "under assault" from the fundamentalist Right under the Bush regime. As such, the politicization/theocratization of the NASCAR imagined sporting community results in part from more concerted efforts to colonize formations of public culture under the domain of the right-wing (and left-wing, for that matter) political ideologues. In this way, NASCAR becomes an essential cultural space through which the cronies of neoliberalism can construct conditions of hegemonic consent, translating the neoconservative "affinities of [sporting] identity" into authorization for Bush-era idioms of citizenship and Christian "values," such as

> the market apologism and scandal mongering of the electronic news media, mobilization drives by the Republican Party and Fox News, administrative edicts to overturn environmentalism and weaken labor, attacks on Social Security, curtailments of minority rights in the name of religious morality, pressure for right-wing appointments to the Supreme Court, support for preemptive wars, tolerance or worse of state practices of torture that flout the Geneva conventions, and propa-

> gation of a climate of fear and loathing against the Islamic world. (Connolly 2005, 870–871)

But how are politics, particularly those of a Bush-era neoconservative bent, so pronounced in the spaces and spectacles of NASCAR Nation? Many commentators have argued that with regard to the North American sporting popular, there is a unique reciprocity, a mutual lovefest if you will, between NASCAR and these political ideologues. "No other professional sport," wrote *CNN Sports Illustrated* journalist Mike Fish, "brags of having *its* guy in the White House. And no other sport—from the offspring of late NASCAR founder Bill France Sr. to the big-name drivers to the wealthy track and team owners—comes down so staunchly on the less-government-is-better Republican side of the aisle" (2001, 1). According to Fish (2001), nearly 90 percent of the money given by individuals affiliated with NASCAR to political campaigns goes to the Republican Party. NASCAR is so unabashed in its support of the Republican Party that in 2004 it hosted a luncheon/voter registration drive at the Republican National Convention. Themed "Race to Victory," the gala featured a number of team owners and popular drivers pledging their support toward President George W. Bush's reelection bid. At the event, popular driver Bill Elliott publicly declared, "The President has done a good job given the circumstances of what he's been through and in my mind his report card's been excellent" (quoted in Grant 2004, 1).

That support came in the form of not only maximal financial donations but public endorsements from the most recognizable of NASCAR's icons: "I was real excited to do it, I look at it as common sense," said former driver Rusty Wallace. "The President came in with all the right things on his mind. He's a tough guy. I believe him. It's pulling for what you know is right and using some common sense about it. I know what I'm pulling for is the right thing to pull for" (quoted in Grant 2004, 1). Those most critical of the Bush regime might suggest that Wallace's use of the notion of "common sense" is a linguistic technique meant (1) to normalize neoconservative assumptions regarding what is "Right," and (2) to reorganize the ontological relations of power with relation to governance and "belief." With regard to the former, that seemingly naturalized, "commonsensical" approach to governance constitutes, and is constituent of, an aggrandized affirmation of the methodologies of the "cause" (a multifarious complex of profitable war, paranoiac discourses of terror, mass privatization, purity of the homeland, and so forth). To such an end, NASCAR team owner Chip Ganassi has been more explicit in his support for the Republican incumbent: "I want to live in a country where I know the President is watching out for the homeland and I want a president who is devoted to protecting our country first and foremost." Ganassi continued, "I want to be behind a party that is not chasing a sound bite on some cable news channel" (quoted in Grant 2004, 1).

And it would be hard to argue against the notion that the sport-polity synchronicity solidified in the public discourse by these stock car celebrities has further normalized "biblical" neoconservative hegemony in NASCAR Nation. As both critics and pundits agree, NASCAR's Southern regional history and aesthetic, hypermasculine, heteronormative, almost exclusively white fan base (and celebrity-driver lexicon), situated in the rhetorical mores of a seemingly harmless Southern "heritage culture," position stock car racing as a sporting extension of what Jim Wright refers to as "traditional American virtues" (2002, 162) and what Kyle Kusz more critically identifies as conservatives' "interest in protecting White male privilege and cultural normativity" (2007, 82). Moreover, while meaning, knowledge, and identities—forged under what Chris Hedges, in his timely, if not necessarily alarmist, book *American Fascists: The Christian Right and the War on America* (2007), describes as the "Dominionism" of the political arms of the Christian Right—are contestable (though seldom contested), the superfluous autonomy granted these performative politicos and their "political politics" are made powerful by the autonomy afforded each. In short, it can be argued that the interplay between neoconservative politicians (falsely) acting out the *will of God* and NASCAR celebrity icons as *representative embodiments* of churchgoing "average folks" (white, masculine, Southern, vitriolic, hetero-obsessive, conservative, God-fearing, patriotic—in sum, "Right") is the proverbial lubricant that oils the political and theocratic cogs in the central engine of Bush-era neoconservatism in NASCAR Nation.

JESUS CHRIST, CORPORATE SPONSOR?

And while the "faithful" have successfully blanketed the narrative spaces of NASCAR Nation with discourses of rapture, terror, and sanctity, they have been equally successful at capitalizing on that "word of God." Indeed, the *holy aesthetic* has become a lucrative link in many of NASCAR's various commodity chains (from merchandising, to sponsorship, to themed experiences, and so on). As if borrowed straight from the script of the Acton Institute's (a neocon think tank) recent documentary *The Call of the Entrepreneur*,[9] there is a prevailing faith among most members of NASCAR Nation in the hegemons of a Jesus-authorized, and indeed theocratically commodified, neoliberal market. In the broader NASCAR Nation, this belief is fueled by the paradoxical bond between social conservatism and economic (neo)liberalism that now holds sway over American life, a shrinking of the gap between Mike Huckabee's faith-based America and Ron Paul's "revolutionary" corporo-market-serving nation-state.[10] Such is the case that "neoconservativism sewn in the soil prepared by neoliberalism breeds a new political form, a specific modality of governance and citizenship" (Brown 2006, 702), whereby political subjects (and the subjectification of identity politics and political politics) are subjected to new forms of devotion (to the market and in fundamentalists' purview for mobilizing the market toward socially and morally just ends) and fear (of rapture, of interference with the "American way of life," and so forth).

As the latest generation of Milton Friedman–inspired free market policy makers has successfully ushered in an age of unfettered capital accumulation and corporate power in the American (and global) economy—in large part due to their theatrics at NASCAR tracks, in and around mercenary machines such as the USS *Abraham Lincoln*,[11] in front of Six Flags over Jesus congregations, and on various other stages—those mouthpieces of social conservatism have been equally successful in grafting a lexicon of fear (of terrorists, of immigrants, of women, of "queers," of liberals, of big government, of socialism, of welfare recipients) and an overprivileging of (white, masculine, heteronormative) "traditions," which in turn give foundational authority to the Bush-era neoliberal/neoconservative ideological package.

Despite what strident neoliberals tell us, this commercialization of fear and the symbolic value of sanctity are essential parts of the consent-manufacturing apparatus that has sustained this failing economic policy (Newman and Giardina 2008). As history is making abundantly clear, the Friedman-inspired free market would long since have collapsed under the weight of a failing housing market, massive consumer credit, unimaginable federal debt, rising global unemployment, and falling wage labor if not for (contradictory) quasipopulist interventions and stimuli, such as the privatization of post-Katrina New

Orleans and the Gulf Coast, the for-profit militaristic exploits in Iraq (and subsequent privatization of public goods such as oil, education, transportation infrastructures, and so forth), the "Republican war on science" (see Mooney 2005) and new windfall for "faith-based and community initiatives," and the massive increase in corporate welfare (which, according even to the neoliberal think tank CATO Institute, taxpayers now underwrite at *ten times* the level of social welfare programs).

And so, this timely collapse of the neoliberal order has forced its hegemons to incorporate (double entendre intended) and proliferate various dimensions of the neoconservative lexicon to sustain a failing market. While students of Milton Friedman turned American politicos, such as George W. Bush, Dick Cheney, and Donald Rumsfeld, have relied on dedemocratic, indeed anti-laissez-faire, measures to ensure growing rates of accumulation, they have concurrently deployed—as Thomas Frank points out in *What's the Matter with Kansas* (2005)—a new strategy of "talk Christ but walk corporate." And as we have argued heretofore, in no other sport is this political- and profit-driven Jesus speak more pronounced than in NASCAR. All this talk of fear, liberty, freedom, and God's will becomes more important in light of the dialectics of commercialization and theocratization. In the first instance, these broader contortions of market and theocracy are brought to life through a number of recent "partnerships" between NASCAR's commodity engines and the commercial organisms of Christianity, each of which simultaneously reconditions the social topography of the sport and reinscribes the capitalist power structure it serves. In very simple terms, God has been good for NASCAR's business.

For example, in 2004 the Interstate Batteries NASCAR racing team formed such a "partnership" with major movie distributor 20th Century Fox to promote the controversial film *The Passion of The Christ*. The movie distributor contracted driver Bobby Labonte and his team to emblazon their #18 Chevrolet Monte Carlo with the film's marketing insignias and images of the film's protagonist, Jesus Christ, for a major NASCAR event prior to the film's release (Maresco 2004).[12] Architect of the deal Norm Miller, chairman of Interstate Batteries, lauded the sponsorship agreement, stating "This outstanding movie factually portrays the most important 12 hours in history. The Bible is clear—Jesus was volunteering when he laid down his life. I don't feel it's near the issue people are trying to make out of it" (quoted in Drehs 2004).

While the joint venture proved to be lucrative for both the racing team and the filmmakers (with the latter grossing over $370 million in the domestic box office alone), the highly publicized, anti-Semitic, slur-spewing, hatemongering rants of the film's traditionalist Catholic director, Mel Gibson, brought the critical gaze back onto the sport's place in the cultural economy of neoconservative Christianity. Rabbi Barry M. Altman, an outspoken critic of the film and the sponsorship, stated, "Really they're not doing anything different than Viagra. I mean, this is a commercial venture. They're putting more dollars into Mel Gibson's pockets" (quoted in Drehs 2004). In spite of this and the detritus of like-themed dissent within the popular media, the consensus among members of NASCAR Nation was (1) that the film's anti-Semitic overtones were merely a "realistic" portrayal of the last hours of the Savior's life, and (2) that the marketization of the deeply proselytizing interpretation was a necessary technology in spreading the "true" story of sacrifices made by the patron of their faith.

By way of contrast, when the Church of Scientology entered into an agreement with a team from NASCAR's "late-model" weekly circuit in California in 2006, there was considerable upheaval within the ruling faction of NASCAR Nation (including "He's nuts" and "Fag" banners littering the raceway when Tom Cruise appeared to promote the race team and defamatory rhetoric spread across NASCAR blogspaces).[13] The deal resulted in a renaming of the team—to the Dianetics Racing Team (named after the influential work of Scientology founder L. Ron Hubbard)—and the emblazoning of the mantra "Ignite Your Potential" on the #27 Ford Taurus (Friaglia and Yeransian 2006). Driver Kenton Gray, himself a follower of L. Ron Hubbard's teachings, praised the business deal: "Through Dianetics I've handled and increased my performance and ability to compete—both on the track and in life" (quoted in Scientology 2006). For two corporations with profit aspirations, the "partnership" was intended to allow both Scientology and NASCAR to "increase their own performances" in the crowded marketplaces of faith and sport. For NASCAR, as spokesman Jim Hunter explained, the proliferation of religious ideology could be boiled down to a simple economic equation: "When you get into philosophies and morals, that's a slippery slope. . . . Not all of our fans agree with some sponsorships, but they do understand that it is imperative for our cars to have sponsors in order to succeed" (quoted in Fryer 2006, 1). And for the "Scientology marketing machine" (Schultz 2006), NASCAR Nation offered a conduit (with mass cultural appeal) through which the company/faith could expand its form of corporatized religion.

In the second instance, and as a consequence of the first, the sport has abetted the rise of neoliberalism by popularizing (and to some extent normalizing) the logics of the "evangelical-capitalist resonance machine" (Connolly 2005), and it has metaphorically, if not materially, extracted sign value from its sporting piety. As popular driver evangelist Darrell Waltrip made clear in a 2000 interview for PBS, "A dangerous, commercialized place is the perfect place for the Lord" (quoted in *Religion and Ethics Newsweekly* 2000). While this contorted logic might be lost on scholars of economic policy or cultural polity, the recent infusion of God into the NASCAR marketplace speaks to a more finite (if less logical) relationship between prophets (in a Christian sense) and profitability. NASCAR's sporting spaces have not only offered fertile ground for advancing the theocratization of the neoliberal market but also served as an imaginary and geometric spatiality dominated by value-added God-signifiers that can transform the religious banal into spectacular commodities.

In some ways, Christianity has been folded into the logotechniques of the NASCAR brand: "NASCAR's alliance with the Christian faith gives the sport a more wholesome, family-oriented image" (Newberry 2004, 2). As part of a recent trend in every major (and minor) North American professional sport, NASCAR hosts "Faith and Family Night" events, Christian rock concerts, and numerous other ancillary Jesus-inspired spectacles, all of which undeniably increase the corporation's bottom line by way of the additional forms of consumption brought to the track by legions of Christians turned race fans. While this explicit commodification of sporting Jesus has thus far eluded the critique of those who might find aberrance in such a market-based relationship with Christ, it has been affective in subjecting members of NASCAR Nation to a "neoliberal political rationality that . . . has prepared the ground for profoundly anti-democratic political ideas and practices to take root in the culture and the subject" (Brown 2006, 702). It could be argued that the media assemblage of the NASCAR lexicon not only "prepares the ground" but fertilizes it with a what Jean Baudrillard (1998) refers to as an "ideological blanket" stitched with the principle that Jesus authorizes neoliberal precepts, such as profit-maximization and the capitalization of faith and culture.

This faith-based market hegemony materializes in many forms, the most pronounced of which are perhaps NASCAR celebrity icon Morgan Shepherd and his #89 "Victory in Jesus" Dodge (Wilkey 2006). While considered by most to be a "fringe operation" due to a lack of sustained capital, the team is nonetheless a "second-favorite" team for many within NASCAR Nation. Originally "reprimanded" by NASCAR for seeking to place an image of Jesus

Christ on the hood of his race car, Shepherd was eventually allowed to add the script "Racing with Jesus" and a crucifix to the hood of the car in 2004 (Drehs 2004). In 2005, ABC's *World News Tonight* ran a piece titled "The Racetrack under God" in which reporters interviewed Shepherd about his sporting godliness. During the interview, the popular NASCAR driver referred to Jesus Christ as "his sponsor" and declared that the team competed as a way of "spreading the word of God" to race fans.

That "word," as has become evident in the rhetorical stylings of Shepherd and former crew chief J. D. Gibbs (son of Joe Gibbs), is one part contextually specific "biblicalism" (Hedges 2007) bound to a "values-based" discourse of postmodern consumption (constructing brand identity around "Christian values") and one part "proselytizing mandate" (Hedges 2007) born of a series of Bush-era evangelical contractions, such as the exercise of power (through white, upper-/middle-class, masculine subjectivities) and the abstinence of guilt therein. With regard to the former, Shepherd implored "corporate America" reciprocate the sport faith- and profit-driven symbiosis by sponsoring his struggling race team:

> Why does corporate America spend so much money . . . supporting things that don't have moral values? Here we are, trying to serve the Lord. There's nothing bad in the Bible. Even if you don't believe in God, if everyone would just live by the Bible and the Ten Commandments, see how much better the world would be. (Quoted in Associated Press 2004b)

Shepherd fails to realize, however, that the free market dictates that its corporate cronies recognize that Jesus, "values," and morality itself are made meaningful not by some deep-seated commitment to righteousness but as dialects of a contextually profitable form of market subjectification.

In other words, and with regard to the lattermost revelation, Jesus Christ has been an important cultural icon that has served NASCAR, its corporate sponsors, its political intermediaries, and various other creatures of the neoliberal order well; yet, at the end of the day, while Shepherd, Gibbs, Gordon, Waltrip, and countless other NASCAR icons prosper under, and sometimes actually *believe in*, the "path of righteousness," these men of faith more consequentially construct a public pedagogy whereby the politics of capital and the accumulation of wealth and material possessions are representative both of God's glory and of the sporting materialities that reflect that glory here on earth.[14]

CODA: WHAT'S THE MATTER WITH DAYTONA?

From Starbucks and McDonald's located inside the heartland's megachurches to the hateful political invective spewed forth from their pulpits, and from the crass deployment of end-times fearmongering to the hyperpontifical proclamations of NASCAR's cruciform-wielding drivers, a new holy trinity of commodified market logics dominating the American consumer-subject in the post–September 11 epoch has emerged: evangelical fundamentalism, hyperaggressive neoconservatism, and predatory neoliberal capitalism. Taken together and in isolation, these three conditions operate as "technologies of enchantment" (Cole 2007, 153) that "activate, confirm, and extend" the normative power of such a discursive iteration. In effect, NASCAR Nation has risen from the proverbial ashes and ascended into triumphal glory at the right hand of the once-mighty dollar: it has been transmogrified from its early days as a regional sporting venture into a complex system of signs, images, and practices that both adheres to the capitalist imperatives of its neoliberal overlords while simultaneously (and paradoxically) promoting a seemingly oppositional rationality as the answer to all that is "wrong" with the world.

It is thus here, in the hypercommodified spaces of the NASCAR spectacle, that Christian nationalism—which, like most other militant ideologies, as Goldberg reminds us, "can exist only in opposition to something" (2007, 69)—has been fomented most assiduously: NASCAR becomes a "visible center" of anti-immigrant, antiblack, antigay, antichoice, antienvironment, anti-Other rhetoric prepackaged and sold hand in hand alongside (an equally commodified) restorative religious fervor delivered on high by celebrity drivers and (right-wing) politicians alike. Couple this with an aggressive, militaristic protofascism masquerading as entertainment (e.g., the U.S. Army Experience tent at NASCAR races or the U.S. Army–sponsored race car, popular Hollywood movies such as *Black Hawk Down* and the latest incarnation of the Rambo series, and evermore realistic, war-themed video games such as *Medal of Honor, Call of Duty,* or *America's Army*), a collapsing U.S. economy (falling U.S. dollar, failed subprime mortgage industry, increasing unemployment, trillions of dollars flushed down the bottomless pit of Iraq "reconstruction"), and the continued exurbanization of America in which "megachurches fill the spiritual and social void, providing atomized residents instant community" (Goldberg 2007, 58), and the turn toward a strong military-industrial-media complex, big-box consumerism, patriarchal family structure, and an almighty God seems all the more naturalized.[15]

Specific to NASCAR, its ruling officials and most faithful Christian drivers-turned-missionaries are selling an integrated spectacle of myths: the myth of infinite growth under neoliberalism, the myth of an endless "American Century," the myth of a commitment to (Southern) cultural heritage, the myth of "NASCAR dad" social conservatism and religious fundamentalism, the myth of Mitt Romney's "conservative" economy, and the myth of the free market's individual freedoms. But this "call" to national redemption and personal salvation is nothing but a false hall of mirrors, an untenable position, another example of the predatory logics of capitalism unleashed. Indeed, NASCAR as religion, framed as such by its most arduous of shepherds, has become yet another vehicle for a mass cultural offertory that has redistributed untold dollars to the Wal-Marts, Exxon-Mobils, and Home Depots of the world—the selling *out* of the soul through the selling *of* the soul.

Notes

1. Consider the cultural import of North American sport's most popular megaevent: the Super Bowl. The economic and cultural impact of that event alone outweighs almost every religious and state holiday in terms of shaping social and consumer activity.

2. It is quite common within the sport and beyond to refer to stock car racing fans as members of NASCAR Nation, as well as to evoke the term in describing the political and cultural trajectory of a national imaginary mesmerized by a strategically controlled, theocratized cultural technology that normalizes the moral, political, economic, and ideological dimensions of George W. Bush's post-9/11 brand of neoliberalism/neoconservatism.

3. Indeed, while ratings numbers for professional football, basketball, and baseball telecasts have taken a sharp downturn in recent years, consumption of NASCAR-related wares and experiences has nearly tripled over the past decade.

4. According to Ministry Watch, "an online database with profiles on more than 400 of the largest churches and parachurch ministries in the United States," MRO had revenues of $1,988,604 against total expenses of $2,088,674. These expenses are recouped by the large-scale communion contributions from driver celebrities and team owners and support from other religious organizations.

5. As Scott Kline argues, "This conservative declaration of 'culture war' was not an attempt to substitute a 'high culture' for philistine politics. It was not, in other words, an attempt to protect a noble or sacred culture from the sullying effects of Realpolitk or mundane political discourse. Rather, it was an attempt to politicize culture and, in the process, instill a *particular* brand of morality-based cultural politics into American political debate" (2007, emphasis added).

6. LaHaye is author of the best-selling *Left Behind* series, which tells stories of apocalyptic fiction that depict the Earth after the pretribulation Rapture (which the author believes will soon occur). The series has been widely derided as misogynistic, homophobic, anti-Catholic, anti-Jewish, theocratic, and apocalyptic.

7. All of this occurred prior to the unveiling of racist subnarratives within his campaign in 2006, including allegations of his repeated use of the word "nigger," controversies surrounding the Confederate flag, his penchant for hanging a noose in his office, and a very public confrontation with an Indian American attendee at one of his campaign events, whom Allen referred to as a "macaca" (a pejorative epithet meaning "monkey," used by francophone colonists in Central Africa in reference to the native population). Taken together, the above events were considered a major factor in Allen's defeat at the hands of Jim Webb.

8. It is inevitable that the battle for position in NASCAR circles plays a substantive role in determining presidential politics, as pundits point out that politicians such as Hillary Clinton and Ralph Nader "would be booed, no doubt about it" (Clarke and Steinberg 2004).

9. *The Call of the Entrepreneur* is a 2007 documentary produced by Acton Media. This film mediates on three stories of people who risked their savings, bet the farm, and defied conventional wisdom by placing their faith in God to achieve economic success. It paints a picture of altruism over greed, the freedom and independence afforded adherents to the free market, the antimoralist role of big government, and the wealth-creating capacity of inventive parishioners.

10. Each of these men created highly visible "grassroots campaigns," which maintained high visibility at NASCAR events during the 2007–2008 primary season.

11. The namesake of which ship, history will prove, was the political and ideological antithesis to the modern-day warmongering protagonist (in terms of militarist conquest, free market capitalism, corporate power, separation of church and state, and so forth).

12. Although they were modest, there were initially two threads of public dissent against the sponsorship maneuver. The first emanated from that faction in NASCAR circles that disagreed with the use of the film's signifiers on the racing vehicles, citing the anti-Semitic overtones of the film. A second, more vocal polemic emerged from the conservative Right, which viewed the commercialization of Jesus (both in cinematic and sporting forms) to be inappropriate.

13. This hegemonic sway of the neoconservative/neoliberal parallax is perhaps no more evident than in the discursive mediations of Scientology's best-known parishioner. The protagonist of the all-time most popular stock car racing film, *Days of Thunder* (where he played bad-boy driver Cole Trickle), became enemy number one for many within NASCAR Nation following Scientology's "intrusion" into the sport.

14. This pedagogy of conspicuous consumption teaches us that $80,000 spent on a new Hummer better represents a close connection to Jesus Christ than would that same sum spent in aiding starvation in Darfur (the logic being that if Darfur's dying children were more vigilant in their commitment to such a corporo-Christian order, they too could share in the fruits of these faith-based "blessings").

15. As Hochschild reminds us, there is a Faustian bargain at play here: "We'll lift your self-respect by putting down women, minorities, immigrants, even those spotter owls. We'll honor the manly fortitude you've shown in taking bad news. But (and this is implicit) don't ask us to do anything to change that bad news" (2003, n.p.).

References

Andrews, D. L. 2002. Coming to terms with cultural studies. *Journal of Sport and Social Issues* 26, no. 1: 110–117.

Associated Press. 2004a. In NASCAR, racing and religion intertwine. NASCAR.com, www.nascar.com/2004/news/headlines/cup/02/10/bc.racing.religion.ap/index.html (accessed January 23, 2008).

______. 2004b. NASCAR blurs lines between racing and religion. ESPN.com. http://sports.espn.go.com/rpm/news/story?id=1733009 (accessed June 20, 2007).

Baudrillard, J. 1998. Simulacra and simulations. In *Jean Baudrillard: Selected writings*, ed. M. Poster, 166–184. Palo Alto, CA: Stanford University Press.

Bochon, D. 2008. Fueled by faith. *Living Light News*, www.livinglightnews.org/vpetty.html (accessed March 4, 2008).

Brown, W. 2006. American nightmare: Neoliberalism, neoconservatism, and dedemocratization. *Political Theory* 34, no. 6: 690–714.

Caldwell, D. 2001. Godspeed: Champion race-car driver Jeff Gordon faithfully examines the daily rewards—and risks—of the sport. Beliefnet, www.beliefnet.com/story/85/story_8550.html (accessed March 2, 2008).

Canfield, J., M. V. Hansen, M. E. Adams, K. Autio, and J. Aubery, eds. 2003. *Chicken soup for the NASCAR soul*. Deerfield Beach, FL: Health Communications.

Clarke, L. 2001. NASCAR races at God's speed: Ministry helps drivers keep faith amid danger. *Washington Post*, April 22, A1.

Clarke, L., and D. Steinberg. 2004. The new language of NASCAR. *Washington Post*, October 6, A1.

Cole, C. L. 2007. Bounding American democracy: Sport, sex, and race. In *Contesting empire, globalizing dissent: Cultural studies after 9/11*, ed. N. K. Denzin and M. D. Giardina, 152–164. Boulder, CO: Paradigm.

Connolly, W. E. 2005. The Evangelical-capitalist resonance machine. *Political Theory* 33, no. 6: 869–886.

De Becker, G. 1998. *The gift of fear and other survival signals that protect us from violence*. New York: Dell Publishing.

Denzin, N. K., and M. D. Giardina. 2007. Introduction: Cultural studies after 9/11. In *Contesting empire, globalizing dissent: Cultural studies after 9/11*, ed. N. K. Denzin and M. D. Giardina, 1–19. Boulder, CO: Paradigm.

Derbyshire, J. 2003. NASCAR nation. *National Review*, November 10, 29–32.

Domke, D. 2004. *God willing? Political fundamentalism in the White House, the "War on Terror," and the echoing press*. London: Pluto Press.

Domke, D., and K. Coe. 2008. *The God strategy: How religion became a political weapon in America*. London: Oxford University Press.

Donnelly, P., ed. 2000. *Taking sport seriously*. Toronto: Thompson Educational Press.

Drehs, W. 2004. Controversy doesn't resonate with NASCAR. ESPN.com. http://sports.espn.go.com/rpm/news/story?id=1732991 (accessed June 25, 2007).

Elder, L., and S. Greene. 2007. The myth of "security moms" and "NASCAR dads": Parenthood, political stereotypes, and the 2004 election. *Social Science Quarterly* 88, no. 1: 1–19.

Faith Motorsports. 2000. Ministry and charity: Morgan's testimony. Faith Motorsports, August 15, http://racewithfaith.com/morgantestimony.php (accessed November 22, 2007).

Fish, M. 2001. The right stuff: NASCAR is a conservative crowd—and proud of it. *CNN Sports Illustrated*, February 28, http://sportsillustrated.cnn.com/motorsports/nascar_plus/news/2001/02/20/nascar_politics (accessed February 17, 2007).

Fotta, M. 2004. God speed—NASCAR: A theological analysis. Unpublished thesis, Boston University.

Frank, T. 2005. *What's the matter with Kansas: How conservatives won the heart of America*. New York: Metropolitan Books.

Friaglia, L., and L. Yeransian. 2006. Scientology goes NASCAR with Dianetics race car. ABC News, http://abcnews.go.com/US/story?id=2044770 (accessed June 23, 2007).

Froymovich, R. 2007. Life in the fast lane: NASCAR driver charges full speed ahead. *Forward: The Jewish Daily*, February 23, www.forward.com/articles/10153 (accessed March 12, 2007).

Fryer, J. 2006. Dianetics to sponsor NASCAR race team. *Washington Post*, June 7, www.washingtonpost.com/wp-dyn/content/article/2006/06/07/AR2006060702520.html (accessed August 12, 2008).

Gibbs, J., and K. Abraham. 2002. *Racing to win: Establish your game plan for success.* Colorado Springs, CO: Multnomah Publishers.

Goldberg, M. 2007. *Kingdom coming: The rise of Christian nationalism.* New York: W. W. Norton.

Gordon, J. 2008. My faith and beliefs. JeffGordon.com, www.jeffgordon.com/about_jeff/default.sps?itype=12225 (accessed February 27, 2008).

Grant, M. E. 2004. RNC joined by NASCAR favorites during voter registration drive at Daytona 500. GOP.com, www.gop.com/News/Read.aspx?ID=3916 (accessed March 3, 2007).

Guttmann, A. 1978. *From ritual to record: The nature of modern sports.* New York: Columbia University Press.

_______. 1986. *Sports spectators.* New York: Columbia University Press.

Hall, S. 1984. The rise of the new Right: The great moving Right show. *New Internationalist*, www.newint.org/issue133/show.htm (accessed November 8, 2004).

Harris, D. 2005. NASCAR takes religion to the raceway. ABC News, May 4, http://abcnews.go.com/WNT/Beliefs/Story?id=727941&page=2 (accessed March 3, 2007).

Hedges, C. 2007. *American fascists: The Christian Right and the war on America.* New York: Free Press.

Higgs, R. J. 1995. *God in the stadium: Sports and religion in America.* Lexington: University of Kentucky Press.

Hochschild, A. 2003. Let them eat war. TomDispatch.com, www.tomdispatch.com/post/986/arlie_hochschild_on_blue_collar_support_for_bush (accessed May 2, 2004).

Hua, V. 2005. Before starting engines, drivers pray: NASCAR racers face danger with ministries' support. *San Francisco Chronicle*, June 27, A1.

Jenkins, C. 2001. Sunday morning service with twist: Motor Racing Outreach provides religious services for racing series. *USA Today*, March 2, 4C.

Kaplan, E. 2005. *With God on their side: George W. Bush and the Christian Right.* New York: New Press.

Kincheloe, J. L., and S. R. Steinberg. 2006. An ideology of miseducation: Countering the pedagogy of empire. *Cultural Studies <> Critical Methodologies* 6, no. 1: 33–51.

Kline, S. 2007. The morality and politics of consumer religion: How consumer religion fuels the culture wars in the United States. *Journal of Religion and Popular Culture* 17, www.usask.ca/relst/jrpc/art17-consumerreligion.html#_edn17 (accessed January 10, 2008).

Kusz, K. 2007. From NASCAR to Pat Tillman: Notes on sport and the politics of white cultural nationalism in post-9/11 America. *Journal of Sport and Social Issues* 31, no. 1: 77–88.

Leitch, W. 2008. *God save the fan: How preening sportscasters, athletes who speak in the third person, and the occasional convicted quarterback have taken the fun out of sports (and how we can get it back).* New York: Harper.

Levy, B.-H. 2006. *American vertigo: Traveling America in the footsteps of Tocqueville.* New York: Random House.

Lipsyte, R. 2001. Auto racing: Wedded to Winston Cup, for better and for worse. *New York Times*, July 22, D7.

MacGregor, J. 2005. *Sunday money: Speed! Lust! Madness! Death! A hot lap around America with NASCAR.* New York: Harper.

Mansfield, S. 2004. *The faith of George W. Bush.* Lake Mary, FL: Charisma House.

Maresco, P. A. 2004. Mel Gibson's *The Passion of The Christ:* Market segmentation, mass marketing and promotion, and the Internet. *Journal of Religion and Popular Culture* 8, www.usask.ca/relst/jrpc/art8-melgibsonmarketing.html (accessed March 1, 2007).

Menzer, J. 2001. *The wildest ride: A history of NASCAR (or how a bunch of good ol' boys built a billion-dollar industry out of wrecking cars).* New York: Simon & Schuster.

Miller, G. W. 2002. *Men and speed: A wild ride through NASCAR's breakout season.* New York: PublicAffairs.

Miller, T. 2001. *Sportsex.* Philadelphia: Temple University Press.

Mooney, C. 2005. *The Republican war on science.* New York: Basic Books.

Morris, M. 1989. Tooth and claw: Tales of survival and "Crocodile Dundee." *Social Text* 21: 105–127.

Nethaway, R. 2006. Scientology off to the NASCAR races. *Waco Tribune-Herald*, June 8, 5.

Newberry, P. 2004. NASCAR mixing religion, racing. *Deseret Morning News*, February 9, 1–2.

Newman, J. I., and M. D. Giardina. 2008. NASCAR and the "Southernization" of America: Spectatorship, subjectivity, and the confederation of identity. *Cultural Studies <> Critical Methodologies* (November).

Putney, C. 2003. *Muscular Christianity: Manhood and sports in Protestant America, 1880–1920.* Cambridge, MA: Harvard University Press.

Religion and Ethics Newsweekly. 2000. Gentlemen start your prayers. Episode no. 408, first aired on October 20 by PBS. Written by R. Lipsyte. Directed by Sue Ann Staake-Wayne.

_______. 2001. NASCAR and religion. Episode no. 426. First broadcast February 23 by PBS. Directed by Sue Ann Staake-Wayne.

Rhee, A. 2005. God and NASCAR: On any given Sunday, drivers pray before they take the track. MSNBC.com, www.msnbc.msn.com/id/7286393 (accessed February 17, 2007).

Richardson, P. J., and R. Darden. 1997. *Wheels of thunder: Top NASCAR and Indy car professionals share how they stay on track.* Nashville, TN: Thomas Nelson Publishers.

Russell, L. D. 2007. *Godspeed: Racing is my religion.* New York: Continuum International.

Scherer, G. 2004. The godly must be crazy. *Grist,* October 27, www.grist.org/news/maindish/2004/10/27/scherer-christian (accessed December 5, 2007).

Schneider, B. 2004. Bush promotes domestic high tech agenda; a look at NASCAR Nation. *CNN Live Today.* First broadcast on April 26 by CNN.

Schultz, J. 2006. Rubbing fenders with religion. *Atlanta Journal-Constitution,* June 8, 6.

Scientology. 2006. Dianetics racing team to join NASCAR circuit. Scientology, www.scientology.org/newsmedia/briefing/2006/dianetics/060525.html (accessed July 27, 2007).

Shaftel, D. 2008a. Amid checkered flags, ministries keep faith. *New York Times,* February 15, D4.

_______. 2008b. Angels in the infield at Daytona. *New York Times,* February 15, D4.

Smith, M. 2001. A renewed faith in the human race. NASCAR.com, www.nascar.com/2001/NEWS/09/27/smith_commentary/index.html (accessed November 27, 2007).

Vavrus, M. D. 2007. The politics of NASCAR dads: Branded media paternity. *Critical Studies in Media Communications* 24, no. 3: 245–261.

Waltrip, D. 2005. Driver testimonial of Darrell Waltrip. TheGoal.com, http://www.thegoal.com/players/autoracing/waltrip_dale/waltrip.html (accessed August 30, 2008).

Warren, L. 2007. NASCAR's Reutimann: Faith-driven. BPSports, www.bpsports.net/bpsports.asp?ID=5552 (accessed October 22, 2007).

Wilkey, L. 2006. NASCAR great Shepherd finds "victory in Jesus." *Associated Baptist Press,* www.abpnews.com/1384.article (accessed January 23, 2006).

Wolf, N. 2007. *The end of America: Letter of warning to a young patriot.* White River Junction, VT: Chelsea Green Publishing.

Wright, J. 2002. *Fixin' to git: One fan's love affair with NASCAR's Winston Cup.* Durham, NC: Duke University Press.

Yates, B. 2005. The NASCAR red state. *American Spectator* 38, no. 3: 12–15.

Zweig, E. 2007. *Drive like hell: NASCAR's best quotes and quips.* Buffalo, NY: Firefly Books.

IV

The Gospel According to Mel Gibson

Critical Reflections on *The Passion of The Christ*[1]

RHONDA HAMMER AND DOUGLAS KELLNER

The February 2004 release of Mel Gibson's *The Passion of The Christ* was a major cultural event. Receiving a tremendous amount of advance publicity due to allegations of anti-Semitism as well as adulatory responses from conservative Christians, who were the first to see it, the film achieved more buzz before its release than any film in recent memory.[2] Gibson himself helped orchestrate the publicity with selective showings of *The Passion* and strategic appearances on TV shows, where he came off as something of a Hollywood eccentric, albeit one who was only too happy to admit to his past sins and to claim that he had achieved "salvation" through his adherence to Christianity. His film, he insisted, was a testament to the truth of Christ and how Christ died so that sinners like Gibson could be saved and enjoy eternal life.[3]

However, many critics argue that Gibson's behavior before and after the film's release demonstrates that the film was more of a testimony to Gibson's own fundamentalist version of Christianity than to what many Christians believe to be the meaning of the doctrine attributed to Jesus Christ. Gibson's claims to truthfulness and telling it as it is (or was) are clearly problematic, given that all films reflect the visions and biases of their writers, directors, and producers. Indeed, it could be argued that *The Passion* represents a reflection of how Gibson perceives himself. In previous film roles and interviews, he presents himself as Christ-like and is constantly referring to persecution and victimization by "Hollywood," the media, and others. As he put it to Rachel Abramowitz of the *Los Angeles Times*, "I'm subjected to religious persecution, persecution as an artist, persecution as an American and persecution as a man."[4]

Moreover, Gibson and his advocates rejected much of the criticism of the film posed by Christian and Jewish theologians, as well as by movie critics and others, by characterizing their views as anti-Christian, claiming, in Gibson's words, "I didn't realize it would be so vicious. . . . The acts against this film started early. As soon as I announced I was doing it, it was 'this dangerous thing.' There is a vehement anti-Christian sentiment out there, and they don't want it. It's vicious. . . . There's a huge war raging, and it's over us!"[5] In this respect, Gibson managed to affirm a conviction shared by many conservative Christians, of all denominations, who believe that they are persecuted in the United States. Even though many would find this viewpoint bizarre, given "how much power they generally have," Austin Cline explains that for Christians this makes perfect sense: "They need to be persecuted as part of their theology. Persecution is a divine sign that they are right and others are wrong."[6] In fact, some argue that the success of Gibson's *The Passion* is due to his exploitation of this myth.[7]

This chapter interrogates both the popularity of the film and the intense controversy it educed. Moreover, we assert that the significance of *The Passion* is demonstrated, firstly, by the arguments over Christianity and the politics of representation encoded in the movie, especially in relation to the depiction of Jews. In addition, critique of the film continues to be relevant because of the wealth of literature over cinematic, political, and theological issues it has provoked in both the academic and popular domains. Indeed, the discussions and commentaries evoked by the media spectacle of Mel Gibson and *The Passion of The Christ* are among the most fascinating and salient consequences of this event.

The film emerged during a period of heated debate and global friction over the Bush/Cheney administration's Iraq intervention, leading to concern over the Manichean vision that informs contemporary Islamic fundamentalism, the Bush/Cheney administration's militarism, and right-wing Christian fundamentalism.[8] The Manicheans, a Gnostic sect emerging in the third century AD and declared heretical by the early Catholic Church, saw the world in terms of a battle between good and evil and the forces of light and darkness.

This dualistic Manichean vision is shared by Osama bin Laden and his followers in Al Qaeda and by the leaders of the Bush/Cheney administration, all of whom see the world in absolute terms of *good versus evil* and *us versus them* whereby each group's "Other" is conceived as corrupt, vile, evil, and to be exterminated. We argue that Gibson's film is part of the reactionary Manicheanism that is fueling religious hatred and violence today, and the film therefore deserves a close reading and political contextualization to discern its meanings, ideologies, and possible effects and uses.

We also argue, however, that Gibson's *The Passion* is a strong propaganda film that uses cinematic techniques to promote Gibson's own theological views and values and that it was brilliantly produced and marketed to sell his own interpretation of Jesus and Christianity.

MEL GIBSON'S VERSION OF CHRISTIANITY

The Passion of The Christ is very much Mel Gibson's construction of Christianity, depicting his vision of Jesus of Nazareth's arrest, prosecution, and crucifixion by recreating of the fourteen stations of the cross marking the sites of Jesus's final journey to his crucifixion and the last twelve hours of his life, involving a set of painful and extremely violent episodes that make up much of the film. The story of *The Passion of The Christ* is part of the gospel of Jesus, focusing on his suffering and death and the sacrifice of God's only son to take upon himself the sinfulness of humanity and provide hope of redemption. In different historical epochs, the story of the Passion, which depicts Christ's suffering and as evidence of God's love for humanity and of the possibility of eternal redemption, has become central to Christianity, revitalizing itself by getting people to identify with Christ's suffering and to join the church in the hope of redeeming their own suffering and finding salvation.

Wasting little time in getting into its sadomasochism, the film begins with the temple guards arresting Jesus in the Garden of Gethsemane, where they savagely beat him and take him to the Jewish high priest Caiaphas. On the way, they suspend Jesus from a bridge, choking him and dangling him over the water, incidents for which there is no Gospel basis. Gibson's version of Christianity is exceptionally violent and bloodthirsty and evokes horror at the magnitude of Christ's suffering and disgust for his tormentors and torturers. There is, to be sure, a small pacifist moment in the film. When the temple guards arrive to arrest Jesus in an early scene, his disciples begin to fight back. Jesus warns that "those who live by the sword shall die by it," ordering his followers to back down. They do, and during the rest of the film, Jesus's disciples are shown as cowardly and supine. While it would have been possible to stress the peace-loving and benevolent aspects of Christ's teaching in more detail, there is but a brief phrase in which he orders his followers to renounce violence; the rest of the film exhibits highly violent and brutal beating and Jesus's crucifixion.

Gibson conveys his messages through images and spectacle, not words, thus undercutting a key aspect of Christianity as a religion of the book and the word. Gibson's film is very sparing in its use of subtitles, and it is the spectacle that most engages viewers. This follows a contemporary trend to promote a culture of image and spectacle but goes against a more traditional Christianity that is suspicious and critical of graven images and relies on "the word" for its teaching. Gibson, however, is clearly a purveyor of graven images, and highly problematic ones at that.

Gibson's narrative of the Passion combines source material from the Gospels, a literary version of the vision of the nineteenth-century nun Anne Catherine Emmerich, and other sources.[9] Anne Catherine Emmerich reportedly had visions of Christ throughout her life, and her hallucinations were put in literary form by the famous German poet Clemens Brentano, whose text *The Dolorous Passion of Our Lord Jesus Christ according to the Meditations of Anne Catherine Emmerich* (1833) was crucial to Gibson's construction of *The Passion*. The anti-Semitic imagery and association of Jews with Satan, closely followed by Gibson, in her text could be ascribed to Brentano, who embellished her stories; hence, Emmerich's 2004 beatification by Pope John Paul II was a highly controversial gesture.

On the whole, Gibson's film takes the form of the notorious Augsburg and Oberammergau medieval passion plays, which themselves have been accused over the centuries of promoting anti-Semitism by presenting Jews as the monstrous killers of Christ.[10] In terms of contemporary cinema, the extent of the violence and blood in Gibson's *The Passion* gives it the aura of a horror film as Jesus is beaten and whipped, and nails are driven through his hands, so that he is covered with lacerations and blood by the end of the film; devils and demons also appear in many scenes throughout the movie, which codes it as a horror film.

The languages used include Aramaic, Latin, and Hebrew, providing both a distancing effect that creates an illusion of realism and a sense of historical otherness and eeriness different from previous Hollywood Jesus films. The use of realist cinematography helps provide a quasidocumentary look and feel, as does the use of languages of the period and sets that appear to capture the atmosphere of the region (though it was filmed in Italy). Yet *The Passion* deploys a variety of cinematic techniques to help capture the strangeness of the story, and while some of the narrative follows the Gospel accounts, there are significant departures that signal the specificity of Gibson's construction of Christianity and view of Christ's death.

Gibson himself allegedly held the hammer that pounded the nail through Jesus's hand, signaling his personal involvement in the film and participation in the sinfulness for which Christ died. Indeed, the film should be named *Mel Gibson's Version of the Passion of The Christ* since, like the Gospels themselves, the film is a highly personal interpretation that represents a specific view of Christianity and the Gospels and other sources dealing with Christ's "sufferings," or "Passion." Gibson's Jesus is a man's man, closely resembling a Mel Gibson action hero. He takes tremendous beatings without a whimper, refuses to be crushed by his enemies, and presents a supremely masculine Jesus, unlike the feminized Jesus of much traditional iconography or the Hollywoodized Christ, who is traditionally handsome and attractive in the Hollywood mode. Gibson's Jesus, by contrast, is played by an off-beat character actor, Jim Caviezel, who seems to have identified with Gibson's version of Christ and plays with intensity the young Galilean carpenter who rounded up a posse of followers and produced a group that founded one of the world's major religions. The Caviezel Jesus is virile, buff, and very macho, representing Gibson's masculine ideal as well as his version of Jesus.

Revealingly, most of the main characters are clearly white and Western—hardly an accurate portrayal of the race and ethnicity of the biblical peoples of the period. Despite some attempts at authenticity, Gibson thus continues a long Western tradition of whitening Christian iconography and presenting images of Jesus and his followers as projections of the white, Western imagination.

Gibson's film has arty and exotic moments, such as the opening scene in the Garden of Gethsemane when Satan tempts Christ, and there are occasional Felliniesque touches in the surreal representations of Satan and exuberant representations of crowds. This inclusion of the devil as a major character, not found in Gospel accounts of the Passion, codes the film as a horror film in *The Exorcist* genre and provides, as we shall see, a major vehicle for the film's anti-Semitism. The music is often eerie, and the sound track powerfully conveys the violence and horrific brutality with the jolting swish and crack of whips. The film borrows from Sam Peckinpah's and Sergio Leone's graphic and balletic depictions of violence, with artful editing, close-ups, and slow-motion sequences of brutality, lavishly garnished with spurts and gushes of blood. The sadomasochistic aesthetic, however, largely focuses on cutting between close-ups of brutal torturers and torn flesh, lacerating wounds, and the manly Jesus's stoic acceptance of his travails, together with edits to leering and jeering Roman soldiers and crowds and Jesus's helpless followers and the two Marys (Mother and Magdalene) looking on in agony. In this sense, the film becomes more of a classic splatter film, masquerading as a theological depiction of Christ's Passion that conveys the fundamental Christian message of Christ's suffering for human redemption.

The representation of the strong and stoic Jesus, manly enough to be beaten to a pulp with nary a whimper, is reminiscent of Clint Eastwood's "Man with No Name" in Sergio Leone's spaghetti westerns and Eastwood's own 1973 film *High Plains Drifter*. The ultramacho bearer of unimaginable violence and torture is also evocative of the Rambo figure and many of Mel Gibson's previous action adventure heroes, such as *Braveheart*'s (1995) stalwart William Wallace (played by Gibson), who is virtually crucified at the end of the film, or any number of other Gibson figures in films like *Ransom*, *Payback*, or *The Patriot*, who are badly beaten but ultimately redeemed.[11]

Structurally, the film opens as a horror film with Jesus's confrontation with Satan and then the frightening arrival of the temple guards, who arrest and torture him. It then morphs into a biblical epic and spectacle of violence with overtones of the splatter film, in which Jesus is tried and battered in the temple, then sent to the Roman courts, where Pontius Pilate tries to appease the bloodthirsty Jewish priests' demand for Christ's death by flogging him. The violence is so extreme that, as Frank Rich points out, "with its laborious build-up to its orgasmic spurting of blood and other bodily fluids, Mr. Gibson's film is constructed like nothing so much as a porn movie, replete with slo-mo climaxes and pounding music for the money shots."[12] Indeed, *The Passion* presents a pornography of violence with savage beatings, brutality, and torture as extreme as any in S&M torture films. The narrative also contains voyeuristic homoeroticism and the fetishism of body parts from the reverently portrayed foot washing to obscenely violent flaying and scourging of flesh. The fact that the violence is being inflicted on a major global religious figure adds to the horror and provides an iconography of violence as extreme as any in cinematic history.

Formally, Gibson's *The Passion* can be read as a postmodern pastiche of different Hollywood genres and conventions, drawing on both European art film and Hollywood biblical epic, action adventure, horror, and other genres. Ideologically, on the whole, Gibson's *The Passion* is a highly problematic version of the arrest, torture, and murder of Jesus, permeated, as we shall demonstrate, with anti-Semitism, sexism, classism, homophobia, and gross historical inaccuracies in the service of promoting Gibson's peculiar version of Catholicism.[13]

Various filmmakers have presented Jesus's life and the story of the Gospels extremely differently in diverse historical epochs. Nicholas Ray's *King of Kings* (1961) presented a pacifist Jesus, and Franco Zefferelli's *Jesus of Nazareth* (1977) focused on Jesus's teachings and good works, while Norman Jewison's *Jesus Christ Superstar* (1973) provided a countercultural Jesus. Although one could present a revolutionary Jesus, as did the Italian filmmaker Pier Paulo Pasolini in his *The Gospel According to Saint Matthew* (1967), which focused on Jesus's relation to his disciples and the common people, Gibson's Christ is presented as largely solitary, and having been betrayed by his followers, he stoically accepts his isolation and harsh fate. Whereas Pasolini stressed Jesus's social gospel, emphasizing Christian love, community, and benevolence, Gibson's gospel is more violent and bloody, with no beatitudes or sympathy for the poor, oppressed, and excluded, who either look to Jesus for miraculous cures in Gibson's film or exult in his suffering and crucifixion.

In contrast to Gibson's version of the Christ story, Martin Scorsese's *The Last Temptation of Christ* (1988), based on the novel by Nikos Kazantzakis, highlights Jesus's ambiguous and conflicted relation with Mary Magdalene and the conflicts between the divine and human in his character. Scorsese presents a much more richly textured and challenging film than Gibson, but because of a right-wing fundamentalist Christian attack on the film, it was quickly pulled from circulation. Gibson's film, by contrast, has become a global success thanks to the support of the same groups who called Scorsese's film blasphemous and worse.[14]

In contrast to previous versions of the life of Jesus, Gibson's *The Passion* thus really takes little interest in the life or teachings of the Christ, focusing instead on the Passion, with very brief flashbacks to episodes in Jesus's early life, the Sermon on the Mount, and the Last Supper. The film has been, somewhat surprisingly, in view of its almost unbearable violence, a global success that seemed to make Gibson one of the hottest figures in film in 2004, when it became a worldwide phenomenon. Helped by all the advanced publicity, many evangelical and fundamentalist Christian churches seemingly organized their congregations to attend together, making the showing of the film a religious event. Many audiences allegedly wept loudly during Jesus's torment and found it a deeply moving and disturbing experience. Many film critics tended to be negative, although there were some positive reviews, and the popular press emphasized the popularity of the film, making it a "must see" cultural phenomenon, which helped put it on the top of the list of the highest-grossing films for week after week.

THE MARKETING OF *THE PASSION OF THE CHRIST*

Although *The Passion* became an instant box office success, it elicited heated controversy, with passionate defenders and sharp critics. Opening widely in the United States on February 25, Ash Wednesday, it had become the tenth-highest-grossing domestic movie of all time by the Easter and Passover holidays in April; by May 22, 2004, it had taken in nearly $369 million in the United States and just over $581 million, adding the worldwide receipts to the U.S. gross. The film eventually allegedly grossed over $600 million worldwide, although the total profits have not been listed on the Icon company website since 2004 due to a pending lawsuit.[15]

Further, the film has also been a great merchandise marketing success, selling books, CDs, DVDs, and various religious items, such as nails resembling those that pierced Jesus. An article on the merchandising of paraphernalia linked with the film notes that the book *The Passion: Photography from the Movie "The Passion of The Christ"* rose to number three on the *New York Times* best-seller list and has sold over 650,000 copies, the CD sound track of the film was highly popular, and the jewelry firm that was the exclusive marketer for the film had sold 150,000 crosses and 125,000 pewter crucifixion nails as of early April 2004.[16]

Hence, Gibson's marketing strategy and the support of Christian churches and audiences may help explain in part the great commercial success of the film. Yet the intense focus on the drama and intensity of Christ's Passion (i.e., his suffering in the Crucifixion) may also explain both the power of the film and the esteem in which it is held with certain audiences. Despite the criticisms of the film that we will develop in the next section, it has become popular with both film culture and religious community audiences.

Reviews indicate that some major film critics responded to *The Passion* very positively as a film, even appreciating its horror-film-like aspects and cinematic violence. Fans of extreme cinema affirmed the cinematography, style, and excessive violence, while religious audiences responded to its Christian themes, and other filmgoers responded to the titanic struggle between good and evil, which is a staple of popular cinema.[17] The Passion story is one of a monumental clash between good and evil, and the monstrousness and horror of the Crucifixion has never been presented in such excruciating detail. For certain audiences, the film's depiction of the unbearable suffering imposed on the Christ and his endurance of the Passion confirms their experience of Christ's divinity and reaffirms that his purpose was to suffer for and redeem "mankind's" sins. Much of the film deals in painful detail with Christ's suffering, and this seems to have provided a powerful experience for some audiences.

"The Scourging at the Pillar," which has no basis in the Gospels, was especially excruciating. Jesus is first caned by two loutish Roman guards and, despite repeated beatings, heroically rises to his feet. He is then beaten with multipronged whips adorned with small iron balls that slash his flesh to ribbons, marking his body with deep wounds and covering it with blood. Repeated facial beatings close one eye, and cumulatively Gibson's spectacle of the Passion produces the bloodiest Christ iconography yet.

Gibson's film crew allegedly focused serious attention on historical detail, and some viewers read this as documentary proof of the authenticity of the Gospels, providing a "you are there" experience of Christ's last hours. The use of natural lighting provides striking contrasts between night and day and exterior and interior scenes. Some of the interior and nighttime scenes achieve a dramatic chiaroscuro quality reminiscent of religious art, while the outdoor scenes have a dusty and sun-drenched Mediterranean look. Lavish care was given to sets, costumes, and designs, making the film much more apparently realistic than many biblical epics.

Thus, the carefully crafted cinematic aspects of the film help account for its power and popularity. The sound track is extremely well produced, providing exotic sounds that both disorient audiences and introduce a sense of the macabre to the story. Like *The Exorcist, The Passion* may well utilize subliminal sounds and images to intensify its effects.[18] All of the tricks of the high-tech horror film are present, with demon and monster children screaming, birds screeching and poking out eyeballs, and people speaking in tongues or strange languages, with few subtitle translations to help anchor meaning. The musical score sweeps up and down in crescendos of (simulated) majesty, cuts to familiar weepy and sentimental orchestrations, and then deploys chanting vocals and non-Western audio effects. And the sound effects of blood spurting, whips lacerating flesh, nails being pounded into hands, and other horrifying details of Christ's crucifixion provide an overpowering audio sound track.

The fast editing and crafted cinematography also contribute to the power of the film for some audiences. Never has there been so much blood and gore in a single film, and the experience of such extreme pain and suffering leaves audiences overwhelmed, susceptible to subliminal messages and ideological massage. The torture scenes often cut to Jesus's point of view with startling close-ups and quick flashbacks to episodes of his life that enable audiences to identify with the character and vicariously undergo his torment. The guttural moaning, groaning, gurgling, and gasping of Jesus during the Passion are interspersed with Mary's agonized face and close-ups of crowds cheering, Roman centurions jeering and hysterically laughing, and Jewish priests looking on smugly. The film rapidly cuts to reaction shots with women, children, and others looking at Christ in wonder and adoration, thus providing a mise-en-scène that suggests Christ's divinity and uniqueness. Yet precisely the intense drama of the Passion, the almost unbearable violence, and the horrific act of the Crucifixion of the alleged Son of God provide an artful cover for some extremely reactionary messages and ideologies, as we will argue in the next section.

THE PASSIONS OF ANTI-SEMITISM AND RIGHT-WING PATRIARCHY

In terms of the film's politics of representation, *The Passion* is deeply sexist and patriarchal, homophobic, classist, and anti-Semitic, although Gibson allegedly toned the latter down in response to early criticism, reluctantly cutting, for instance, the English subtitles for the inflammatory passage in Matthew 27:25, in which Jews take responsibility for killing Jesus by asserting, after Pontius Pilate has washed his hands of the matter, "His blood be on us, and on our children." The phrase is kept, however, in the Aramaic, and the film's anti-Semitism goes beyond the biblical sources in both subtle and overt ways.[19]

Throughout the film, there are imagistic and narrative connections between Jews and the devil, a highly polymorphus and sexually ambiguous figure in Gibson's narrative. Opening images show Jesus praying in the blue-lit and fog-shrouded Garden of Gethsemane while an androgynous devil appears to tempt him (played by actress Rosalinda Celentano with shaved eyebrows and a dubbed voice). Jesus resists the devil, stomping on a snake that slithers toward him as one of Satan's apparitions. Unlike Adam, who is tempted by the snake in the Garden of Eden, bringing sin and death into the world, Gibson's Jesus triumphs over evil and temptation (as does *First Blood*'s [1984] Rambo, who crushes a snake in his hand).

No devil appears in the Gospel accounts of Jesus's meditation and arrest, where Satan appears to cast him as the embodiment of evil, a figure that will be associated with Jews throughout the film. The story of Satan in the garden and his struggle with Jesus during the entire Passion is the literary invention of the nineteenth-century nun and notorious anti-Semitic Anne Catherine Emmerich, whose narrative Gibson faithfully follows in his version of Christ's Passion.[20] The scene cuts to the temple where Judas accepts the Jewish priests' bribe to betray Jesus, and in a flashback scene where Judas bestows his fateful kiss on Jesus, one again hears the snake hissing. And as the temple guards haul Jesus away, there is another quick glimpse of Satan and an ominous hiss. When Jesus is brought before Caiaphas and the priests, once again Satan appears. As Jewish crowds chant to kill Christ and the Jewish priests smugly look on, again images of a smirking, demonic figure appear. Throughout the scenes of Jesus being beaten, the Satan figure smirks at the brutality and appears near the end when Caiaphas mocks Jesus crucified on the cross to register pleasure in the seeming defeat of Jesus.

Thus, the images, spectacle, and narrative of the film associate Jews with Satan and evil, going far beyond Gospel accounts. Moreover, Gibson deploys horror-film iconography throughout the narrative. For instance, after his betrayal of Jesus, Judas is confronted with a hissing devil face, and then monster Jewish children with devilish eyes mock him, driving him to suicide. A baby carried by Satan reveals itself to be a demon, and Satan takes different forms in the film, producing a sense that evil is afoot in the world and is associated with Jews and the killing of Jesus. Taken before Caiaphas and his sinister cadre of Jewish priests,[21] Christ is mocked, insulted, hit, spat upon, and abused to the great delight of the sadistic priestly caste and much of the temple crowd. As Katha Pollit puts it,

> The high priest Caiaphas and his faction are not just bad, they fit neatly into ancient Christian stereotypes: They are rich, arrogant and gaudily dressed; they plot and scheme and bribe; they cleverly manipulate the brutal but straightforward Romans; they are gratuitously "cruel" and "hard-hearted," to quote Anne Catherine Emmerich, the nineteenth-century German nun whose visions of the Passion Gibson relied on for some of the more disgusting tortures he inflicts on Jesus. Physically, they are anti-Semitic cartoons: The priests have big noses and gnarly faces, lumpish bodies, yellow teeth; . . . The "good Jews" look like Italian movie stars (Magdalene actually *is* an Italian movie star, the lovely Monica Bellucci); Mary, who would have been around 50 and appeared 70, could pass for a ripe 35. These visual characterizations follow not just the Oberammergau Passion Play that Hitler found so touching but a long tradition of Christian New Testament iconography in which the villains look Semitic and the heroes, although equally Jewish, look Northern European.[22]

To prolong the suspense and agony, Caiaphas turns Jesus over to the Romans and Pontius Pilate, who personally finds no fault with Christ. But in the face of a hostile, angry mob and the Jewish priest's insistence upon his guilt, Pilate has Jesus flogged mercilessly and then turns him over to King Herod, the Jewish authority in collaboration with the Romans. Herod is presented as highly effeminate, and the members of his court are overtly homosexual, promiscuous, and debauched. The brief Herod sequences produce images of Jewish decadence and sensuality, consistent with right-wing views of pagan pre-Christian culture, yet without explicit biblical grounding, revealing again the highly constructed and problematic nature of Gibson's interpretation, which links decadent Jews with homosexuality, apparently two of his personal obsessions.[23]

The Passion is thus deeply and insidiously anti-Semitic, as the film systematically produces a series of associations between Jews, Satan, and Christ's arrest and crucifixion, going well beyond Gospel accounts of Jews' connection with Christ's death by associating the episode with Satan in a Manicheanism as pronounced as that of George W. Bush and Osama bin Laden. Since Satan does not appear in any of the Gospel accounts of Christ's Passion, this obvious departure from the scriptures and association of Jews with Satan together give away Gibson's biases and undermine his claims that he is just following the Gospels.

Jon Meacham writes in a *Newsweek* cover story titled "Who Killed Jesus?" that Gibson put Satan in such a prominent role to underscore that the world is in the grip of evil and that Christ must make the ultimate sacrifice to save humanity from its sins.[24] Since throughout the film Satan hovers in and out of scenes that prominently feature Jews and Christ's Passion, the implication is that Jews are a source of the world's evil, that they are in the grips of Satan and thus minions of the devil. This appalling view has been used to justify extermination of Jews over the centuries and is embedded in the iconography and mise-en-scène of Gibson's film, if not explicitly argued and presented in the text.

Gibson insists that he presents good Jews in his narrative, for instance, individuals in crowd scenes who respond favorably to Christ's teaching and then show sympathy for Jesus during the Passion, such as the woman who gives him water and the man who helps carry Jesus's cross after he has been beaten to a pulp. This is a weak defense, however, for Jesus and his disciples were in fact Jews, and Gibson's distinction between "good" and "bad" Jews exhibits both his fundamental Manicheanism and his bad faith in presenting strongly negative and anti-Semitic representations of Jews, associations of Jews with Satan, and the Jew's responsibility for the death of Jesus in his narrative. In fact, the only good Jews depicted in Gibson's *The Passion* are Jesus and his followers or those Jews who appear ready to covert to Jesus's teaching as they watch him bear his cross during the Passion.

Many purely Gibsonian fictions make evident his departure from the Gospels and construction of his own version of Jesus. In a flashback scene that shows Jesus building a very modern table, taller and sleeker than standard ones of his day, his mother Mary says, "It'll never catch on," a phrase with a completely contemporary ring. The notion that the Galilean carpenter is too advanced for the times and that his furniture innovations will not be accepted is an obviously constructed representation of Jesus as forward-looking and avant-garde for which there is no biblical reference, once again signaling Gibson's departure from the scriptures to produce his own idiosyncratic story. Indeed, the inventive, ahead-of-his-time Jesus is perhaps another Gibson projection of his self-image as a daring filmmaker willing to take on novel creative projects, just as his depiction of Jesus as ultramasculine is a Gibson action-hero self-projection.

On the whole, the women in the film represent a conservative patriarch's fantasy of how women are put on earth to serve and adore men. The main women in the film, Mary Magdalene and Jesus's mother Mary, look at Jesus in adoration during the Passion episode, hold each other and weep, and say little during the entire film. Like Jesus, they are stoic and largely silent during the unrelenting violence inflicted on Christ, exhibiting no agency or resistance, other than crying and holding each other, rather than shouting out, protesting, or screaming, as one might well respond to seeing such brutality inflicted on a loved one. One scene shows Mary grasping Jesus's bloodied foot with almost erotic urgency, a symbol of female submission in the service of men, if not outright foot fetishism.

The Passion follows conventional patriarchal iconography, evident in Clint Eastwood films like *High Plains Drifter* (1973) and *Pale Rider* (1985), which highlight close-ups of adoring women looking on at the major male character. There are no strong female characters in *The Passion*, and women are largely part of a faceless crowd, sadistically enthusing during Christ's systematic abuse and torture or looking on helplessly. Mary and Magdalene are attired in what appear to be nun's habits during the Passion and appear to embody Gibson's feminine ideal: women who are saintly, pure, quiet, and reverential toward men.

The film is also highly individualist, with Jesus as the ultimate Mel Gibson superhero, focusing relentlessly on Christ and showing his disciples and followers to be weak, timid, and pusillanimous. While many versions of the Gospel play up the Christian community and Jesus's close and loving relation with his disciples, in Gibson's version, the disciples are uniformly cowardly and craven, raising questions as to why one would want to join such an organization and undermining notions of Christian community and solidarity that have been so important over the centuries. None of Jesus's followers stands out or speaks up; nor does the Judas episode in Gibson's version probe into why his supposed friend betrays him. Further, the contemptuous looks of the Jewish priests who buy Judas and the loud clink of the money thrown to him dismiss Judas as a sellout rather than explore Judas's motivations. Interestingly, by contrast, *Jesus Christ Superstar* (1973) paints Judas as a resistance fighter who breaks with Jesus because the Nazarene sells out and gives up the revolutionary cause for celebrity status and a decadent lifestyle, while an ABC TV movie shown at the time of *The Passion's* opening in 2004 presents Judas as a revolutionary disappointed in Jesus's pacifism and desirous of a more vigorous response to Roman oppression. Yet Gibson has no interest in Judas beyond associating him with the devil, money, jealousy, betrayal, and Jews.

Although the Jews are largely shown as corrupt, decadent, and the cause of Christ's death or as ignorant masses calling for Christ's crucifixion, the Romans, by contrast, are depicted as ruled by noble leaders like Pontius Pilate, who twice refuses to condemn Christ despite pressures from the Jewish priests and the crowd, as well as suggestions that in light of the widespread calling for Jesus's punishment, Caesar will punish him if another rebellion occurs. Pilate philosophizes, posing the fabled query "What is truth?" in response to claims of Jesus's blasphemy and loudly proclaims, "Behold the man!" when Jesus is presented to the crowd before his condemnation. Pilate lavishly washes his hands to signal his distance from Jesus's persecution and then proposes that he pardon a criminal in the traditional fashion, providing another avenue of escape for Jesus. But in the face of repeated calls by Caiaphas and the Jewish mob to "crucify him!" and calls by Caiaphas and the crowd to spare Barabbas instead of Jesus, Pilate reluctantly signals that the mob can have its way and take Jesus. Crucially, it is Caiaphas who prompts the crowd to release Barabbas and not Jesus when Pilate offers mercy to one of the two individuals up for crucifixion. Moreover, Caiaphas is the first to repeatedly shout out "Crucify him!," which pins Jesus's crucifixion largely on the Jews. Importantly, neither of these interventions is depicted in the Gospels, and historical sources indicate that Pilate and the Romans were responsible for the crucifixion, not the Jews, revealing again Gibson's anti-Semitic biases in the narration.[25]

Further, Pilate's wife, Claudia, is idealized as a noble Roman who comes to recognize Jesus's divinity. When Pilate is first confronted with deciding what to do with the prophet Jesus, whom Caiaphas and his clique have arrested and charged with blasphemy, Claudia recommends that Pilate not persecute the Nazarene and gazes sympathetically on Jesus throughout. She is an admirable partner to Pilate, who confides his political dilemmas to her, although, once again, her supposed nobility is not found in any Gospel accounts and comes from Anne Catherine Emmerich's literary version. Curiously, Pilate and Claudia are perhaps the only two characters beyond Jesus who have any character or depth in Gibson's narrative, with most figures appearing as caricatures and cartoons.

While the noble Romans are depicted as sensitive and caring, Pilate's underlings, who ultimately carry out the scourging and crucifixion of Christ, are represented as sadistic thugs who revel in abuse and torture. Earlier, the Jewish guards who arrested Christ in the Garden were shown as brutish and thuggish, a consistently negative view of lower-class functionaries in the film. But it is the Roman police who carry out the most brutal beatings in unbearably long sequences of sadistic detail, which signals a deep misogyny and sadism in Gibson's imaginary, as well as contempt for the underclass, depicted as a bloodthirsty rabble.[26]

Gibson is obviously engaging in historical revisionism here, letting the Roman leaders off the hook for their oppression of the Jews and Jesus. Most reliable historians, starting with Philo of Alexandria and Josephus, present Pontius Pilate and his accomplices as brutal figures, who systematically persecuted and killed thousands of Jews, including, according to many accounts, Jesus and his followers.[27] Gibson's Pontius Pilate, by contrast, is the noble Roman, a Brutus/Caesar hybrid who intones noble sentiments and philosophical utterances and tries his best to keep his hands clean of the act of condemning the Christ.

Caiaphas and the Jewish priests, by contrast, are shown as dark, sinister, and corrupt, taking payoffs from the Romans and becoming angry when Jesus attacks the money changers in the temple, depriving them of some of their bounty as collaborators. Jewish mobs are also shown as a frenzied collective, given to bloodlust for punishment and calling for Christ to be crucified. At the end of the film, as Jesus seems to die on the cross, there is a set of fragmented and mysterious spectacles that include the cracking and collapse of the temple, which Jesus had prophesized, and the unmasking and humiliation of Satan, whose shroud falls off, revealing a bald-headed and screaming monster, producing another subtle association between the defeat of Satan and the fall of the temple.

Thus, in terms of the appropriation of the structure of the medieval passion play, the sources of the iconography, the specific representation of Jews, the narrative role in ascribing Christ's death to Jews, the association of Jews with Satan, specific breaks with the Gospel's account of the Crucifixion, and the historical inaccuracy of whitewashing Pilate and the Romans, Gibson's *The Passion* is deeply anti-Semitic, and his version of the Passion is highly problematic.[28] It is also, as noted, reactionary in many other ways, and we can easily imagine smug Christian philistines leaving the film convinced that Jews killed Christ and are in league with Satan; gays are corrupt and decadent; working-class louts are brutal, stupid, and violent; and in the light of the evil rampant in the world, the church, state, and police need more power.

CRUSADING FUNDAMENTALISM, MILITARISM, AND CONTESTATION OVER CHRISTIANITY

To assess the resonance and significance of *The Passion* in the contemporary moment properly, we suggest that the film be read in the context of the politics of an era marked by post–September 11 fear and a war of religious fundamentalisms, militarism, and accelerating societal violence and turbulence. Since the collapse of the Soviet Union, there has been a wave of religious fervor in former Communist regions, and in the United States, with George W. Bush's ascension to the presidency, Christian fundamentalists have received high positions in government. At least part of Bush's War on Terror policy and invasion of Iraq was fuelled by a sense of crusade.[29] In his response to Bob Woodward's question as to whether he had consulted his father, former president George H. W. Bush, before invading Iraq, Bush Junior admonished Woodward, saying that he had consulted his heavenly father and hoped that he was worthy to be "God's messenger."[30]

Ironically, many neoconservative and pro-Israel Jews in the Bush administration have been among the most aggressive militarists, revealing the complex intermixing of religious and political passions in the Bush/Cheney administration.[31] In this context, there is clearly danger of a surge of irrationalist religious fervor that can take violent forms, such as Al Qaeda's attack on the infidel West, Bush/Cheney's retaliatory militarist response in Afghanistan and Iraq, and Israel's escalating attacks on the Palestinians and its enemies in the region. Films like *The Passion of The Christ* fuel this religious fervor and are thus dangerous cultural forces that should be taken seriously by those interested in political and cultural critique.

Right-wing militarist culture, represented by such products as the Gibson film or the *Left Behind* novels and films, has its analogue in the crusading Christian militarists in Iraq.[32] Yet today, in 2008, seven years after the September 11 tragedy and five years into the invasion and occupation of Iraq, right-wing extremism and the hard-right policies of the Bush/Cheney administration have been more contested. Before 2004, criticisms of the Bush/Cheney regime's actions were more likely to be characterized as unpatriotic and even treasonous within the dominant societal institutions and corporate media. Indeed, the United States has radically changed in the wake of September 11, and not for the better; many experts argue, the very tenets of the U.S. Constitution and the democratic principles it expresses are being transgressed, eroded, and dismantled.

As Naomi Klein so insightfully writes in her best-selling book *The Shock Doctrine* (2007), people often become so traumatized after a personal or collective disaster that they are incapable of "rational thought" and lose their ability to "make sense out of the world."[33] And this is an apt depiction of the state of mind of millions of Americans after the shock of the September 11 terrorist attacks on the World Trade Center and Pentagon. Klein goes on to argue that the Bush administration exploited this large-scale state of shock to implement radical economic and legislative policies, as well as to wage costly and unwarranted wars, which would be unthinkable and sharply opposed in other circumstances. "Like the terrorized prisoner who gives up the names of comrades and renounces his faith, shocked societies often give up things they would otherwise fiercely protect" (Klein 2007, 17).

Rather than providing Americans with the necessary background information needed to understand the attacks and assuaging some of their fears, the Bush/Cheney regime, in conjunction with the corporate media (and lobbyists), engaged in a propaganda campaign designed to further shock and intensify panic and hysteria in order to pursue the administration's conservative agenda. Hence, a culture of fear, which already permeated mainstream news media and U.S. politics, was further exaggerated and employed to distract the public from urgent problems, which included the deterioration of the infrastructure and mounting economic troubles on the domestic front. Moreover, it was during this public disorientation, less than one month after September 11, that Bush signed into law the Patriot Act, which undermined civil liberties and allowed for unilateral increases in military spending, war profiteering, and the powers of the executive branch, as well as the implementation of Bush's "radical vision of a hollow government in which everything from war fighting to disaster response was a for-profit venture" (Klein 2007, 298). The success of this fearmongering found much of its basis in the ideological rhetoric through which the Bush administration, in collusion with the mainstream mass media, manipulated fear of terrorism. As Klein puts it, "A new army of experts instantly materialized to write new and beautiful words on the receptive canvas of our post-trauma consciousness: 'clash of civilizations' ... 'axis of evil,' 'Islamofascism,' 'homeland security'" (Klein 2007, 17). Noted sociologist Barry Glassner points out that "fearmongering depends, in large part, upon people with fancy titles and professional narrators to transform something implausible into something believable" (1999, 207).[34]

After September 11, the public now appeared ripe to welcome and embrace a reductionist, bifurcated, either-or ideologically propagandistic view of the world that distorts the complexities of reality in an oversimplified, oppositional discourse that posits, basically, that there are only two sides to every issue: right and wrong, good and evil, black and white with no shades of grey. It is a *Star Wars* fairy tale version of the world, where the forces of good defend themselves against an evil empire. And the effectiveness of this kind of philosophy is that any person, organization, group, race, ethnicity, or nation can stand in for the tyrannical Darth Vader and the psychopathic puppet-master emperor who determines his actions by pulling his strings.

It is in this context that Mel Gibson's *The Passion of The Christ* takes on its political function. Like the Bush/Cheney administration, Gibson's film contributes to a culture of fear and a Manichean sensibility that good (white Christians) is under attack by the forces of evil. Fortunately for Jews, in the conservative imaginary Arabs came to serve as the embodiment of contemporary evil, so Gibson's vilification of Jews in *The Passion* seems not to have had major effects in terms of outbreaks of anti-Semitic violence. Yet the Manichean vision in Gibson's *The Passion* calls attention to a dualistic absolutism in the contemporary conservative imagination that sees the world in the simplistic terms of a fight between good and evil, which promotes a psychological underpinning for crusading militarism and a politics of fear.

Like the Bush/Cheney administration, Gibson's *The Passion* employs tactics of shock and awe to overpower its audience. It overwhelms rational faculties with its intense and horrific images, unrelenting violence, and seductive music. Like every great work of propaganda, it manipulates its audience into its traps, in this case a fundamentalist Manicheanism and primitivist Christianity. Christian evangelicals were extremely excited about the "event" of *The*

Passion, which they believed would be a great recruiting tool, although there is no evidence that its results are as spectacular as anticipated.[35] It is significant that Gibson's *The Passion* works on a visceral level of emotion rather than thought, which seems highly foreign to Gibson's mind-set. Gibson, like George W. Bush, is disdainful of intellectuals and critical thinking, privileging emotion and faith over reason, operating through a visceral "gut" level.

Indeed, there is a series of interesting similarities between George W. Bush and Mel Gibson. Bush has famously declared that Jesus is his favorite philosopher, and part of Gibson's highly effective publicity for the film stressed his deep Christian beliefs, which drove him, despite the controversy, to make and market the film. Both Gibson and Bush Junior are born-again Christians who overcame struggles with drugs and alcohol to embrace a highly fundamentalist Christianity (albeit of different denominations and with mixed results, as we will see below). Both are Manichean to the core, see themselves on the side of good, and view their enemies and adversaries as evil. For both, you're either with us or against us; Gibson and his followers attacked critics of *The Passion* as anti-Christian and even minions of Satan. Both Bush and Gibson are morally righteous and accept redemptive violence in the struggle for good. Both are extremely megalomaniacal, seeing themselves as chosen vehicles of God, yet themselves often appear addled and inarticulate when confronted with difficult questions (possibly due to years of excessive drug and alcohol abuse that impaired their cognitive faculties). Each deploys his political or cultural power to advance the ends of his conservative version of Christianity, arguably with highly controversial effects. And both have been accused of mendacity and a purely instrumental relation to truth, using language to justify themselves, whatever the veracity of their claims.[36] And as a popular joke has it, the similarities between Jesus Christ and George W. Bush are evident in that both believe that they are appendages of God and each owes his job to his father.

Mel Gibson is a great hater, and his films *Braveheart* and *The Passion* radiate with hatred for the British, Jews, and homosexuals, as well as with contempt for "the mob." Crucially, *The Passion of The Christ* promotes fear and hate through its relentless Manicheanism and caricatures of evil Jews and Roman soldiers who condemn, torture, and brutally kill Jesus. The film projects a vision that violence is prevalent in the world and that Christ is the savior who will put the world aright. Its violent torture scenes induced horror in its mass audiences, which could have led to support for violent militarism against those accused of being forces of evil and helped nurture support for the Bush/ Cheney "War on Terror." What, then, from our vantage point, have been the effects of the film, and how does it now appear in retrospect?

THE AFTERMATH OF *THE PASSION OF THE CHRIST* AND THE QUESTION OF MEL GIBSON'S ANTI-SEMITISM

While Christian evangelists hoped that Gibson's *The Passion* would trigger mass conversion to Christianity and Jews feared that it would incite violent anti-Semitism, it is not clear that the film had such a dramatic impact. While it allegedly produced conversion experiences for Christians, induced criminals to confess their crimes, and triggered some anti-Semitic manifestations, it appears to have produced neither the dramatically positive effects that its champions predicted nor the dangerous negative effects its critics feared.[37] At the time of *The Passion's* release, the Lovingway United Pentecostal Church in Denver posted a marquee reading "Jews Killed the Lord Jesus." A Georgia couple got into a violent theological dispute after seeing the film, police were called, and the couple spent the night in jail, both charged with battery. Illustrating the contradictory effects a media culture artifact can have, a twenty-one-year-old Texas man admitted, after seeing Gibson's film, to killing his pregnant lover and making it look like a suicide (although he later pleaded innocent).[38] An Arizona burglar and a Norwegian neo-Nazi allegedly confessed to unsolved bombings. Jewish school children were reportedly accused of being Christ killers, and an Italian actor who played one of the Roman soldiers who tormented Jesus said that he had been spit on and cursed in the streets, that his daughters had been harassed in schools, and that a priest had insulted him.[39]

Ultimately, *The Passion of The Christ* may or may not significantly contribute to the spread of right-wing crusading Christian fundamentalism and militarism or violent anti-Semitism. There are important countervailing factors to the aggressive religious militarism in the Pentagon and White House, such as outspoken criticism of right-wing Christian fundamentalism in the name of a more progressive Christianity.[40] The failure of the Bush/Cheney invasion and occupation of Iraq called into question crusading militarism, and the regime's various failures called into question the role of ideologues and

Christian extremists in politics, while emboldening progressive Christians to criticize reactionary ones like Mel Gibson.

In addition, while Gibson's version of Christianity is strongly masculine, there are attempts to stress the "feminine" side of Christianity, with a series of studies stressing the importance of Mary Magdalene in early Christianity after lost Gnostic texts were discovered containing an alleged Gospel by her. Furthermore, popular strands of Christian revisionist history are finding articulation in the best-selling novel by Dan Brown, *The Da Vinci Code* (2003),[41] and the 2006 movie based on the book. While Gibson's version reinforces and upholds an unquestioning patriarchal and violent interpretation of Judeo-Christian politics and beliefs, *The Da Vinci Code* provides a damning critique of the conservatism of both the Catholic Church and the kinds of misanthropic, misogynist, and fundamentalist Christianity advanced in Gibson's film.

Drawing on a number of controversial theological arguments and scholarly sources (which include the Gnostic Gospels discovered in Egypt in 1945), Brown's story articulates alternative and resistant accounts of a far more egalitarian Christianity, which celebrates a feminine/masculine dialectic and attributes status to Mary Magdalene as the thirteenth—and most important—apostle of Christ's teachings. Part of the plot centers on attempts by the Catholic Church and Opus Dei to suppress documentation that not only attests to Mary Magdalene's, and women's, active contributions to and importance in early Christianity but also the nature of Mary Magdalene's (spiritual and physical) relationship with Jesus.

Brown's novel is important for its documentation of the constructed nature of the Gospels, with the church choosing some texts of the period and rejecting others. Moreover, Brown's accurate identification of Opus Dei as a wealthy, elitist, fundamentalist, and right-wing international sect of the Catholic Church provokes a recontextualization of current dilemmas in contemporary institutionalized Christianity, especially concerning the corruption, secrecy, and revelations of widespread abuse related to the Catholic Church. Given Gibson's fundamentalist beliefs, it is hardly surprising that the reactionary politics of Catholicism, like Opus Dei's extreme patriarchy, are reflected in his film.

After the controversy over *The Passion of The Christ* died down, many people were probably willing to accept Mel Gibson's protestations that he harbored no anti-Semitic feelings or beliefs, although a shocking DUI incident re-opened the question. On July 28, 2006, Gibson was arrested on suspicion of driving under the influence of alcohol after being stopped for speeding on the Pacific Coast Highway in Malibu, California. The day after the arrest the website TMZ.com posted a detailed account of Gibson's arrest and claimed it had a copy, later released, of the eight-page arrest report, which alleged Gibson stated upon being arrested, "Fucking Jews . . . Jews are responsible for all the wars in the world," and asked the arresting deputy James Mee, "Are you a Jew?" While there were reports that the Los Angeles County Sheriff's Department was trying to cover up the story, the release of the arrest report and nondenial by the Los Angeles police opened a firestorm of controversy and media reports that forced Gibson to write a profuse apology, blaming his anti-Semitic tirade on alcoholism. He quickly entered a Malibu outpatient addiction-recovery clinic and, when formally charged with misdemeanor drunken driving, entered Alcoholics Anonymous counseling programs, enrolled in an alcoholic-abuse program, and agreed to do public service announcements on the hazards of drinking and driving.[42]

Gibson also wrote a public apology to the Jewish community and met with Jewish leaders and friends to help him deal with his anti-Semitism. On October 13, 2006, Gibson broke his media silence, and in an interview with Diane Sawyer for ABC's *Good Morning America,* he admitted he was ashamed of his remarks, which he characterized as "the stupid ramblings of a drunkard." Ultimately, however, Mel Gibson will be judged according to his work and deeds and not his exculpatory sound bites.

In conclusion, Gibson's version of *The Passion* deflects us from alternative kinds of religions and spirituality, which embrace social justice and egalitarian social relations. Gibson's *The Passion* has revealed itself to be a highly propagandistic instrument for a certain Manichean view of the world and traditionalist Catholic version of Christianity that puts a heavy burden on Jews as killers of Christ. Finally, the fact that an extremely unpleasant and widely upsetting film could become such a major cultural phenomenon calls attention to the power of both the culture industry and religion in the contemporary world. Despite centuries of enlightenment, many people still adhere to fundamentalist religion, even in the mecca of consumer capitalism and materialism, the United States. Obviously, serious social problems and conflicts exist that drive individuals and entire societies to find religious solutions to their deepest problems. Critical social theory and cultural studies thus face the challenge to decode major cultural phenomena like the worldwide success of *The Passion of The Christ* to unravel what it tells us about contemporary culture and society and what problems need to be confronted and dealt with to create a freer and happier world.

Notes

1. A shorter version of this chapter was previously published as "Critical Reflections on Mel Gibson's *The Passion of the Christ,*" *Logos* 3, no. 1 (spring 2004), www.logosjournal.com/hammer_kellner.htm (accessed September 4, 2008). For this text, we have updated our analysis in the light of subsequent scholarship and events, more cogently contextualized the event within the Bush-Cheney administration's "War on Terror," and sharpened our critique of the film.

2. For a detailed account of the prerelease controversy and Gibson's deeply committed marketing of the film, see Peter J. Boyer, "The Jesus War: Mel Gibson and '*The Passion,*'" *New Yorker,* September 15, 2003, www.wcnet.org/~bgcc/Gibson.htm (accessed September 4, 2008). To some extent, Gibson himself fuelled the issue of whether the film was anti-Semitic through his passionate disclaimers and attempted to present the film as faithfully following Gospel teaching. This promotion strategy helped bring in both flocks of Christians and others curious as to what the controversy was about. As we will show, the obvious departures from Gospel sources provide clues to Gibson's biases and politics.

3. Gibson told journalist and religious scholar Peter J. Boyer in an interview before the release of the film that "his script for '*The Passion*' was the New Testament, and that the film was directed by the Holy Ghost. . . . 'I wanted to bring you there,' he says, 'and I wanted to be true to the Gospels. That has never been done'" (Boyer, "The Jesus War"). Gibson repeatedly claimed after its release that his film faithfully followed the Gospel accounts and provided a true version of the events portrayed, stating in an interview, "I think it's just meant to tell the truth. I want to be as truthful as possible" (*Globe and Mail,* February 4, 2004, www.theglobeandmail.com/servlet/story/RTGAM.20040204.wupassion04/BNStory/Entertainment (accessed September 4, 2008). As we shall argue, however, many scholars have pointed out that Gibson draws on multiple sources and adds many fictional aspects to the film that go beyond the established biblical and historical record.

4. Gary Wills, "God in the Hands of Angry Sinners," *New York Review of Books,* April 8, 2004, www.mafhoum.com/press7/186C33.htm (accessed June 26, 2008).

5. In Gary Wills, "God in the Hands."

6. Austin Cline, "Religious Persecution."

7. Sarah Hagelin, "*The Passion of the Christ* and the Lust for Certitude," in *Passionate Dialogues: Critical Perspectives on Mel Gibson's* Passion of the Christ, edited by Daniel Burston and Rebecca I. Denova (Pittsburgh: Mise, 2005), 149–167. As media scholar Sarah Hagelin puts it, "Gibson indulges his audience's lust for certitude, not sex, using the audience's visceral reaction to the culturally-fraught image of a man being tied to a post, stripped, almost naked, and whipped. Viewers are trained by culture to read the image of a man on the cross as religious, and trained to see whipping in terms of power—specifically racial oppression. This connection to power animates not only the lust for certitude but also the way Gibson tries to reframe the cultural debate about Christianity in public and cultural life. Gibson addresses an American Christian audience that is socially, economically, and culturally dominant but whose central religious texts frame them as a persecuted minority. The film is an attempt to obscure this reality, to form Christianity's primal scene in pain, not in power—in being oppressed, not the oppressor" (Hagelin 2005, 153).

8. On the "clash of fundamentalisms" between Al Qaeda jihadism and Bush/Cheney administration militarism, see Tariq Ali, *The Clash of Fundamentalisms* (London and New York: Verso, 2002). For detailed critique of Bush/Cheney administration ideology and policies, see Douglas Kellner, *From 9/11 to Terror War: Dangers of the Bush Legacy* (Lanham, MD: Rowman & Littlefield, 2003). We use the term *Bush-Cheney administration* to call attention to the extraordinary role of Dick Cheney and his associates during the Bush Junior years. A series in the *Washington Post* under the rubric "Angler" documents the unprecedented role Dick Cheney has played in the Bush presidency, justifying speaking of the "Bush-Cheney administration." See http://blog.washingtonpost.com/cheney.

9. See Philip A. Cunningham, "Commentary: The Beatification of Anne Catherine Emmerich," October 7, 2004, www.bc.edu/research/cjl/meta-elements/texts/cjrelations/topics/commentary_emmerich.htm (accessed June 25, 2008). Gibson detailed to Peter J. Boyer in "The Jesus War" the importance of Anne Catherine Emmerich for his vision of the Passion and during an interview showed Diane Sawyer a piece of cloth allegedly belonging to her.

10. As Jessica Winter puts it, "The earliest passion plays, medieval pageants that brandished repulsive caricatures of homicidal Jews, fanned anti-Semitism and encouraged mob violence against so-called 'Christ-killers.' The most famous passion production, the seven-hour Oberammergau Passion Play in Bavaria (first home of the Nazi party), won Adolf Hitler's admiration after he attended its 300th anniversary in 1934; he later called the play a 'precious tool' in the fight against Judaism and reserved special plaudits for its Pontius Pilate, who 'stands out like a

firm, clean rock in the middle of the whole muck and mire of Jewry.' (The play is still performed every 10 years, having undergone substantial revisions in 1990 and 2000.)" See Winter, "Mel Gibson's Jesus Christ Pose," *Village Voice*, November 5–11, 2003, www.villagevoice.com/news/0345,winter,48380,1.html (accessed June 26, 2008).

11. On how previous Mel Gibson characters and films anticipate *The Passion*, see Winter, "Mel Gibson's Jesus Christ Pose."

12. Frank Rich, "Mel Gibson Forgives Us for His Sins," *New York Times*, March 7, 2004, www.theglobeandmail.com/servlet/story/RTGAM.20040204.wupassion04/BNStory/Entertainment/# (accessed on September 4, 2008). Rich wrote a series of articles before the release of the film discussing dangers of anti-Semitism in Gibson's highly publicized film and concerned Jewish reactions. Gibson was allegedly enraged by the accusations and told a *New Yorker* writer producing a story on the phenomenon, "I want to kill him [Frank Rich]. I want his intestines on a stick. . . . I want to kill his dog" (see Boyer, "The Jesus War"). Gibson later used his psychotically intemperate remarks to affirm his Christian forgiveness of his tormentor. Rich remains worried and concerned: "The fracas over 'The Passion' has made me feel less secure as a Jew in America than ever before" (Rich, "Gibson Forgives Us for His Sins").

13. Mel Gibson and his father Hutton Gibson are widely reported to be adherents of traditionalist Catholicism who reject the reforms of the Second Vatican Council (1962–1965), which include legislation concerning performing Mass in vernacular languages rather than Latin, liberalizing church doctrine, including the mandate to refrain from eating meat on Friday, and, crucially in this context, absolving Jews from responsibility for killing Christ. Gibson's father has been identified as a "sedevacantist," an extreme form of traditionalist Catholicism, whose adherents regard the pope and the bishops of the "official" church as having fallen into heresy and therefore forfeited their authority. Gibson's father has also been identified as a Holocaust denier and extreme anti-Semite. Wikipedia's entry on Hutton Gibson has a full account of his religious views and anti-Semitism at http://en.wikipedia.org/wiki/Hutton_Gibson (accessed June 25, 2008).

Gibson himself has contributed money to traditionalist Catholic causes, as well as built and had consecrated a private traditionalist Catholic Church of the Holy Family in Malibu in February 2007, and thus is a committed activist in the traditionalist Catholic movement of which his film, as we demonstrate, is propaganda. As Tim Rutten points out, "The World Faith Foundation, of which Gibson is a principal benefactor, has purchased a church complex in Greenburg, Pennsylvania, near Pittsburgh, for $750,000. This existing church will be converted into a traditional Catholic Church which will serve as a regional center for the Traditional Latin Mass and Sacraments. . . . The producer-director's father, Hutton

Gibson, a traditional Catholic writer and publisher associated with the WFF, has already moved to the Greenburg area to oversee the complex for the foundation." (Rutten, "Clues Dismissed in Time of 'Passion,'" *Los Angeles Times*, August 5, 2006, E1).

On Gibson's specific version of Catholicism, see Boyer, "The Jesus War," Wills, "God in the Hands," and the studies in Burston and Denova, *Passionate Dialogues*.

14. *Monty Python's Life of Brian* (1979) was also attacked as blasphemous by right-wing Christian audiences for its satire of Hollywood versions of the life of Christ. Ironically, the popularity of *The Passion* led to *Life of Brian*'s rerelease in some markets as an antidote to Gibson's toxins.

15. The coauthor of the screenplay for the film, Benedict Fitzgerald, is suing the company, claiming that he has not been adequately paid or given an accounting of the film's profits. See WENN, "Gibson Wants Passion Records Sealed," www.imdb.com/title/tt0335345/news#ni0123388 (accessed on June 25, 2008). For the partial box office receipts, whose recording was stopped in 2004, see the Icon production site at www.imdb.com/title/tt0335345/business (accessed June 25, 2008). Evidently, Gibson is as sleazy a businessman as he is an interpreter of the Gospel.

16. See Anne Thompson, "Holy Week Pilgrims Flock to 'Passion.' Film Is Selling Books, CDs and Jewelry, Too," *New York Times*, April 12, 2004, http://query.nytimes.com/gst/fullpage.html?res=9F02E1DC1138F931A25757C0A9629C8B63 (accessed September 4, 2008). The article also notes that part of the marketing strategy was to open the film on Ash Wednesday and keep up marketing momentum through Easter, to bring in big crowds during the Christian holy season.

17. The Internet Movie Data Base contains a variety of reviews, listing the most accessed and popular reviews at the beginning of its "external review" list (see www.imdb.com/title/tt0335345/externalreviews (accessed June 25, 2008). Roger Ebert gave the film four stars and praised it cinematically but claimed, "This is the most violent film I have ever seen" and worried about its effects on children in the audience (see Roger Ebert, Review of *The Passion of The Christ*, *Chicago Sun-Times*, February 24, 2004, http://rogerebert.suntimes.com/apps/pbcs.dll/article?AID=/20040224/REVIEWS/402240301/1023 (accessed May 23, 2004). *Guardian* reviewer Mark Kermode unabashedly affirmed *The Passion* as a horror film and example of extreme cinema; see Kermode, "Drenched in the Blood of Christ," *Guardian*, February 29, 2004, http://film.guardian.co.uk/News_Story/Critic_Review/Observer_review/0,,1158620,00.html (accessed June 25, 2008). As of 2004, almost 2,000 user comments were posted on the Internet Movie Data Base user comments board (see www.imdb.com/title/tt0335345/usercomments [accessed May 23, 2004]); by June 2008, there were 2,677 user comments at www.imdb.com/title/tt0335345/usercomments (accessed June 25, 2008). These often-revealing

commentaries provide testimony to the tremendous interest in the film globally and the passionate controversies it has created. It was disheartening, however, to find so few cogent critiques of the film's theology from the Christian religious community in the mainstream media, though we found some good critiques on Internet sources, including a Christian minister who noted the film's departure from scriptures; see Rev. Dr. Stephen R. Montgomery's review, "The Gospel Truth," at www.explorefaith.org/homiliesLent/20040303.html (accessed September 4, 2008). See also the critique by Fr. John T. Pawlikowski and Rabbi David Sandmel, "What Christians Must Watch for in 'The Passion,'" at www.beliefnet.com/story/140/story_14030.html (accessed May 24, 2004). A webpage of material is found at the Boston College Center for Christian-Jewish Learning at www.bc.edu/research/cjl/meta-elements/texts/education/PASSION_resources.htm#passion%20 (accessed May 24, 2004), and we draw on other scholarly material throughout this study.

18. *The Exorcist* (1973), like *The Passion*, evoked extremely strong responses from its audiences, who exhibited symptoms of hysteria and later attested to nightmares and anxiety attacks. The film used frightening sounds, like bees buzzing, birds screeching, and children shrieking, as well as incantations of satanic texts, spoken backwards or translated into ancient languages. On *The Exorcist* controversy and how it provided ideologies of right-wing Christianity and attacks on feminism and liberalism, see Douglas Kellner and Michael Ryan, *Camera Politica: The Politics and Ideology of Contemporary Hollywood Film* (Bloomington: Indiana University Press, 1988).

19. Gibson told Peter J. Boyer in an interview,

> In Matthew, that gesture is followed by a shout from the crowd: "His blood be on us, and on our children." This passage, which is depicted only in Matthew, is one of the sources of the notion of collective Jewish guilt for the death of Jesus. Gibson shot the scene, but with Caiaphas alone calling the curse down. Wright, Gibson's editor, strongly objected to including even that version. "I just think you're asking for trouble if you leave it in," he said. "For people who are undecided about the film, that would be the thing that turned them against it."
>
> Gibson yielded, but he has had some regrets. "I wanted it in," he says. "My brother said I was wimping out if I didn't include it. It happened; it was said. But, man, if I included that in there, they'd be coming after me at my house, they'd come kill me." (Boyer, "The Jesus War")

We have some idea as to who "they" are, and as it turns out, the film contains Caiaphas's blood curse on the Jews, but not the English subtitle that translates it.

20. See note 9. Noting the anti-Semitic sources of Gibson's representation of the Passion, Stephen Montgomery remarks in "The Gospel Truth" that there are "over 30 scenes and lines in the movie" that are directly from nineteenth-century nun and rabid anti-Semitic Anne Catherine Emmerich, "virtually all of them depicting Jews as malevolent and blood-thirsty, and picturing a God short of forgiveness and long on sadism. There is one scene towards the end where the thief on the cross ridicules Jesus, and a raven settles on the cross and starts pecking the thief's eye out in gory detail. That wasn't from scripture. That was from Emmerich."

21. Scholars indicate that High Temple priests would not congregate for a trial on the first night of Passover and that such proceedings would not be open to the public; see Rebecca I. Denova, "An Historical and Literary Understanding of the Passion Narratives in the Gospel," who writes, "Historically, both the arrest and the subsequent 'trials' are problematic. Consider the timing. If this is the first evening of Passover, the authorities in question had spent a long day in preparation, as only priests could slaughter the lambs for hundreds of thousands of pilgrims. That evening, they would have been home with their own families observing Passover. Nothing short of a revolution could have compelled them to leave their homes that night. And according to Jewish Law, trials and official meetings were forbidden during the festival" (in Burston and Denova, *Passionate Dialogues*, 27).

22. Katha Pollit, "The Protocols of Mel Gibson," *The Nation*, March 29, 2004, www.thenation.com/doc.mhtml%3Fi=20040329&s=pollitt (accessed April 14, 2004). Another reading of the priests is to see them as allegorical representatives of the Roman Catholic Church, whose bureaucracy and concessions to liberalism Gibson and his father scorn for a more conservative and traditionalist view of Catholicism.

23. The Wikipedia entry on Mel Gibson has a section titled "Allegations of homophobia," as well as discussion of his anti-Semitism, at http://en.wikipedia.org/wiki/Mel_Gibson (accessed June 25, 2008). Gibson's film *Braveheart* (1995) features a gay son of the villainous King Edward of England who has a gay friend whom the king, in a moment of wrath, throws out the window of a castle, as if gays were to be arbitrarily executed at will; the gay Herod and his entourage provide negative images of homosexuals in *The Passion*.

24. Jon Meacham, "Who Killed Jesus?" *Newsweek*, February 16, 2004, www.newsweek.com/id/53129?tid=relatedcl (accessed March 1, 2004).

25. Jon Meacham, "Who Killed Jesus?" noted, "In fact, in the age of Roman domination, only Rome crucified. The crime was sedition, not blasphemy—a civil crime, not a religious one. The two men who were killed along with Jesus are identified in some translations as 'thieves,' but the word can also mean 'insurgents,' supporting the idea that crucifixion was a political weapon used to send a message

to those still living: beware of revolution or riot, or Rome will do this to you, too. The two earliest and most reliable extra-Biblical references to Jesus—those of the historians Josephus and Tacitus—say Jesus was executed by Pilate. The Roman prefect was Caiaphas's political superior and even controlled when the Jewish priests could wear their vestments and thus conduct Jewish rites in the Temple. Pilate was not the humane figure Gibson depicts. According to Philo of Alexandria, the prefect was of 'inflexible, stubborn, and cruel disposition,' and known to execute troublemakers without trial." Barabbas was also presented in the Gospels as a political insurgent, and not just as a "notorious thief," as in Gibson's fantasy version, which abstracts completely from the sociopolitical context of the time to present a version of the Passion that supports his own religious beliefs.

26. The view that military/police underlings explode out of control and engage in brutal torture and abuse is startlingly parallel to right-wing readings of the Iraqi abuse scandal, which unfolded in the media in May 2004 with the release of the Abu Ghraib torture images. These readings blamed the scandal on callow youth lost in a culture of pornography and media sadism, who betrayed their noble leaders. This view, however, was undercut by subsequent exposes by Seymour Hersh and *Newsweek* writers who see the source of Iraqi prisoner abuse as directed from top echelons of the Pentagon and Bush administration. See Seymour Hersh, "The Grey Zone," *New Yorker*, May 15, 2004, www.newyorker.com/fact/content/?040524fa_fact (accessed September 4, 2008); see also John Barry, Michael Hirsh, and Michael Isikoff, "The Roots of Torture," *Newsweek*, May 24, 2004, www.newsweek.com/id/105387?tid=relatedcl<(accessed September 4, 2008). Hersh updates his critique, which squarely blames the torture policy on upper echelons of the Bush/Cheney administration, in *Chain of Command: The Road from 9/11 to Abu Ghraib* (New York: HarperCollins, 2004).

27. Professor John Pawlikowski, director of the Catholic-Jewish studies program at Chicago's Catholic Theological Union, noted, "The main storyline of *The Passion* puts the responsibility for Jesus Christ's death squarely on a Jewish cabal led by Caiaphas [the Jewish high priest], who, at one point, is described in the script as 'bloodthirsty' and who succeeds in blackmailing Pilate into putting Jesus to death. . . . We know from recent Catholic documents and from modern biblical scholarship that this was not the case, that Pilate was the bloodthirsty one and that he, rather than the Jews, played the central role in putting Jesus to death." See Lawrence Donegan, "Christ in the Crossfire," *Observer*, September 28, 2003, www.guardian.co.uk/film/2003/sep/28/features.review1 (accessed on September 4, 2008). On Gibson's distortion of history, see also Meacham, "Who Killed Jesus?"; David Remnick's interview with Elaine Pagels, "Passions, Past and Present," *New Yorker*, March 8, 2004, www.newyorker.com/archive/2004/03/08/040308ta_talk_remnick (accessed on September 4, 2008); and studies in Burston and Denova, *Passionate Dialogues*.

28. We thus agree with Mahlon H. Smith, a renowned scholar and professor of religion at Rutgers University, who lists and documents a multiplicity of problems with the film:

> Now, as I emerge from witnessing two unrelenting hours of sadistic torture and psychological agony, I am convinced that what is *most* problematic about this film is not its brutally vivid presentation of the Passion narratives but rather Gibson's pretense that he has accurately represented the gospel accounts. He has not. Rather he has projected a pastiche of snippets of scenes and dialog arbitrarily cut from various texts and pasted in a collage informed less by their original gospel context than by the imaginative inventions and distortions of late medieval Latin piety. Gibson has simply resurrected many of the popular misconceptions and grotesqueries of the 15th century Passion plays, polishing and updating an element here or there to impress a cinematically sophisticated 21st century audience. The spirituality that informs this vision of Christ is not that of the canonical gospels but the worldview of the neo-Manichean Cathari and the flagellants. Much of Gibson's script comes from the fanciful meditation of Anne Catherine Emmerich—a 19th c. anti-Jewish German nun—entitled *The Dolorous Passion of Our Lord Jesus Christ*. Much of the rest is the product of the director's own brooding fantasies. (Mahlon H. Smith, "Gibson Agonistes: Anatomy of a Neo-Manichean Vision of Jesus," Virtual Religion Network, http://virtualreligion.net/forum/passion2.html [accessed June 26, 2008].)

29. On the horrors of the Bush/Cheney administration, see Douglas Kellner, *Grand Theft 2000: Media Spectacle and a Stolen Election* (Lanham, MD: Rowman & Littlefield, 2001), Kellner, *From 9/11 to Terror War*, and Kellner, *Media Spectacle and the Crisis of Democracy* (Boulder, CO: Paradigm, 2005).

30. See Bob Woodward, *Plan of Attack* (New York: Simon and Schuster, 2004).

31. On the neoconservatives in the Bush administration, see Kellner, *From 9/11 to Terror War*, and other articles in the issue of *Logos* where we originally published our article on *The Passion of the Christ* (see *Logos* 3, no. 1 [spring 2004], www.logosjournal.com (accessed on September 4, 2008)).

32. Right-wing militarist culture, like that represented by Gibson's *The Passion* or the *Left Behind* novels, has its analogue in crusading Christian militarists in Iraq. In October 2003, Gen. William G. Boykin received brief press coverage when it was revealed that the deputy undersecretary of defense for intelligence had been regularly appearing at evangelical revivals preaching that the

United States was in a holy war as a "Christian nation" battling "Satan." General Boykin revealed the insight that his battle with the forces of evil was a crusade between his "true God" and "the false one." Boykin insisted, "I knew that my God was bigger than his. I knew that my God was a real God and his was an idol." Sidney Blumenthal noted, "Just before Boykin was put in charge of the hunt for Osama bin Laden and then inserted into Iraqi prison reform, he was a circuit rider for the religious right. He allied himself with a small group called the Faith Force Multiplier that advocates applying military principles to evangelism. Its manifesto—Warrior Message—summons 'warriors in this spiritual war for souls of this nation and the world'" (Blumenthal, "The Religious Warrior of Abu Ghraib," *Guardian*, May 20, 2004, www.guardian.co.uk/world/2004/may/20/usa.iraq2 (accessed on September 4, 2008). Mel Gibson is obviously a member of a similar Warrior Messenger cadre, and the message entails a violent and bloody crusade against the forces of evil.

33. See Naomi Klein, *The Shock Doctrine: The Rise of Disaster Capitalism* (New York: Metropolitan Books, 2007).

34. See Barry Glassner, *The Culture of Fear* (New York: Basic Books, 1999).

35. For very revealing insight into right-wing Christian manipulation of Mel Gibson's film, see Tim Chey's "documentary" *Impact: The Passion of the Christ* (2004), available on DVD in a two-disk set. The film puts on display the propagandistic mind-set of Gibson and his followers and their combining of Christianity with hucksterism, as they sell themselves and their ideology. The "documentary" is pure propaganda for Gibson and his film, but it shows how excited evangelicals were to use the film as a tool for recruitment, which could help explain why they would overlook some of the more problematic theological elements and Gibson's own problematic anti-Semitism and drinking problem, which would erupt to embarrass his fans and promoters, who had set him up as the Second Coming of Jesus. The gushing over *The Passion* and Mel Gibson and interviewees' vehement defense of Gibson and his film against charges of anti-Semitism appear both comic and pathetic in retrospect.

36. On the Bush-Cheney administration's systematic use of a politics of lying, see Douglas Kellner, "Bushspeak and the Politics of Lying: Presidential Rhetoric in the 'War on Terror,'" in *Presidential Rhetoric*, special issue, edited by Robert Ivie, *Presidential Studies Quarterly* 37, no. 4 (December 2007): 622–645. As note 3 indicates, Gibson falsely claimed that he was basing *The Passion* on the Gospels and vehemently denied anti-Semitic motives in producing the film, as well as claimed that the Holy Ghost was directing the film, as if he were the vessel of God. We and many other scholars have noted how *The Passion* departs from standard Gospel accounts throughout this study, and in a concluding section, we discuss Gibson's outburst of anti-Semitic ravings during a DUI incident in 2006.

37. An article published several months after the release of the film indicated that it had failed to produce the predicted dramatic effects. See Roy Rivenburg, "The Furor, the Fizzle," *Los Angeles Times*, July 19, 2004, E1. In an introduction to a book on *The Passion* controversy about a year after the release of the film, coeditor Daniel Burston concludes that while *The Passion* has promoted some productive interfaith discussion and did not have the feared effect of inciting explosions of anti-Semitic violence, it has also polarized sides and "*thinned the ranks* of Christians and Jews who will be willing and able to embrace this sacred mission in the future" (Burston and Denova, *Passionate Dialogues*, 7).

38. See "Mel's Passion Too Much for Georgia Couple," *Guardian*, March 19, 2004, www.guardian.co.uk/film/2004/mar/19/news.melgibson (accessed on September 4, 2008) Scott Gold and Lianne Hart, "'Passion' Prompts Man to Confess," *Los Angeles Times*, March 26, 2004, A17; and "Uproar Over Mel's Pride and Passion," *Globe*, March 15, 2004, 12. The latter claims that an opening-day viewer suffered a fatal heart attack; that psychiatrists reported that the film had induced nightmares and warned that viewers might suffer severe, long-lasting emotional problems; and that an Israeli leader called for Israel to put Mel Gibson on trial for slandering the Jewish people.

39. See Rivenburg, "The Furor, the Fizzle."

40. For an account of the rebirth of progressive evangelical Christianity standing up to and criticizing the conservative Christian Right that has supported the Bush-Cheney administration, see Caryle Murphy, "Evangelical Author Puts Progressive Spin on Traditional Faith," *Washington Post*, September 10, 2006, A1, and the work of the Sojourners/Call to Renewal at www.sojo.net (accessed June 25, 2008).

41. See Dan Brown, *The Da Vinci Code* (New York: Doubleday, 2003). The novel has been a publishing phenomenon, selling over five million copies and heading the *New York Times* best-seller list for almost a year. A search through amazon.com reveals that there is already a small library of at least fifteen books commenting positively or negatively on *The Da Vinci Code*, attesting to the contestation of Christianity currently underway. Interestingly, critics of the book are the same right-wing Christians who uncritically embraced *The Passion*, so that Gibson's film and Brown's novel represent two sides of the contestation of Christianity in contemporary U.S. media culture. This is not, however, to endorse the version of Christianity in the novel and film that was drawn from various contemporary books; for a sharp critique of the *Da Vinci Code* phenomenon, see Laura Miller, "The Da Vinci Crock," *Salon*, December 29, 2004, http://dir.salon.com/story/books/feature/2004/12/29/da_vinci_code/index.html (accessed June 27, 2008).

42. See the report on Gibson's arrest and documents at www.tmz.com/2006/07/28/gibsons-anti-semitic-tirade-alleged-cover-up (accessed June 27, 2008).

V

Convertoons?

VeggieTales for Young Souls

MICHAEL HOECHSMANN

For the first time in human history, children are hearing most of the stories, most of the time, not from their parents or school or churches or neighbors, but from a handful of global conglomerates that have something to sell. It is impossible to overestimate the radical effect that this has on the way our children grow up, the way we live, and the way we conduct our affairs.

—George Gerbner (1994)

In Beverley Hills, they don't throw their garbage away—they make it into television shows.

—Woody Allen, as quoted on www.philvischer.com

Bob the Tomato and Larry the Cucumber might not have the name recognition of Spiderman, Barbie, or Mickey Mouse, but they are a force to reckon with in some sectors, household names in the Christian community and beyond. In fact, these stars of the *VeggieTales* series have helped to account for the remarkable success of a media franchise that holds down the record for highest sales in the United States of straight-to-VHS/DVD media productions. Bob, Larry, and the rest of the cast of veggie eccentrics are animated characters that embark on a series of adventures and misadventures under the guidance of the God of their understanding, a compassionate and understanding Christian God who provides them with moments of insight when they most need it and helps them see the unfolding of the universe in simple, understandable terms. Taken alongside the mind-numbing stream of cotton candy dreck served up regularly to children on the major networks, the *VeggieTales* fare appears to be thoughtful, holistic entertainment for children, and to some extent it is. However, *VeggieTales* is hardly culturally neutral; it is in fact a controversial set of programs both for some members of the Christian Right and for many secular critics. Scratch below the surface of Bob and Larry's adventures and you find an exemplary tale of the culture wars alive today in contemporary America: a sociocultural tale of religion, values, and media messaging, as well as a media industry story of narrowcast programming in an era of corporate control. The story of *VeggieTales* is ultimately rather nuanced and complex, without clear boundaries of right and wrong or good and bad, but it is an account too of the risks of proselytizing versus taking care of business, of letting ideology (or theology) trump common sense.

To make sense of this media franchise and its role in the contemporary cultural contexts of North America, we need to draw on a comprehensive paradigm of analysis. I will draw on Richard Johnson's (1996) heuristic for cultural studies, an approach to cultural analysis that links questions of production, text, audience, and lived culture in a dynamic tension. Johnson's model is illustrated as a circle, or circuit, with four topoi (places of analysis), resembling the east, north, west, and south points of a compass. The four points of the circuit, all of them interconnected, are (1) production, (2) textual or material form, (3) reception, and (4) influence on lived culture. Included under production are questions of authorship, complicated and complex matters in an era of corporate media. To tease out the full range of problems associated with authorship in the age of the media corporation means looking at corporate governance and economy, alongside the agency of the creative personalities involved in authorship, or production. At the site of the textual or material form, we analyze the object under study, drawing on forms of analysis from literary and semiotic analysis. At the third site, reception, we conduct an audit of audience reactions or readings of the particular text or set of texts. Finally, we examine the influence of the preceding three sites on lived culture to come to an understanding of how culture is reflected and inflected by the phenomenon at hand. As Johnson describes it, each box represents a moment in the circuit, each moment depends on the others but is also distinct, and each is indispensable to the study of the cultural form as a whole. The model demands a holistic mode of inquiry that takes into consideration all four elements. The conceptual framework Johnson lays out does not presume a narrowcasting of media "effects" or media manipulation; rather, it sets cultural texts into a set of relationships that enable sometimes contradictory insights to emerge from the same text. In other words, we cannot simply interpret conditions of production, textual forms and practices, and audience readings as resonant sites of meaning without some consideration of the interplay between them and the broader social and cultural contexts in which they are made meaningful. The final stage in Johnson's framework considers how cultural forms affect everyday cultural life and how cultural change feeds back on the moment of production. An analysis of a contemporary media phenomenon such as *VeggieTales*, as well as some of the cultural and historical factors surrounding it, helps to exemplify this feedback loop.

PRODUCING VEGGIES

What better way to introduce *VeggieTales* than to turn to Rotten Tomatoes? The rottentomatoes.com website aggregates movie reviews from newspapers and other media from around North America. This one-stop shop provides a quick snapshot of informed opinion on the merits of particular movies, rating them on the "tomatometer" scale of one to one hundred. Alongside many shorter DVD productions, Big Idea, the media production house that developed the *VeggieTales* franchise, produced two feature-length films, *Jonah: A VeggieTales Movie* (2002) and *The Pirates Who Won't Do Anything: A Veggie Tales Movie* (2008). These movies were intended to take *VeggieTales* over the top, to make the franchise a household name across the United States and beyond. As is explained below, this foray into feature-film making proved to be the unraveling of the Big Idea production company, but regardless of the financial impact on Big Idea, these films remain two testaments to the big idea, two media texts that reflect the values and stories that *VeggieTales* stand for. Reactions to these films are varied, as a brief scan of Rotten Tomato reviews will show. The tomatometer ranks the percentage of reviewers from major media outlets who give a movie a positive review. The first *VeggieTales* feature film, *Jonah,* received a solid score of 66 percent. *The Pirates* had a less stellar rating of 44 percent. More significantly, *Jonah* brought in a box office total of just under $25.5 million (all monetary figures are in U.S. dollars), while *The Pirates* received just over $12.5 million. To demonstrate the mediocre box office showings of these two films, we must seek contemporary cognates, and there is a robust crop of successful films, such as *Monster's Inc.* (2001; 95 percent; $255.5 million), *Shrek* (2001; 89 percent; $266.5 million), *Finding Nemo* (2003; 98 percent; $339.5 million), *Shark Tales* (2004; 34 percent; $160.5 million), *Madagascar* (2005; 55 percent; $193 million), *Robots* (2005; 63 percent; $128 million), *Ratatouille* (2007; 88 percent; $206 million), to name only a few. That the movies with the lowest tomatometer readings of the group, *Shark Tale* and *Robots,* each brought in over $100 million more than *Jonah,* the best showing of *VeggieTales,* illustrates these films' lack of popularity. Big Idea's productions are, it appears, narrowcast to a young, Christian audience, preaching to the in-the-process-of-conversion set, and are willfully neglected by a wider audience. In an era when the family audience for feature-length movies was ripe for the picking, *VeggieTales* missed the boat.

The competition for the hearts and minds of the preschool set is an intense one in contemporary media, but while new forms of convergent media reach down to the ages of their older school-bound peers, the youngest, freshest media consumers are still primarily captivated by the twentieth-century media of television (and all of its assorted delivery mechanisms, such as VHS, DVD, and TiVo), feature films, and intertextual product tie-ins, such as toys and clothes. For this reason, feature films, packaged media (VHS and DVD), and product tie-ins targeted at audiences under six years old are big business. To compete in this marketplace is not easy for a small production house, a lesson that the team at Big Idea learned the hard way. The trend in media ownership is toward convergent platforms and vehicles and the consolidation of media properties by a small number of global media behemoths. An example of this is the highly successful Disney corporation, the world's largest purveyor of children's entertainment and currently the third-ranked media conglomerate in the global marketplace. Despite the odds against it, Big Idea was a small production company that emerged in the early 1990s to produce Christian media for young children. Seeing the rapid success of the *VeggieTales* made-for-DVD release offerings, its CEO, Phil Vischer, was soon swept up in the enthusiasm of an expanding media franchise and the hubris of success.

One of the main creative forces behind the *VeggieTales* franchise, Vischer has chronicled the story of the rise and fall of Big Idea on his blog (2004, www.philvischer.com/index.php/?p=38). In 1997, Vischer recounts, he entertained the idea that his company might become the next Disney. Company profits were growing exponentially in this period, from $1.3 million in 1996 to $44 million in 1999, and continuing growth appeared inevitable, even part of the master plan. Through a set of poor business decisions—a rapid expansion with a concomitant overextension of credit—and a stubborn plan to produce *Jonah* as a feature film, Vischer saw the Big Idea disappear before his eyes despite his best efforts. The company lost a lawsuit with U.K.-based HIT Entertainment (the owners of *Barney, Thomas & Friends, Pingu,* and *Bob the Builder,* among other franchises) over the distribution rights to videocassette versions of *VeggieTales* videos, and this proved to be its undoing. A subsequent bankruptcy proceeding resulted in Bob and Larry's finding a new home, first with Classic Media in the United States and subsequently with another U.K.-based company, Entertainment Rights. Told with humility and sincerity, Vischer's account—a breath of fresh air compared with the bombast that usually fills the Hollywood vanity press—lays out a clear mea culpa and a set of lessons learned. That he draws on his Christian God to guide his path should come as no surprise. His faith gives him the capacity to recognize his own human folly, albeit after the fact, and to put his foibles into a learning framework. It also allows him to accept both responsibility for his own actions and the idea that his actions were part of some bigger plan. Ultimately, his God allowed him to close the chapter on the *VeggieTales* experience and to move on with another part of his life.

TEXTING JONAH

While the story of Big Idea involves many subplots and twists, a string of successful made-for-VHS/DVD *VeggieTales* productions, a foray into television with NBC, and other successful franchises like 3-2-1 Penguins, the focus of this analysis will remain on Big Idea's megaproject, the big fish that brought the company down, *Jonah: A VeggieTales Movie.* Before we enter into a discussion of one particular film, however, it is necessary that we focus some attention on the kids-appeal characters created by the *VeggieTales*/Big Idea team. The stars of *VeggieTales* are animated cartoons of vegetables that simulate the human condition and form without the aid of limbs (arms and legs). They are caricaturized morphs of head and body, blobs of folly and inspiration that appear to have lifelike mobility and move with the flexibility of humans but with the traction of slugs. The key to the kiddie appeal of the *VeggieTales* characters lies in the facial morphology. It's all in the eyes and the smile. Just like the facial bonding that occurs between parent and child, the semiotic appeal of big, open eyes and a corresponding smile makes these characters lovable and worthy of extended interest for the youngest members of society. That this sort of introduction to media forms, whether through VHS/DVD, television programming, or feature film, preys on the yet uninitiated kinder-consumer is not surprising.

To appeal to the youngest premedia set, it is important to speak a linguistic and semiotic language that they can relate to. Simultaneously with Big Idea, and digging further down the demographic ladder, the frontier of kiddie programming began to extend to the diaper set in the 1990s with programs such as *Teletubbies* (Ragdoll Productions, 1997–2001). Addictive media offerings for toddlers, such as the prelinguistic *Teletubbies*, set out to bring new and early converts to media forms. Rather than articulating real words, the *Teletubbies* characters communicate in guttural blatherings. The programs do not rely on conventional narrative form but rather on impressionistic action and temporal shifts of scene. The contribution made to media consumption by *Teletubbies* is one of recruitment. If a child is old enough to view moving images on a screen accompanied by a simple sound track, the same child can begin his or her couch potato career through the recognition of sound, image, and movement. Just a small step up the kiddie-consumption media continuum is the contents of the *VeggieTales* archive. The narrative convention of *VeggieTales* requires a prerequisite linguistic ability, but the subtext of the programs is just as readily available in the simple rendering of human communication as a set of wide eyes and a smile. The characters are a set of lovable vegetables, limbless creatures with expressive faces and irrepressible personalities. The cast of characters is headed by Bob the Tomato and Larry the Cucumber but backed up by a diverse team including Archibald Asparagus, Mr. Lunt (a gourd), Laura Carrot, and Anne the Scallion, among others. Animated vegetables are clearly good for you when packaged as Saturday morning television with Sunday morning values, but it takes the imagination of a very young child to suspend disbelief and accept a vegetable as a fully functioning creature, complete with linguistic ability and physical mobility.

Despite the tremendous flight of fancy required to accept these characters as animate beings, they are very well-designed, irrepressible dynamos that share a sense of agency, purpose, and fallibility with humankind while retaining their distinct vegetative forms.

Jonah: A VeggieTales Movie is an animated feature film with great production values and a multilayered story that returns in several ways to the central theme of compassion, forgiveness, and second chances for those who make mistakes in judgment. In relation to the moral of the story, this film does not differ from the majority of kinder-flicks. Tales of folly and redemption are standard kiddie fare, though the notion that the enemy is within is a particularly religious trope of overcoming human fallibility. External struggles can intervene in the life of a Veggie, but there is no greater goal than redeeming and transforming one's own character and assisting others in this quest. Working the faith for others' benefit is an admirable goal and a pleasant enough subtext for a group of Veggie friends, but when it comes to treating the Other, *Jonah* surrenders to another Christian trope, that of missionary zeal and conversion. Not to spoil the story, *Jonah* retells the biblical story of the prophet Jonah and his reluctant attempt to save the people of the Assyrian city of Nineveh from an unknown peril. As Nineveh is an ancient settlement close to the present day city of Mosul in Iraq, this story must be seen as another entry into the broad corpus of Eurocentric literature and representation. The historical moment of the film's release, with a second U.S. military incursion into Iraq in full swing, dooms the Veggie adventure as yet another narrative of historical denial, cultural superiority, and latent racism. While adhering as faithfully as possible to the biblical story may be Christian creed, it should be unnecessary to the broader theme of the film to tread into the cultural politics of the Iraq War, but there is no question that saving the Ninevites, while secondary to saving the souls of the central characters, is Jonah's destiny and God's choice for him. Though the subtext of the Iraq War is not articulated and even the referent of Nineveh is left vague, this film initiates the toddler troopers into one of the central struggles of our times, whether they are ready to piece the story together yet or not. This subtle, or not so subtle, engendering of a historical narrative that marks "us" from "them" is a first step in the not-so-long journey to ethnocentricity and xenophobia.

Jonah: A VeggieTales Movie begins with a much more innocent setting, a first story starring Bob the Tomato and a few of the other Veggies that sets up the later tale of Jonah. The movie opens with a scene as surreal as a bunch of Veggies driving in a Volkswagen van should seem. Bob is taking several of the characters on an outing to see a concert performed by an artist called Twippo. As on a typical family car trip, conflict reigns, and tensions run high. Laura Carrot is the only one of the bunch with a backstage pass to meet Twippo, and she torments the others with her good fortune. Add to the chaos a guitar-playing Asparagus, and you have a recipe for disaster, which happens when Dad Asparagus whacks Bob with the guitar, and Bob loses control of the van, which hits a porcupine and careens off the highway. By the time the van comes to a stop, Laura has lost her backstage pass, and the Veggie friends have lost their sense of unity. The unhappy group has the good fortune to find a local restaurant in which to take shelter. Junior Asparagus happens upon a band of pirates (the eventual heroes of *The Pirates Who Don't Do Anything*), who have a moral fable to share that will help our heroes to resolve their conflict. Thus begins the story within a story, the tale of Jonah the prophet.

The story the pirates tell holds quite faithfully to the biblical narrative of Jonah. A messenger for God, Jonah is given a difficult assignment to go to Nineveh and teach the Ninevites to quit whacking one another with fish. The idea that the Ninevites have nothing more to trouble them than internal squabbles and the odd sport of hitting one another with fish is the playful resolution of a more complex set of stories for a child audience and may be an homage to the British comedy troupe Monty Python. Whatever the case, Jonah sets off on his mission reluctantly, questioning God's plan for him and first trying to escape his fate by going elsewhere. When he eventually finds himself on a ship heading toward Nineveh, a ship crewed by the "Pirates Who Don't Do Anything," he meets the character who becomes his companion and cultural intermediary, Khalil the Caterpillar. As the cultural broker between East and West, Khalil steps into the time-honored role of trusted servant, the Ariel/Caliban to Shakespeare's Prospero or Friday to Defoe's Robinson Crusoe. Khalil praises Jonah for his renowned talents, which serves to further torment this unhappy servant of God. In short order, the ship is enveloped by a terrific storm, and the crew determines that God must be angry at someone on board. A tense game of cards finds Jonah holding the last card, and he confesses that God is angry with him. In order to spare the ship and the crew, Jonah is forced to walk the plank, and the storm immediately abates.

Though every effort is made to save Jonah, he is swallowed by a whale, as is Khalil, who was mistakenly sent off the ship in the fracas. Inside the belly of the whale, Jonah is met by God's messengers, who are able to impress upon him the importance of his mission. God is characterized as compassionate and forgiving and convinces Jonah to repent for his errant ways. Once absolved of his sins, Jonah gets a second chance, and with Khalil he is delivered to the shore. Despite his recognition of the good word of the Lord, Jonah is an unhappy camper, a reluctant messenger who will turn tail given the thinnest excuse. The plot strays significantly from the biblical story when Jonah is refused entrance to the city of Nineveh. "The Pirates Who Don't Do Anything" have also made their way to Nineveh to claim a prize for winning the Mr. Twisty's Twisted Cheese Curls Sweepstakes, a bizarre aside and a fictional product tie-in that references the contemporary consumption of snack food. The pirates smuggle Jonah into the city, but the whole group is arrested on trumped up charges of stealing Twisted Cheese Curls. Given a chance to explain his story to the king of Nineveh, Jonah is able to impress the royal sovereign with his tale of surviving in a whale's belly. So taken is the king with Jonah's feat that he accepts the message from God to reform his people, who must repent and stop slapping each other with fish. Not satisfied with the resolution of his quest, Jonah goes through an existential bout of religious doubt. Khalil tries to help him see the light, but Jonah is left on the outskirts of Nineveh suffering with his inner turmoil.

Having heard the great story of Jonah, the Veggies realize their good fortune and the great possibility that resides in forgiveness and second chances. To add to the great vibes in the restaurant, Twippo himself walks in and treats the Veggies to an impromptu musical performance. This earnest narrative of goodwill and compassion is, of course, the type of fare that make parents and children smile as they leave the movie theater. The kids know that they can redeem any damage they have done in the eyes of their forgiving parents and the God who guides them, and the parents are given the chance to go one up on Jonah, to forgive and to forget, to redeem themselves in the eyes of God by giving their kiddies plenty of second chances. That this confluence of good tidings involves the imaginary infantilization of the Other—the Ninevites/Iraqis as hapless children motif—presumably flies well below the radar of the movie-consuming public, not because they lack the intelligence to recognize Eurocentrism in narrative but because they are not trained to do so. The disturbing absence of a public debate on the deep history of cultural relations between the ancient civilizations around the Mediterranean basin and to the east thereof has resulted in an impoverished and imaginary discourse of East/West relations that trades on stereotypes and a critical lacunae of intercultural understanding. That a Christian moviegoing public in North America should bear the burden of correcting historical accounts that operate on multiple registers and through a broad range of key tropes might be beyond the expectations that can be placed on them. Nonetheless, the communion of popcorn, family entertainment, and righteous "Christian values" in no way should preclude an analysis and awareness of the histories of xenophobia and racism, as well as the profound lack of understanding of the cultural contributions of present-day Iraq to world cultures.

EATING (READING) VEGGIES IN CONTEMPORARY AMERICA

The various *VeggieTales* productions are not uniformly received by Christians or non-Christians. It appears that stories such as *Jonah* are not sufficiently Christian to offend nonadherents or Christian enough to please the more orthodox Christian Right. In a send up on the orthodox reaction, the satirical Landover Baptist Church (2008, www.landoverbaptist.org) published a story on the product release of the Larry the Cucumber toy. It is worth quoting the story at length:

> "We don't want to state the obvious here," said Pastor Deacon Fred at a recent press conference. "To put it simply, we're concerned that a battery operated cucumber is being marketed to young children. We just think it's in poor taste for a Christian organization to put such a product on the shelf." In reviews of the product, the secular media jokes, "adults enjoy the toy even more than their children." . . . "It's not just the dancing green penis that we are concerned about," said Dr. Jonathan Edwards. "The VeggieTales corporation is watering down scripture and promoting a lack of respect for the sanctity of God's Holy Word by producing videos where a talking head of lettuce with a New York accent skips through uncomfortable Bible passages in order to make a story more appealing to children." (Landover Baptist Church 2008)

Tongue-in-cheek, and clearly over the top, the Landover commentary does however raise the key point of the Christian critique of the *VeggieTales* stories.

The core texts of Christianity are not easily opened for interpretation by those who adhere closely to them, and the liberties taken by *VeggieTales* in the recounting of biblical stories such as that of Jonah render them unfaithful to the originals. While even the Christian press tends to support the *VeggieTales* series as a breath of fresh air or even a necessary distortion to promote the Christian faith, the groundswell of criticism is apparent in the blogosphere, where individuals can express their concerns freely. Reflecting the unease with which the series is greeted, bloggers raise concerns about the popularity of the videos and movies in non-Christian environments and over the loose adherence to traditional Christian narratives.

On the other hand, the flexible Christian politics of *VeggieTales* accounts for the muted response of secular critics. As *Time* magazine points out, the series' relative commercial success is a product of its irreverence and the melding of contemporary production with Christian lore. Says Belinda Luscombe of *Time,*

> Although the series is based on sacred texts, the popularity of the videos rests largely on their irreverence. . . . But the irreverence has limits. "We will not portray Jesus as a vegetable," says Phil Vischer, 35, the Billy Graham–Bill Gates hybrid who made the first video in 1993 with fellow Bible-college dropout Mike Nawrocki. ("We failed chapel," Vischer says, because they were always up late the night before writing puppet skits.) Raised on a cultural diet of church and MTV, they wanted to create something that combined family and production values. (2002)

This hybrid Christian oeuvre is sufficiently palatable to the Christian market to have been picked up by megaretailers that pride themselves on so-called family values such as Wal-Mart. The biggest controversy that the series has faced came from the other side of the fence when NBC picked up the series for Saturday morning television. As Phil Vischer recounts on his blog, NBC wanted to pick up *VeggieTales* as values programming but would not allow the inclusion of the statement "God made you special and he loves you very much." He states that "while some *VeggieTales* shows work fine without overt references to God or the Bible . . . most of the shows I wrote in the pre-bankruptcy days don't really teach lessons about values at all, but rather about God. And those shows don't hold up very well if you try to take God out" (World Net Daily 2006). The programs picked up by NBC aired without the key phrase that Vischer had staked his creative work upon. Again, the blogosphere was ripe with outraged commentary, particularly over the perceived hypocrisy of NBC's airing of live footage of Madonna's Confessions Tour, where she parodies Christ on the cross. Led by the American Family Association, a grassroots campaign emerged to stop NBC from airing the footage, something the network was unwilling to do. Often set in direct contrast to the censoring of *VeggieTales*, the broadcast of Madonna evoked a strong sense of persecution among segments of the Christian community.

The controversy over NBC's censorship of *VeggieTales* struck a raw chord among Christians frustrated with an inability to infiltrate the mainstream media with content that they deem appropriate. The sense of doom and persecution felt by some is indicative of a deep cultural rift that threatens contemporary America, one that often follows political lines as well as religious ones. The story of *VeggieTales* and its reception is an exemplary one in this context because it stokes the fires of discontent among alienated Christians, including many adherents of the Christian Right who might otherwise not be disposed to consider the irreverent *VeggieTales* favorably. It may be tempting to suggest that this same lobby ignores the strong institutional support for Christianity in America, both historically and in contemporary terms, but this dismisses the reality that this very same lobby claims a right to speech predicated on the very history of Christianity in America. In other words, Christian pride is predicated on a deep sense of a historical mission that goes right back to the founding of the United States. In a contemporary multicultural and polytheistic society, orthodox Christians are easily drawn to a culture of discontent and a defensive position based on a feeling of persecution. Bob and Larry cannot, and could not, correct this sentiment, but that these Veggies may have emerged as pseudomartyrs is unfortunate. The very innocence and innocuousness of *VeggieTales* might have been sufficient for a public broadcaster such as NBC to turn a blind eye, but this too would have been a policy position and political stance with consequences, however subtle, for the public debate that rages in contemporary America. At the end of the day, Phil Vischer and his creative crew have conducted themselves as directed by their consciences and have produced media that responds to some of the more vapid and offensive elements of kiddie programming with messaging that includes the values of compassion and hope. That they cloaked these messages in Christian clothing and invoked a God that is not of everyone's choosing was a political choice that places *VeggieTales* in the tumultuous ebb and flow of the present-day culture wars over the place of the Christian religion in America. These vegetables have legs after all.

References

Gerbner, George. 1994. Reclaiming our cultural mythology. *In Context, The ecology of justice* 38 (spring): 40, www.context.org/ICLIB/IC38/Gerbner.htm (accessed March 21, 2008).

Johnson, R. 1996. What is cultural studies anyway? In *What is cultural studies? A reader*, ed. J. Storey, 75–114. London: Arnold.

Jonah: A VeggieTales Movie. 2002. Directed by Mike Nawrocki and Phil Vischer. Franklin, TN: Big Idea Productions.

Landover Baptist Church. 2008. *VeggieTales* releases product in poor taste. Landover Baptist Church, www.landoverbaptist.org/news0502/veggietales.html (accessed March 21, 2008).

Luscombe, Belinda. 2002. Finding God in a pickle. *Time*, May 26, www.time.com/time/magazine/article/0,9171,1101020603-250037,00.html (accessed March 21, 2008).

Vischer, Phil. 2004. What happened to Big Idea? philvischer.com, November 15, www.philvischer.com/index.php/?p=38 (accessed March 21, 2008).

———. 2006. Update: The latest on *Veggie* edits on NBC. philvischer.com, September 21, www.philvischer.com/index.php/?p=55 (accessed March 21, 2008).

World Net Daily. 2006. "Madonna as Jesus" to be aired on NBC. *World Net Daily*, September 20, www.wnd.com/news/article.asp?ARTICLE_ID=52049 (accessed March 21, 2008).

VI

Screening Jesus
Hollywood and Christonormativity

SHIRLEY R. STEINBERG

Hi Shirley, my name is _____, I'm the communications and web coordinator for the _____ Faculty of Education.

I know people are looking forward to your talk. I just have one point I'd like to work out—I received the blurb for your talk entitled "Christotainment: Selling Jesus Through Popular Culture." It currently reads:

North Americans have experienced a turn to religious fundamentalism in the past two decades. However, it is evangelical Christians who lead the path to zealotry. Not only have mega-churches cluttered the landscape, but all forms of media, children's toys, clothing, sports, and even holiday destinations have become Christianized. Along with corporate think tanks, religious leaders have found marketing Jesus through popular culture to be lucrative not only in conversations, but in building heaven's bank accounts.

Our goal with the _____ Faculty site is to create a welcoming environment and that includes involving everyone in the discussion. I think statements like your first sentence could be misinterpreted as a blanket statement that North Americans are becoming more religiously fundamentalist. Also, zealotry has a negative connotation which I believe would be offensive to many Christians.

I believe the phrase "building heaven's bank accounts" could be interpreted as a bit sacrilegious. We don't strive to avoid offending everyone (as that can lead to a bland academic environment), but also don't want to seem disrespectful about anyone's beliefs.

Although I am not a religious person myself, I feel like a part of my job is to ensure our faculty website speaks with a voice of tolerance and empathy for all beliefs, which includes the various denominations of Christianity.

It's challenging to be provocative and tolerant at the same time—but I think it's worth it to do so, since controversy is not a bad thing in itself. I'd be happy to work with you to ensure that your talk is communicated in a way that everyone is happy with.

Regards,

______, July, 2008

I RECEIVED THE ABOVE E-MAIL JUST AS I BEGAN TO WRITE THIS CHAPTER. As a writer, I am always looking for a *hook* with which to begin my work. The e-mail spoke to me as the perfect example to explain what I call "Christonormativity." Understanding normativity as *how things should be* (not always what they are), we know that dominant culture prescribes the normal way, the expected way, to negotiate the world. Normalized culture is that which is invisibly dictated, creating a hegemonic agreement between different individuals on what *it* is supposed to be. Christianizing is different from Christonormativizing. When attempts are made to proselytize and convert, the overt nature of missionary work is apparent. However, when a mainstream normalizing culture includes themes and messages assumed to be acceptable by populations, there is a different outcome.

The well-intentioned e-mail presents the position of a mainstream person who sees Christianity as an invisible norm. The author makes an assumption that "many Christians" will be offended by a cultural studies reading of fundamentalist Christianity. The writer is alarmed that the statement is "blanket" and states that "zealotry has a negative connotation which would be offensive to many Christians." The writer is alarmed that a phrase could be "a bit sacrilegious." To imply that something is sacrilegious assumes that belief exists in the particular religion. The note is completed by a thinly veiled accusation that my presentation somehow lacks tolerance and empathy. After receiving the e-mail, I considered the language used by the writer and concluded that without a Christonormative society, this e-mail would not have been written. The e-mail is grounded in the belief that presenting a critical reading of one particular group of Christians would be inappropriate even in an academic situation. Christianity is the invisible norm by which all else is measured; consequently, any critique of the norm becomes a critique of *all* people in the category of Christianity.

In this chapter, I examine the screening of Jesus on TV and in film. There are two models of Christotained films and television programs: one includes films and television programs that directly represent Christian fundamentalism and are consequently created to teach, convert, reaffirm beliefs, and save. The second model features works that are produced on mainstream screens, created for the viewing public, without any outward inscription of Christianity but nonetheless represent assumptions of Christonormativity. Within these two models, I focus on the Rapture screen, examining the television series *Revelations* and the *Left Behind* film trilogy. I investigate the moralistic screen as I look at four network television shows and several commercial films. I discuss the reflected themes and how they inscribe and perpetuate the growing industry of Christotainment.

THE RAPTURE SCREEN

Left Behind, Right Ahead: Rapture Politics—Christotainment and the Ideology of Fear

The Apocalypse and the Rapture are central dimensions of the political fundamentalist and Dominionist cosmology. The producers of Christotainment in this eerie context turn out novels, films, video games, music, and other artifacts that portray horrendous images of earth's inevitable end. When six in ten Americans, according to a *Time*/CNN poll (McAlister 2003), believe that particular fundamentalist interpretations of the book of Revelation will come to pass, the influence of political fundamentalist and Dominionist theopolitics is not something to dismiss simply as the ravings of a small group of crackpots. Reviewing the prevailing contemporary view of the Apocalypse, Jesus returns to earth to "deal with" the Antichrist and the billions of people who have rejected the word of God. According to a majority of fundamentalists, Jesus kills around 2.5 billion people in the Jezreel Valley in Israel. The carnage, fundamentalist theologians, such as the world's best-selling living author, Tim LaHaye, argue, will create a two-hundred-mile-long river of human blood that is 4.5 feet deep. One would conclude that this qualifies as an ideology of fear.

LaHaye and those who buy into a similar theological reading of the Bible present this Dominionist fundamentalist interpretation of the book of Revelation as beyond dispute. Tim LaHaye, the most influential evangelical of our time, takes a series of unrelated Bible verses and seamlessly places them in a clear narrative that never reflects on the multiple ways that any one of the passages could be interpreted and the narrative constructed. To LaHaye's and coauthor Jerry Jenkins' credit, the narrative they produce is easily readable, simple to comprehend, eminently marketable, and highly influential. At the time of the Rapture, Jesus brings the saved to heaven. The nonbelievers and people from other religious traditions suffer through seven years of war, famine, disease, and pestilence referred to as the Tribulation. Then, of course, Jesus returns to settle age-old scores.

As with any piece of fiction or scripture, the literal interpretation of the book of Revelation promoted by LaHaye and the Dominionists cannot be read outside of the backgrounds of those who have constructed this interpretation. LaHaye and the Dominionists are the storm troopers of the cultural wars of the last three decades. In this sociohistorical context, it is not unusual that they might read the Bible and the book of Revelation through the lens of their present struggle. They want revenge against the hated intellectuals, scientists, liberals/leftists, homosexuals, secularists, Muslims, mainline Christians, and other enemies who have, in the Dominionists' eyes, worked to destroy true Christianity, murdered millions and millions of children in their support of abortion, and undermined the traditional family by supporting sexual promiscuity, feminism, and the homosexual agenda.

The trilogy of *Left Behind* movies replicate on film what LaHaye and Jenkins originally published in their enormously popular book series. To suggest that the *Left Behind* books are successful would be an understatement at best. Selling nearly 70 million copies of the original book, *Left Behind*, and millions of the succeeding books, the set narrates an eschatological (pertaining to the end of days) scenario of the looming future of earth. The films, while popular on DVD, never made much of a mark in theaters; consequently, the revenues earned are even grander. The first film, *Left Behind: The Movie* (2000), starred Kirk Cameron, the darling of the Christian Right, originally featured as Michael on *Growing Pains*.

Cameron plays Buck Williams, an eager young reporter who works in Israel investigating a new way to grow food. As he reports, Syrian armed forces send in an air attack, and God destroys the troops—this replicates the biblical promise that the promised land, Israel, would be guarded by God. Airline Pilot Rayford Steele, a married man with a newly wandering eye, attempts to fly to New York; however, people (passengers and staff) disappear from the flight—not everyone, just a selection. Summing up the plot, it is apparent that the Rapture has taken place, and the worthy believers have been removed to above. Left behind are the unbelievers and the undecided. Buck eventually connects with Rayford, who goes home to find his family missing (they were raptured) and reads the Bible for solace. He visits a minister in his neighborhood and aligns with him to attempt to understand the Rapture (this clergyman was not faithful enough to have been spirited away). During all of this, the Antichrist is manifest in the persona of Nicolae Carpathia. As the film closes, Steele's left-behind daughter accepts Christ, as does Steele, but Buck remains unconvinced. Buck finds his way to the church and notes that Nicolae has proclaimed seven years of peace (as predicted in Revelation) and that only faith will save them.

The second film, *Left Behind II: Tribulation Force,* debuted in late 2002 and included the same cast as the original film. The third film, *Left Behind: World at War* (2005) stars Lou Gossett Jr. as President Fitzhugh and was released to churches as the sites for the premiere. The three films cover the first two books in the series. Following the ushering in of the Rapture, World War III, and the creation of the global community, forces battle with the power of Carpathia. I assume the trilogy will be followed by additional films, covering the entirety of the series.

Following the amazing success of the books, a *Left Behind* youth book series was created, and the written texts resulted in *Left Behind: Eternal Forces,* a video game in which players use prayer to increase the strength of fighting forces and attempt to save citizens from evildoers and the Antichrist. Noted by critics as a violent game, *Eternal Forces* is often found in the youth areas of many churches.

Revelations: Christotainment by NBC

In 2005, NBC featured a miniseries starring Bill Pullman as Harvard astrophysicist Richard Massey, a grieving father whose only daughter has been savagely murdered by a Satanist. After securing the capture of the murderer, Isaiah, the embodiment of evil, Massey returns home a defeated nonbeliever.

His company and advice is sought by Sister Josepha Montafiore, a spirited young nun who is dangerously close to excommunication due to her insistence on following signs that she believes will usher in the end of times, the Apocalypse. Sister Josepha is tracing the birth of a male baby to a virgin nun in Greece; she is convinced of the virgin birth and seeks the child, whom she believes to be Christ. The baby has vanished, and the young mother (the virgin nun) has been confined to an institution.

Tortured by Isaiah, Massey is threatened by not only his own destruction but that of all human beings who do not bow to Isaiah. Soon after Massey returns home and meets Sister Josepha, a young Miami girl is struck by lightning and presumed to be brain dead. While evil doctors and hospital administrators argue about the possibility of harvesting her organs, she begins to speak in Latin and to draw and write messages. (The plot segues here to include a Terry Schiavo-esque debate and editorial.) As the nun and astrophysicist try to unravel the tangles of a very confusing plot (which attempts to follow the book of Revelation quite literally), Massey's daughter's stepbrother/best friend, Hawk (né Henry), is kidnapped by the ever-growing forces led by Isaiah and trained to become the heir and son to Isaiah. Isaiah begins to convert forces of convicts to his legions, escapes prison, and starts to build an empire that sports scores of upside-down crosses and followers in black-hooded robes. Massey and Sister Josepha follow leads all over Europe, end up in the Middle East after following the directions of the comatose little girl (who is finally murdered by Isaiah's men), interpret clues that coincide with the apocalyptic visions of John the Revelator, and eventually save the day by killing Isaiah with a dead exorcist's dagger and rescuing the boy, Hawk. The two separate as great friends, Sister Josepha ever faithful and Massey apparently now a believer. The series ends with a close-up of the little baby, who was rescued by an excommunicated priest. The baby is surrounded by light, and heavenly voices accompany the concluding shots of the boy on a carpet in the middle of a desert, guarded by the priest.

Throughout the series, Bible verses separate significant scenes, all dealing with prophecy and the end of days. Additionally, interspersed within the six episodes are two beautiful raven-haired women who are only spotted by Massey. Alternating with the two stunning women are two black cats with gleaming yellow eyes. One can only assume that the women/cats are closely watching Massey. The astrophysicist notices the women/cats, yet never mentions them, always pausing with a clouded recognition whenever he spies them.

Revelations was written and created by David Seltzer (*The Omen*), a conservative Jew who insists he had no religious agenda in creating the series. He considers the series a fantasy/drama and was asked by Gavin Palone to create the series given the current issues plaguing the earth. Palone wanted to address the increasing violence, environmental issues, and wars via the book of Revelation. In an article in the *New York Times*, Palone stated that "his personal interest in religion and Armageddon stems from a long-ago summer spent at an evangelical Christian camp" (*New York Times* 2005). Seltzer discussed the film with UPI reporter Pat Nason, maintaining "*Revelations* would not cover the same ground as the 'Left Behind' books have—tribulation. Followed by the rapture. We are in no way following a fundamentalist track" (*New York Times* 2005).

Palone told Nason in the same interview that he would not discuss his own personal religious beliefs, but that he showed the pilot to

> friends of mine who are deeply religious and Christian, and wanted to make sure that they felt comfortable with it. And what I got back from them uniformly, among everyone that I showed it to, was a certain gratitude for expressing faith in a specific sectarian manner.
>
> I think that the fact that the religion in this show is so clearly Christian, and that we are talking about the New Testament—and willing to take that somewhat sectarian stance—is something that was embraced by everyone that I showed it to. I think people wanted to see some specificity in faith as they see it on television. (*New York Times* 2005)

Seltzer claims that the series deals with a man and a woman and the struggles within their lives. He asked the press to not continue asking questions about his faith as he saw no connection between his own religious beliefs and his fantasy creation. Matt Sullivan of *In Touch Weekly* endorses the DVD box set: "If you're a fan of *The Da Vinci Code, Left Behind* and the *X-Files*, you'll love this six-part series."

The Da Vinci Code, while centering on a biblically inspired plot, never comes across as a conversion or repentance device. The *X-Files* deal with the fantastic, yet lack any hint of Christotainment. Missing in both of these contemporary examples are the normative assumptions of Christianity, moralistic platitudes, fearsome threats of the end of the world, and a savior who must be acknowledged and worshipped to achieve eternal life. Sullivan's endorsement thinly veils Seltzer's intent to keep the series as a fantasy, not a religious tool. Seltzer failed.

Revelations in Being *Left Behind*

As fundamentalist Dominionist authors and clergy, LaHaye and Jenkins are clear in their intent in the *Left Behind* books. It is their duty to warn readers of the coming of the last days and the advent of the millennium. The *Left Behind* books clearly act as conversion tools, and their presence in even the most unlikely places accentuates the growing Christotained reading audience. Stores like Wal-Mart and Sam's Club create mountainous displays of new book releases and find it difficult to keep them in stock. Airport bookstores prominently display the editions, and many airports include entire "inspirational" sections featuring *Left Behind* volumes.

Rapture politics, so adeptly laid out in the *Left Behind* series, with its end-of-times retribution scenario is now a major dimension of the foreign policy discourse in the United States. The cultural politics of the Rapture are central to a wide array of fundamentalist lobbying groups in the nation's capital and in think tanks and assorted organizations throughout the country. The *Revelations* miniseries and *Left Behind* books position the Rapture and the coming of the Apocalypse as the inevitable outcome for the citizens of earth. However, many experts discount the possibility that such bizarre "literal" interpretations of the Bible could influence major social, diplomatic, or military policy decisions.

It has many times been possible for Dominionists to slip under the radar of cosmopolitan academics and veteran career diplomats, simply because such individuals couldn't believe that the ideas they promoted could be taken seriously by large numbers of people. The fundamentalist media empire, the coalition with other right-wing groups, and, of course, Christotainment have helped disseminate Dominionist ideas. In short, at the end of the first decade of the twenty-first century, political fundamentalist interpretations of biblical prophecy are molding decision making in a variety of domains. Indeed, the efforts by Dominionists to gain this level of influence and the details of their agenda are not state secrets. Leaders such as LaHaye and James Dobson have openly discussed and published their ideas about these issues for decades. As

LaHaye, for example, has written, good Christians can no longer view secularists as benign individuals who choose not to accept Jesus or attend church.

In a direct and unequivocal statement, LaHaye (1980) proposed that Dominionists eliminate all secularists from political office and replace them with political operatives who are moral Christians. It is important to note that LaHaye is not talking about replacing these leaders with anyone who falls under the wide umbrella of self-proclaimed Christianity. Much to the contrary, he's calling for these positions to be filled with a particular variety of Christian who believes, as does LaHaye, in the strict precepts of Dominionism. The black-and-white Manicheanism here is sobering: in LaHaye's Rapture politics, the virtuous will be taken to heaven when the time arrives; "the rest" either are tacitly in league with the Antichrist because of their belief structures or consciously support him and his work. If one believes that his or her political opponent is working for Satan and wants to bring only misery to the planet, then the chance of a productive, respectful democratic dialogue is seriously undermined (LaHaye 1980; McAlister 2003; Frykholm 2005; Unger 2005).

When the Dominionist-dominated National Religious Broadcasters (NRB) met in 2005, a major theme of the convention involved the effort to take political control of as much of the world as possible as soon as possible. As speaker after speaker made reference to the Islamic effort to take over the world, the general consensus that emerged from participants was that they weren't opposed to religious zealots establishing a theocratic society, just to an Islamic group of zealots engineering such a maneuver. One seminar led by Raul Justiniano, the Bolivian president of the Confederation of Ibero-American Communicators (the Latin American *brother* organization of the NRB), was titled "Taking Over Cities for Christ: The Thousand Day Plan." In his presentation, Justiniano delineated his strategy "to invade" the major cities of Latin America by establishing cells in individual churches and, with this base, to make a move to take over all public and private dimensions of each city (Blumenthal 2005; Hedges 2006).

While traditional forms of fundamentalism, and even evangelicalism in general, hold in common several of the characteristics of this new, more virulent and violent form of fundamentalism, old-time fundamentalists and most evangelicals never attempted to inflict their dogmas on those who didn't share their theopolitical perspectives. Make no mistake, evangelicals, fundamentalists, and Dominionists all believe in submitting to a patriarchal hierarchy that declares its frequent conversations with the deity, a lesser or greater degree of intolerance toward the unsaved, and a gnawing discomfort with intellectual analysis. But when the Dominionists proclaim their intent to transform the civic realm into a domain of their church, they break with many in the evangelical and fundamentalist camps. As part of the neoliberal free marketers and colonialist neoconservatives, they are a prized group in the right-wing phalange of American politics. With their ability to turn out voters and the enthusiasm of their political volunteers, Dominionists gain access to funds from wealthy allies.

We find that the theoretical basis for one of the most powerful movements in contemporary American politics and theology is based on an antidemocratic, theocratic set of precepts. These precepts echo the Nazis and the eugenics movement, and Dominionist goals include visions of global conquest for Jesus. Promoting a Christian nation and God's kingdom on earth, Dominionists preach a Rapture politics that lets Muslims and other nonbelievers know that *they are the enemy* who must be destroyed before God's will on earth can be done. It is not hard to understand, when the U.S. government and military are employing these concepts, why Muslims would interpret Rapture politics as a call for their ultimate destruction. The Dominionist ideology of fear has profound consequences. Never before has the United States been viewed by various peoples around the world as such a frightening threat not simply to their well-being but to their survival itself. Conversations with individuals around the world illustrate the depth of this fear of the Dominionist vision of the U.S. military as the army of the vengeful Christian God (Thomas 2005; Hedges 2006).

Depictions of Muslims and Arabs in the *Left Behind* series and in the *Revelations* TV miniseries reinscribe current fear and loathing exhibited by many North Americans and the media. By using the Rapture screen, Islamophobia increases, thus confirming biblical proclamations. While the *Left Behind* series is decidedly religious in content and intent, *Revelations,* a so-called secular production, is NBC's contribution to Rapture politics. The elements of Christotainment are the same in both productions; fundamentalist evangelical predictions fill the screens, without doubt, critique, or even the possibility that the narrative is mythical. *Revelations* follows the script laid out by John the Revelator in the book of Revelation, and the *Left Behind* films appear as well to frighten members of the audience into belief and salvation. Many viewers of both series watch the films without knowing that they are Christian in nature.

By assuming the Christonormative belief that the world is destined to end with the coming of the Antichrist and his eventual defeat by Jesus Christ, Rapture politics serves to support the continued escalation of a U.S. neocolonial military force.

As a postscript to the ideological underpinnings of the two series, as a media critic, I saw both series as expensive production undertakings, resulting ironically in naïve and simplistic products, confusing scripts, over- or underacting, and poor lighting, cinematography, and overall cohesiveness. Both series had elements common to undergraduate film students, lacked sophistication, and were hard-pressed to sustain any interest other than academic-type analysis in over sixteen hours of film. These dynamics tend to play themselves out in many religious films, somehow demanding that the audience view the texts through a lens of innocence, even ignorance. In the next section of this chapter, I draw the same conclusions based on my screening of all films discussed. I propose that audiences consider the notion that this naïveté is deliberate and echoes simplistic Sunday school lessons and repeated sermons that do not go beyond the literal in fundamentalist churches. When one becomes "like a child" and, thus, is open to the spirit, this imposed innocence prevents analysis, challenge, and doubt.

THE MORALISTIC SCREEN

Born-again TV: *Touched by an Angel* in *7th Heaven* while Seeking *Joan of Arcadia* on the *Highway to Heaven*[1]

Network television has a long history of producing all-American family fare. From the saccharine days of *Father Knows Best, Family,* and *Eight Is Enough,* to the nonreligiously inscribed religious dramas of *Highway to Heaven, Touched by an Angel, 7th Heaven,* and *Joan of Arcadia,* tacit themes thread through concerning what is expected of an American family. Of the 109th U.S. Congress (2005–2006), 89.2 percent was Christian, and according to the most recent census data (2001), 76.7 percent of all Americans are Christian. While the earlier family shows did not openly articulate a specific denomination, it was always apparent that every family was somehow Christian, most probably Protestant. Only in *The Waltons* is the viewer clearly aware that the family is "churchgoing." Later shows, such as *Highway to Heaven, 7th Heaven, Touched by an Angel,* and *Joan of Arcadia* all assist in identifying what is expected from Christian behavior. Television shows with overarching Christian themes address the audience with an expectation that Christianity is the norm—they are all Christonormative.

Even though Christianity makes up 76.7 percent of our population in the United States, Christians only make up 33 percent of the world's population, according to adherents.com. Still, at 33 percent Christianity is the largest religion in the world, though it is followed closely by Islam (21 percent), then those who identify as nonreligious, such as atheists and agnostics (16 percent), Hinduism (14 percent), primal-indigenous (6 percent), Chinese traditional (6 percent), and Buddhism at (6 percent). The four television shows are globally syndicated with large audiences. Rarely, if ever, are they referred to as religious or Christian.

Highway to Heaven

The earliest distinctly Christonormative drama, *Highway to Heaven,* aired for five years (111 episodes). The late Michael Landon plays an angel, Jonathan Smith, sent to earth by God, referred to as "The Boss." Jonathan's duty is to team up with Mark Gordon, played by Victor French, to assist people in helping one another or finding a better life for themselves and their loved ones. Human failure is a prevalent theme, as people exhibit greed, anger, and ego. Some episodes deal with realistic issues like cancer and racism.

The series was very popular, and its cancellation is believed to have been due to the death of Victor French in 1989. The show had an overarching lesson in each episode: the "highway to heaven" is open to all that choose it.

Touched by an Angel

As does *Highway to Heaven, Touched by an Angel* brings messages directly from God to its characters. Each show revolves around a person or group wrestling with a problem or undergoing a crisis. Angels appear in order to help those in need. The supervising angel, Tess, played by Gospel singer Della Reese, and her apprentice Monica, played by Roma Downey, aid those Christians who have lost their way. Each week they deliver messages of hope directly from God to those who have no hope.

Two other characters that become regulars on the show are Andrew, played by John Dye, and Gloria, played by Valerie Bertinelli. Andrew is the Angel of

Death; he takes those who have died to either heaven or hell. Gloria is a novice angel who learns about being human, sometimes adding comic relief.

The show labels itself nondenominationally as "Christian," a theme that plays itself out continually. The opening theme song, sung by Della Reese, praises God for helping those in need: "When you walk down the road. Heavy burden, heavy load. I will rise, and I will walk with you. I'll walk with you till the sun don't even shine. Walk with you, every time. I'll tell ya, I'll walk with you. Believe me, I'll walk with you." The song offers solace and is an obvious marketing tool. The marketing is slick; the message sells well.

The show enjoyed global popularity and is now syndicated worldwide. Running nine years, the series had many celebrity guest stars, including Muhammad Ali, Maya Angelou, Carol Burnett, Bill Cosby, Kirsten Dunst, Faith Hill, Rosa Parks, John Ritter, and Luther Vandross, among others; all except Ali self-identify as Christian. The show's fan base is large and includes both young and old.

Touched by an Angel's episodes vary in depth, sending a final message of hope at the end of each. Ironically, while definitively Christian, the show does not exude a sense of perfection in the manner of other Christian TV shows. There is no sense of condemnation or guilt imposed upon the "sinner." Death is a predominant theme, and one is always aware of its inevitability. This is also the only Christian-themed program (whether implied or defined) that includes black actors and has any indication of cultural diversity. There is no confusion among viewers as to the Christian nature of the show; yet critics consistently ignored this religiosity, and the show was highly successful.

7th Heaven

7th Heaven is a good example of a nonreligious, yet overtly Christian, show. The series follows a minister, his wife, their seven children, a loveable dog, a happy home, and a wholesome community. The long-running series of eleven seasons features a Protestant cleric, Reverend Eric Camden, and his family, who deal week after week with "everyday life." Eric Camden, played by Stephen Collins, and his wife Annie, played by Catherine Hicks, initially have five children of varying ages. The oldest two, Matt and Mary, played by Barry Watson and Jessica Biel, are high school students. Simon and Lucy, played by David Gallagher and Beverly Mitchell, are in junior high, and the youngest Camden, Ruthie, played by Mackenzie Rosman, is just beginning school.

During the third season, however, the show's producers decided to add two more babies to the Camden family, Sam and David, played by Nikolas and Lorenzo Brino. The fact that the family is Protestant is rarely stated in the show but is inscribed on every scene.

Just as most other Christian-based shows shy away from most controversial topics, so does *7th Heaven*. The most heated issues are alcoholism (preacher's sister) and premarital sex (preacher's daughter); however, topics like homosexuality and abortion are never mentioned. Each week the Camden family endures "typical" American problems, traumas like not having a date for the homecoming dance, knee surgery, a mean teacher, and not getting the perfect job. Everything turns out well in the end, and family solidarity remains intact. *7th Heaven* is a wholesome television show that never fails to warm the heart. It portrays the *average* (white, middle-class, Christian) family as the *perfect* family. In fact, the show is so wholesome that even the villains are somewhat benevolent.

The topics and show always relate to conservative Christian beliefs and ideologies. It comes as no surprise that producers asked Jessica Biel, who plays eldest daughter Mary, to leave the show after she posed seminude for *Gear* magazine. Biel reportedly posed for the magazine precisely to combat her wholesome image on the show, which made it more difficult to get diverse parts in Hollywood. Producers needed a wholesome feminine representation for their program, so they had to get rid of the "fallen" starlet.

Joan of Arcadia

God speaks to sixteen-year-old Joan Girardi, played by Amber Tamblyn. Joan goes to high school, has family problems like other girls, and worries about the same things as other girls, but God approaches her each week in a different person's body and tells her to what to do. Recalling the premise of *Oh, God!*, in which George Burns plays God and John Denver his somewhat hesitant servant, *Joan of Arcadia* ran for three years. God appears to Joan in the form of an elderly lady, a teenage boy, a little girl, a street vendor, the school mascot, an amateur stand-up comic, and a stoner at school, and other unlikely characters, and asks her to do complete a task. Joan questions, pretends not to hear, and argues with God. In one episode, as God gets on Joan's nerves, she proclaims, "So many people pray to see you; if they only knew." The audience is engaged in a more contemporary Christian discourse. With Joan's teenage persona, ABC hoped her contrarian attitude would invite a younger, hipper audience.

Joan of Arcadia takes on a new dynamic when trying to help the viewers "see the world," and simple, blind faith is not relied upon.

The show's popularity was astounding. *Joan of Arcadia* won a People's Choice Award and was one of the few shows in its first season to be nominated for an Emmy. In its first season, 10.1 million viewers watched the show each week. The popularity of the show was accredited to its being considered spiritual though not judgmental or too religious. The production team and viewers were shocked when the hugely popular show was cancelled after only two seasons. Fans wrote letters, sent e-mails, and made telephone calls to CBS in order to have the show put back on the air, but their efforts were in vain as CBS claimed it wanted to target a younger audience.

Joan of Arcadia does not solve all problems in every episode. Some issues span several episodes, and others are never resolved due to the show's abrupt cancellation. The supporting cast consists of sympathetic and diverse characters: Joan's father, Will, played by Joe Mantegna, is a police officer, and her older brother, Kevin, played by Jason Ritter, is a paraplegic. Each episode ends with a moral, always noted by "God"; for example, "How you see the world, how you deal with it—that determines your real wealth," and "Growth is a process."

Born-again TV

These four television dramas all created a Christonormative discourse. While Christianity was rarely, if ever, articulated, the shows were laden with assumptions that a North American audience was receptive to and expected Christian values and morals. Banal, ordinary, and simplistic, most shows catered to the socially and theologically uninformed and depended heavily on sentimentality. As they were all network programs, the production quality in all shows was high, and each had a large budget. The inability to convert or "turn" a subject was never considered, and even through death, the unseen Jesus influenced participants. The whiteness of three of the dramas also emphasized the Norman Rockwellian context of American middle-class Christianity. The climate that allowed these shows to thrive indicates a lack of resistance and questioning regarding the issues engaged. Rather, all the programs were well accepted and considered wholesome and mainstream. Most involved in production would still declare that the shows were neither religious in nature nor promoted any particular agenda.

Mundane Moralistic Movies

It is a mystery to me why one cannot convert or be saved in a sophisticated manner. In my weeks, days, and hours of research, I was unable to find a film or television series with Christian content or intent that manifested some degree of complex narrative, production, and conclusion. I rearticulate my previous comment that somehow the ordinary, simplistic plots and productions engage an audience to be open to the suggestion of repentance, conversion, and guilt. The following films deal with both tacit and overt Christonormative values and intent. None of them provides any hint that there are alternative paths to salvation or diverse roads to Christianity. Being a true believer is the only way to be saved.

Interestingly, Hollywood has a tradition of blockbuster religious-themed films, but even considering the content of these films, none of them falls within the Christotainment realm. Films like *King of Kings, The Silver Chalice, Spartacus, Ben-Hur,* and *The Greatest Story Ever Told* manage to cross over to audiences as serious dramas, Christian in theme, yet not proselytizing in intent. The following films are not of the blockbuster genre and are rather modest in scope; yet, they purvey a distinctly missionary zeal and fundamentalist posture.

The Cross and the Switchblade

David Wilkerson, played by an untanned Pat Boone, is a bumbling preacher who means well. He feels called to New York to do God's work. The first of the Christoconversion genre, *The Cross and the Switchblade* (1970) tells the tale of a young Latino gangbanger played by Erik Estrada (Ponch from *CHIPS*). Reverend Wilkerson is not wanted when he invades the *bad neighborhood:* "Don't be layin' that God stuff on me." He retorts, "There's somebody who cares about you people. . . . In fact, he loves you just the way you are." The young pastor does not ask, nor does God, that the gang members change, merely that they give themselves to God and believe. "God'll get you high, but he won't let you down. God sent me." Wilkerson appears whenever there are problems and conflicts, preaching the need to get to heaven. "You just don't know what heaven's like, Preach." Wilkerson/Boone responds, "I don't have any magic cure." He tells the kids that he is just a "simple preacher" but continues to involve himself in opining about their futures.

Laced with god-awful rock music, the film takes us through a rumble, prostitution, heroin addiction, and stabbings. Renting a theater with the local church group, the reverend asks two rival gangs to take up the collection. To prove to him that they can be trusted, the kids collect the money and give every cent to the preacher. Estrada's character rises, cries, and receives the spirit as Wilkerson preaches, "Jesus Christ was perfect, and they crucified him. When he died on that cross, he was a man." At this point, the gang leader receives the lord, and when told that the macho Jesus had a "spike drove into his feet," he is able to relate to this manly deity. Conversion is complete as he is invited to be saved: "It's free. All you have to do is accept it. Let Jesus Christ come in."

As a young tween, I remember my mother giving me a book, *Twixt Twelve and Twenty*, followed by *Between You, Me, and the Gatepost*, both written by Reverend Wilkerson's alter ego, Pat Boone. I remember reading the books with absolute shock, wondering why my mother had given them to me. The books preached purity of spirit and body and were laden with advice for young women. I remember telling Mom that they were Christian books, and she didn't believe me. How could the white-bucked 1950s star turn into a Bible thumper? When I watched *The Cross and the Switchblade*, I couldn't get those two books out of my mind. At any rate, the film ends with glory to God, converted gang bangers, a few dead bad guys, and lots of happy people of color following their newly anointed leader.

Hometown Legend

Terry O'Quinn of *LOST* (in which he plays John Locke) stars in this modest-budget film from 2002. Produced by Jerry Jenkins, coauthor of the *Left Behind* books, the film follows a coach who rediscovers Jesus Christ. Since the coach's kid was killed in a football game, the coach has lost his faith. In Athens, Alabama, it is said that the only two things anyone cares about are God and football, and in this film, the statement is true. The coach returns to lead the team for one last year since the school is going to be closed—he wants to help the team win. The retired jerseys of the "Crusaders" are brought out for the game, and as you can guess, God wins the game for the team, and the coach finds the path to Jesus Christ again. His son, however, remains dead.

Flywheel

In this 2003 film, Max is a used-car salesman who attends a megachurch with his family, runs a business, and exhibits confidence to his employees. However, Max isn't an honest man. Driven by debt and greed, he insists on charging customers more than cars are worth and pockets large profits. His saved pregnant wife and son are disappointed in Max and pray for him to find Jesus. Facing certain financial ruin, he takes the advice of an evangelist on TV: "Your marriage is in the shape it is in today because of the choices you have made. You are in financial bondage today because of the choices you have made." He knows that he is a failure and wants to pray for himself, yet says, "I don't think God would listen to me right now. He knows I'm not an honest man." Falling on his knees (with the American flag behind him), he learns to manage money, be honest, and pay attention to his wife and son. He acknowledges that "my pride got in the way, but when I let the lord tell me how to run my life," things got better. After a long search, Max acquires a valuable flywheel for his car and is able to have his vintage MG repaired. The moral is clear: a car can be a great car, but without a flywheel, it won't go anywhere. Max's car gets the flywheel; the lord gets Max.

Facing the Giants

Facing the Giants (2006) was produced by members of a local Georgia church. Using extravagant music reminiscent of old biblical films, the story opens on the first day of school at Shiloh Christian Academy. Another football film, the coach is grumpy, his life sucks, his wife can't get pregnant, the car doesn't run, and the house has a bad odor. The team is on a losing streak, and he is in a deep depression. Falling on his knees, the coach prays, "You're my god. You're on the throne.... Lord, give me something, show me something." Meanwhile, the kicker of the team is challenged to kick a field goal twenty yards further than he ever has before. As he gets ready to attempt the kick, his crippled father pulls himself out of his wheelchair to inspire his son. The kicker sees his father and knows that the lord is with him. The kick is made, and the game is won. Jesus is lord.

The coach is able to save his job, his wife finds she can get pregnant, the stink in the house was only a dead mouse, and in a coincidental plot twist, the coach is admonished, "Your attitude is like the aroma of your heart. If your attitude stinks, it means your heart's not right." Now *that* is Christotainment.

CONCLUDING ON ONE'S KNEES: THE GETHSEMANE-IZATION OF WHITE MEN

In the way too many films that have been made claiming conversion and change of heart, common themes wind through the reels: men losing their way, men falling on their knees, men finding God, and men winning football games or getting their cars fixed. I didn't find any films dealing with females losing faith and regaining it; instead, each reiterates the need for the *man*, the dad or husband, to step up and take charge by rededicating himself to God and letting God take over. The man, in turn, takes over the family. White male desperation is always caused by unavoidable outside forces: losing seasons, losing jobs, losing honesty, or losing family members. By regaining God, men are able to retrieve their rightful patriarchal roles and find their places at the head of the family.

Other contemporary films assume Christianity and its belief system, while not centering the plot on Christ or conversion. The big-budget movie *World Trade Center* deals with two surviving rescue workers who are caught beneath September 11 rubble at Ground Zero. They are saved by a man who is called by God while sitting in church. Drawn to New York, he sneaks over the barricades and goes directly to rescue the two men. Never mentioning God or Christ in a direct manner, the film cuts to rays of light appearing along with cross-shaped metal at the site of the destroyed Twin Towers. An implied holiness and godly presence underlies the film, while not overtly demanding adherence to the word. The Christonormative nature of this film is subtle, but there is no doubt that it is the Christian God whose hand is made manifest (at least to two rescued workers). Interestingly, God doesn't rescue the other hundreds of workers from Ground Zero or the nearly three thousand people who jumped from the Twin Towers or were incinerated in the attacks.

Whether it is explicitly noted that a film is a product of, for example, Christian Cinema.com or Epiphany Films, there is no doubt that cinematic and televised Christotainment exist within million-dollar industries. Not particularly striving for Oscar- or Emmy-winning performances or productions, these films and television shows depend on a naïve audience settling for moralistic and threatening narratives. Viewers are able to identify with the fragile nature of fallen men and find comfort in the fact that by falling on their knees and giving themselves up to God, they will be saved. The goal of Christotainment, aside from marketing, is to prepare for the end of days and eventually get to heaven.

With the increase of heaven-bound viewers, the last three years has seen Neveah as one of the most popular baby girls' names. Spell it backwards. Media works.

Notes

1. This section was written with the collaboration of Dr. Ruthann Mayes-Elma, research associate.

References

Blumenthal, M. 2005. Air Jesus. MediaTransparency, http://mediatransparency.org/story.php?storyID=16 (accessed August 29, 2008).

Frykholm, A. 2004. *Rapture culture:* Left Behind *in evangelical America.* Oxford: Oxford University Press.

_______. 2005. The gender dynamics of the *Left Behind* series. In *Religion and popular culture in America,* ed. B. Forbes and J. Mahan. 2nd ed. Berkeley: University of California Press.

Hedges, C. 2006. *American fascists: The Christian Right and the war on America.* New York: Free Press.

Hendershot, H. 2004. *Shaking the world for Jesus: Media and conservative evangelical culture.* Chicago: University of Chicago Press.

LaHaye, T. 1980. *The battle for the mind.* Old Tappan, NJ: Fleming H. Revell.

LaHaye, T., and Jerry B. Jenkins. 1995. *Left Behind.* Carol Stream, IL: Tyndale House.

McAlister, M. 2003. An empire of their own. *Nation,* September 4, www.thenation.com/doc/20030922/mcalister (accessed August 29, 2008).

McAuliffe, J. 2008. An interview with R. J. Rushdoony. *The Forerunner,* www.forerunner.com/revolution/rush.html (accessed August 29, 2008).

NationMaster. 2008. Biography of Rushdoony. NationMaster.com, www.nationmaster.com/news/2006/fellowship_church (accessed July 2, 2008).

New York Times. 2005. Gavin Palone with UPI reporter, Pat Nason. *New York Times,* March 20.

Thomas, P. 2005. Christian fundamentalism and the media. WACC, www.wacc.org.uk/wacc/publications/media_development/2005_2christian_fundamentalism_and_the_media (accessed August 29, 2008).

Unger, C. 2005. American rapture. *Vanity Fair,* December, www.vanityfair.com/politics/features/2005/12/rapture200512 (accessed August 29, 2008).

Filmography

7th Heaven. 1996–2007. Created and produced by B. Hampton. WB Television/CW Television Network.

Facing the Giants. 2006. Directed by A. Kendrick. Albany, GA: Sherwood Pictures.

Highway to Heaven. 1984–1989. Directed by K. Inch. Written by E. Barnham and C. Beaumont. NBC Universal Television.

Hometown Legend. 2002. Directed by J. Anderson. Foley, AL: Jenkins Entertainment.
Joan of Arcadia. 2003–2005. Created by B. Hall. CBS Television.
Left Behind: The Movie. 2000. Directed by V. Sarin. Columbia Tri-Star Pictures.
Left Behind: Tribulation Force. 2002. Directed by B. Corcoran. Cloud Ten Pictures and Namesake Entertainment.
Left Behind: World at War. 2005. Directed by C. Baxley. Cloud Ten Pictures.
Revelations. 2005. Created by D. Seltzer. NBC Universal Television.
The Cross and the Switchblade. 1970. Directed by D. Murray. New York: Gateway Productions.

VII

"The Battle for the Toybox"

Christogimmicks and Christian Consumer Culture

CHRISTINE M. QUAIL

On a recent trip to Florida, I bumped into a group of twenty-somethings waiting at the airport check-in counter. They were dressed in hipster T-shirts and shorts, with suitcases and guitars in tow. The guitars were covered with Jesus stickers. The eldest in the group had a What Would Jesus Do (WWJD) badge holder around his neck and sported a lime-green T-shirt painted with two saltshakers, reading "salt of the earth, missions 2006." Later that day, I got stranded at the Philadelphia airport due to an overbooked flight. As I sat on the floor with my two daughters, two little girls shared some Scooby snacks with my kids and invited them to watch their music DVD. The kids on the DVD sang about the power of God and the blood of the lamb, with hand motions reminiscent of both Black Power and a slaughtering. The kids knew the words; my kids seemed interested in something so different from *Blue's Clues*. The mother, who was very nice and very generous in sharing the snacks, crayons and paper, and DVD with my kids, said that she'd bought it at Vacation Bible School. "Camp, not school," her younger daughter corrected her. With a wink, she said her kids had to leave "camp" early, so she bought the DVD hoping that it would serve the same purpose as being there. It seems to be working, she confided, as the kids got up and performed the songs and Disney-style tween dances for people sitting around us. Is that true? Is the DVD the same as "being there" at Bible school and even better? Why all the T-shirts, stickers, and jewelry about Jesus? Why the explosion of Christian toys, clothing, and merchandise? Christogimmicks? What does it mean to wear one's faith or carry a Jesus or Mary doll around? How does this shape kids' identities?

This chapter situates these questions in the history, rationale, and mechanics of marketing, advertising, and branding. It establishes several core concepts, such as the notions of the "demographic" and the "niche market," that are used to identify and sell to consumers. It then discusses the development of Christian consumerism before performing a discursive analysis of several key Christogimmicks.

It is important to note that throughout the chapter, layers of analysis are present, moving between a thick description and an interpretive analysis. Attention is given to different levels of cultural life, beginning with the cultural artifacts at hand. Understanding the complexities of these artifacts as processes and experiences necessitates an anthropological dimension and respect for the uses and reception of goods and practices. However, this does not mean that these practices are not situated more sociologically within economic and political and, in this case, religious contexts that should be ignored or subsumed by the moment of consumption itself. Here, attempts are made to move back and forth through Stuart Hall's encoding/decoding model of cultural analysis, where texts/discourses are analyzed as artifacts, as produced goods with intended meanings and purposes, and as polysemic texts that are open to interpretation.

CONSUMER CULTURE: SHOP TIL YOU DROP

One might take for granted the fact that North American life is largely invested in "consuming in mass quantities." It would not shock us to drive around a developing neighborhood in a sprawling community and see rows of strip malls, box stores, and chain restaurants. It's sometimes a matter not of *whether* to go to the mall but *which* mall—the strip mall with the Dollar Store, tobacco shop, and tanning salon, the old mall with the food court and anchor stores JCPenney and Sears, or the upscale mall with anchors Neiman Marcus and a scaled-down version of Saks 5th Avenue. Or maybe we would choose to take a trip out to the outlet malls or to Wal-Mart or Target. There are approximately forty-six thousand shopping centers in the United States, and the numbers are increasing (Schor 2004, 9). Forget about Main Street, as many towns' local shops are disappearing due to a slowing economy and the economic prowess of vertically integrated chains that aggressively underprice and outsell their competition, putting them out of business with strategies that should be investigated through antitrust regulations as predatory and unfair in nature. If, however, we explore shopping and consuming as cultural practices situated in a specific historical context, we can better understand the push and pull of shopping, consuming, and leisure time as a commodity-filled pursuit.

Theorists such as Karl Marx and Jean Baudrillard have critiqued this cultural moment. For Marx, the concept of "commodity fetishism" encapsulates the state of relating to others based on the consumption of commodities and ceasing to view these commodities as products of a particular time and place with political implications (1992). Baudrillard writes that

> we have reached the point where "consumption" has grasped the whole of life; where all activities are sequenced in the same combinatorial mode; where the schedule of gratification is outlined in advance, one hour at a time; and where the environment is complete, completely climatized, furnished, and culturalized. In the phenomenology of consumption the general climatization of life, of goods, objects, services, behaviors, and social relations represents the perfected, "consummated," stage of evolution which, through articulated networks of objects, ascends from pure and simple abundance to a complete conditioning of action and time, and finally to the systematic organization of ambiance, which is characteristic of the drugstores, the shopping malls, or the modern airports in our futuristic cities. (1999, 37)

In such a world, consumption is the raison d'être, and it is in fact a duty to participate and support the conspicuously consuming society. How did we get here?

Stewart Ewan's seminal work *Captains of Consciousness: Advertising and the Roots of Consumer Culture* (1976) provides a critical history of the development of consumer culture. With roots in capitalism itself, the rise of a specific consumer culture can be correlated to burgeoning industrialization at the turn of the twentieth century. As mass production became possible, more goods became available in mass quantities. The rise of the concept and the lived experience of the "mass"—the masses, mass society, mass media—were enabled by urbanization, industrialization, and even the development of mass transportation: transcontinental railroads enabled the shipment of goods over vast terrain, making it possible for a person in New York and a person in Kansas to read the same magazines, buy the same soap, and eventually watch the same television shows and view the same commercials. As the twentieth century progressed, gains in the labor movement inspired a new conception of leisure time, as the forty-hour week and the minimum wage system (or "family wage") were established. Taking a historical tour through two world wars, Ewan also cites the demilitarization of the industrial war machine as a final impetus for full-fledged consumer culture, as American and some European industries were tooled to continue mass production, not of bullets and tanks but of dolls and cars. Cultural historians further identify the interstate highway system, suburbanization, and the rise of the privatized nuclear family as leading contributors to the success of consumer culture—as families became more self-sufficient and moved farther from work, Main Street, and friends and neighbors, more goods could be consumed, especially cars, houses, and innovative, time-saving devices like the washer and dryer. It might be easy to criticize consumer culture and its excesses, but it is important to note that benefits also ensue. To wit: One could lament the loss of the pastoral handwashing and line-drying of clothes and critique the environmental costs of inefficient electric devices such as the washer and dryer. On the other hand, one could celebrate a woman's freedom from having to spend an entire day scrubbing soiled clothes, allowing her perhaps to spend a few minutes on herself or on other work. The gendered, racialized, and classed implications of a changing consumer society are addressed by key articles in Lawrence Glickman's (1999) collection on consumer society and have informed this chapter.

Consumer culture, in historical development and contemporary expression, involves an overarching ideology that shopping, buying, and the capitalist, postindustrial economic system that produces the goods that we buy are natural, useful, necessary, and central to an American lifestyle. It is even considered patriotic to consume—slogans such as "buy American" and "American-made," as well as the call to "not let terrorists win" by staying home from malls after September 11, reveal how consumer ideology has been sutured into the American psyche. These ideologies, if a corporate manager were to get a hold of them—and they have, as we will see later—might be referred to as "core values." Business language and culture has found a way to discuss ideology without using such a loaded word, one that is often associated with duping the public and has ties to the red scare and anti-Soviet thinking of the Cold War. Hence, "core values" is corporate-speak for "ideology" and what a company "stands for" with its "mission statement" or brand identities. So do corporate America, consumer culture, and Christians share the same "core values"? This question is taken up in a later section.

MARKETING, ADVERTISING, AND BRANDING: FROM SELLING CONSUMER CULTURE TO SELLING IDENTITY

Advertising arose alongside consumer culture. The previous discussion of consumer culture suggests that the overproduction of goods creates the need to produce consumers, hence the development of marketing and advertising as the persuasive—some might say propagandistic—tools of consumer pedagogy. Critical approaches to advertising, especially from a political economic perspective, chart the rise of these persuasive industries alongside mass production of consumer goods and a growing mass media (as well as concentration of ownership in media and cultural products, which favor large, ideologically similar companies) (Bagdikian 2000; Ewan 1976; Berger 2007). While marketers say that advertising only alerts people to a product, its price, or its features, critics of advertising and marketing psychology hold that ads create a need that the product will meet. Theorists like the renowned Jean Kilbourne (1999) write that ads create a sense of lack or inferiority that the product will fulfill or fix—a transference, if you will, of the need.

Today, we are bombarded with advertising. Naomi Klein (1999) charts the steady increase in ad expenditures in the United States across the twentieth century. Over $200 billion a year is spent on advertising, $15 billion of which is spent marketing directly to children (Linn 2004, 1). Advertising is a tax write-off in the United States, so the fistfuls of cash spent are worth the effort. Newspapers, radio, magazines, and television are plastered with increasing amounts of ad space relative to editorial copy (Bagdikian 2000). Advertising has become so ubiquitous that some researchers estimate that the average American will spend approximately one entire year of her or his life watching TV commercials (Berger 2007). In addition to the typical venues for advertising, increasing amounts of space are becoming vehicles for these messages, with public schools (Giroux 2000) and other public spaces, such as busses, toilet stalls, and stadiums (Klein 1999), being commercialized at breakneck speed. Because of the slippage of commercial culture, it is difficult to even estimate how many commercial messages we are exposed to.

Advertisers aren't just trying to reach random consumers though. They don't want just any audience; they want the "right" audience, one with a will and a way to consume—in other words, consumers with spending money and the desire to spend it with abandon. The idea of the "target market" is the idea that ads are specifically targeted to a particular slice of the market, which has become fragmented by marketers attempting to anticipate, thus exploit, what a particular group gets excited about. The particular slice of the market, the target audience, is defined by "demographics," or aggregate data that encapsulates the "average" or typical consumer in that market. Men aged eighteen to thirty-four, women aged forty-five to fifty-nine, and tweens (preteens) are all demographics. Once the proper demographic is identified for a product, advertising houses and marketing departments employ teams of researchers to determine the desires and fears of that market and find the cutting edge within it. "Cool hunting" has become a lucrative venture, where teams of "cool hunters" set out to capture the homegrown practices of cutting-edge teens in order to use images and slang to market jeans, music, and even Taco Bell burritos. Once the cutting edge is made mainstream, it loses its cool factor, and a new cool is already on the horizon. In this giant feedback loop, the continuous drive to find the up-and-coming, cutting-edge band, musical genre, fashion, or even author or toy results in the cycling through of these goods and consumers' need to continuously confront the new gimmick being marketed to them (*Frontline* 2001).

An even smaller slice of a particular demographic can be located in the niche market—one that might not contain as many members as a more broadly defined demographic but that can be defined, understood, and marketed to as well, though with more specialized products and services for that smaller, yet well-defined, market. For example, "gay," "urban," "African American women," and "Goth kids" are all niche markets. Identity politics and rights movements unwittingly play into bringing into the consumer-culture fold previously excluded, or seemingly excluded, groups of people. When all models in fashion ads are white, companies are sending the message that their products are for a white audience. The increasingly diverse faces seen in ads, increasing number of ad campaigns created specifically for minority markets, and increasing number of advertising dollars being spent in minority publications illustrate marketers' desire to convince more, and more diverse, people that the company values them and will fulfill their lack because they can identify with the product or company.

Even the demographic of children is becoming more integrated into the world of corporate ploys and marketing. Shirley Steinberg and Joe Kincheloe (2004) examine this "corporate construction of childhood," in which children are savvy consumers hailed by corporate parents. Juliet Schor (2004, 31) demonstrates that kids spend five times as much time shopping than playing sports. Polling shows that parents think that marketing causes children to become materialistic and to value consumption over other activities (Linn 2004, 8). With all the toys, websites, clothing, and other cultural products being marketed and used to market themselves and other products, we are currently living in a state of hypercommercialization in which, as mentioned, people as young as six months old are being hailed as consumers (Linn 2004; Schor 2004).

As consumers have become savvy in the world of hypercommercialization—the last few generations having grown up in a media-saturated world, largely understanding of and critical toward the messages and appeals of advertising—and as more space becomes commercialized, resulting in "ad clutter," marketers have developed new strategies to reach the target audience: product placement, merchandising and tie-ins, and branding. A brand is a way to differentiate products that are essentially or almost the same. What actually differentiates Wonder white bread from Stroehmann white bread from Sunbeam white bread? Not too much. The central difference is the brand name of the item. Branding functions in a more complex manner than ads—the brand itself is anthropomorphized, ascribed characteristics that the company wants to project. Marketers attempt to create brand loyalty for more efficient marketing. It will take more work to lure away a consumer loyal to Coke than a person who will buy whichever cola. And the earlier consumers become loyal, the longer the brand has become a part of their identities, making them all the more difficult to lure away—meaning more profits and less work for Coca-Cola. One strategy is to try to monopolize a consumer's buying power by "cradle-to-grave" marketing: getting a baby hooked on Disney by putting Winnie the Pooh on the diaper will serve the company well when the six-month-old (who can actually identify a brand logo, such as Pooh or the Golden Arches), recognizes the character on toys, clothing, sheets, books, and DVDs and becomes a lifelong consumer (Linn 2004). Klein (1999) writes of "brand tribes," groups of consumers so loyal to a brand, such as Disney, that they heavily identify with that brand to the point of feeling that they are part of the brand's family. Within this drive to create brand tribes, "buzz" must be circulated about a product—old-fashioned word of mouth and press about a product that will break through the commercial clutter and appear more authentic.

THE CHRISTIAN DEMOGRAPHIC AND NICHE MARKET

Much like "women aged twenty-five to forty-nine," "African Americans," "golf enthusiasts," and "urban youth," "Christians" have become a demographic, and Christian consumers are creating "brand tribes" and "buzz" around wildly popular Christian consumer products, such as the What Would Jesus Do (WWJD) Christogimmicks or Fully Rely on God (F.R.O.G.) bracelets. The concept of demographic flattens every identity into a market segment so that the identity can become a marketing tool. Thirty years ago the discussion of demographics was reserved for marketing and advertising gurus setting out to research and define their target audiences to better craft their messages—the world of persuasive communication dutifully studied its audience in much the same way a speechwriter crafts her rhetoric to touch the hearts and minds of a politician's constituency. Today, demographics have become so ingrained in popular discourse that my university students, rather than saying "people my age," or "my friends and I," refer to themselves as "our demographic." The rise of the "tween" demographic has also been highly successful. People aged seven to twelve have been crafted by a marketing guru as a unique band of kids "in between" childhood and teenage years in order to create products that are necessary to this group and to craft marketing messages directed at them. The term is now commonly used to refer to kids in this age group—whether we need a new word for an eight-year-old or not (Mitchell and Reid-Walsh 2005). This seemingly inane phrase indicates a sea change in the internalization of marketing and consumer culture. In order to be useful, the demographic needs to be clearly defined; in my students' case, they simply mean "young adults." However, transposing "young adults" into "my demographic" indicates their willingness to submit to marketers' desires to flatten that category and overgeneralize the likes, dislikes, and ultimately buying behaviors and identity of that category. The same flattening happens when any group loses the power to define itself and becomes a marketers' demographic.

In this case, we are considering the "demographic" and niche market of Christian consumers. Surely, this category, consisting of billions of people, has some dissimilar likes, dislikes, and buying behaviors, not to mention an array of religious beliefs and political positions. Despite the differences in this group, the demographic has been utilized to try to market both religious and secular products.

The rise of Christians as a demographic and niche market must be understood vis-à-vis the history of religious marketing. Christian holidays themselves could be considered a form of religious marketing, as product differentiation against the pagan rituals occurring at the same time. Both Mara Einstein (2008) and James Twitchell (2007) chart the history of religious marketing, especially in America. Twitchell's book reproduces a political comic strip from the 1800s depicting each religious denomination setting up a booth at a carnival, each calling to passersby, just like carnival or boardwalk hucksters. Einstein (2008) writes that Americans have always been able to choose their religion, which might cause religions to market their "product" (be it their religion or denomination or their specific church or congregation) in order to attract "consumers" (worshippers). Despite the legal right to choose, most Americans used to adopt the religion of their parents; converting was not a popular activity. Now, however, with the growth of nondenominational churches, megachurches, or revivalist "born-again Christian" churches, many more people are more flexible about their religious affiliation—some people find themselves "shopping for God" (as Twitchell titles his book on the subject) in much the same way they shop for a car, a pair of tennis shoes, or a bar of soap. This is not to equate the products just listed. Religious affiliation is usually undertaken very seriously, with great introspection and commitment. I don't mean to be flip in comparing religion to soap, but some similarities in product differentiation, branding, and marketing do exist. Twitchell calls this type of thinking "supply-side religion," which is useful in linking this discussion to the previous discussion of consumer culture.

Einstein notes that media saturation has allowed the proliferation of all types of media content: "the simple fact that there is more media means that there is more religious media" (2008, 7). In a 2005 U.S. Census Bureau study,

Americans reported spending approximately 3,649 hours per year with TV, radio, music, magazines, video games, Internet, videos, newspapers, and other media (Berger 2007, 63). Some of this time is spent with religious media. The use of so much media, secular and religious, Einstein also notes, leads to increased advertising, and with media saturation and increased advertising comes increased religious marketing—especially that which attempts to attract people based on fun and entertainment (Einstein 2008, 7). What is new, however, is the intensity of the marketing, the context of the messages, and the political and personal implications in today's world to be branded Christian, especially Dominionist of the Christian conservative right wing.

IT'S ALL ABOUT JESUS: BUYING CHRISTIANITY TODAY

Marketing religion goes hand in hand with merchandising religion. This, too, is not a new endeavor. Crosses, crucifixes, statues, and Russian icons have existed for many centuries. What is different now, then, with Christian consumer culture and gimmicks? In the 1980s, the growth of megachurches, many of which have stores in the church itself, prompted both the need to differentiate the church and/or the religion from others. An article in *Newsweek* from 1986 provides evidence that Christian toys were still not very widespread. The article says that the JCPenney catalogue contains Christian toys for the "increasing, if still small, segment of the market," capitalizing on the trend's upswing (*Newsweek* 1986). Today, the Christian market segment is massive. According to studies, 85 percent of Americans consider themselves to be Christian; 60 percent of the world's Christians see themselves as evangelical; and in the United States, 88 million people consider themselves "born again." Born-again Christians constitute 39 percent of the adult population in the United States (Twitchell 2007, 22–23) and have an extreme amount of influence in politics, particularly in the Republican party, including the White House. It is criminal to ignore a market or "demographic" this large and powerful from a marketing perspective.

Einstein proposes, "Not only are Americans religious, or spiritual as some prefer to call it, but we readily buy products and services that relate to our faith. We do this because . . . traditional religious institutions are not the primary source of spiritual sustenance for most people anymore. . . . 60 percent of Americans get their faith from something other than a religious institution"

(Einstein 2008, 5), especially in online formats, such as beliefnet. And people are buying that spiritual sustenance: in 2006, over $5 billion was spent on Christian consumer products (Righton 2007). One estimate suggests that "nearly 12% of Americans spend more than $50 a month on religious products, and another 11% spend $25 to $29, according to a national survey of 1,721 adults by Baylor University, out in September" of 2006 (Grossman 2006). Further, "one in three Americans surveyed made at least one purchase in a Christian bookstore in 2005," says Baylor sociologist Jerry Park. They're buying books, music, DVDs, toys, gifts, home decor and 'witness wear' such as jewelry, T-shirts and more" (Grossman 2006).

Even specialty retailers serve the Christian market, such as the Family Values Center or Family Christian Stores. "With 304 stores nationwide, Family Christian is already the world's largest Christian chain and is adding more stores . . . says [Cliff] Bartow," president of Family Christian Stores. "It competes with big-box stores and Internet sites in breadth of selection (25,000 items) and a presentation 'focused on people's needs,' says Bartow"(Grossman 2006). Coming after the specialty shops, Wal-Mart and Target (and other retailers, such as Shoe Dept, Toys R Us, Virgin Records, and even Urban Outfitters) have introduced Christian product lines onto their shelves beyond the typical Christian books that are sold at practically every bookstore. The legitimation toys and clothing get from being featured at these popular stores cannot be underestimated. The reach of these stores is huge and extends to broader segments of the population that may not choose to shop at a Christian Family Store but is now exposed to a product at Wal-Mart.

Churches themselves are used as marketplaces, as megachurches contain stores and are able to capitalize on this spending. Besides the actual church store, church itself is a way to feature new products in the course of a sermon and during other activities. Mel Gibson's *The Passion of The Christ* was marketed to preachers, who bought blocks of tickets in theaters in advance, helping boost box office sales. The apocalyptic book series turned movie franchise, *Left Behind*, did one better: *Left Behind: World at War* "was the first film ever to open only in churches, not theaters" (Twitchell 2007, 7). The producers of John Milton's *Paradise Lost* have adopted the same strategy and will release the film to churches that pay a licensing fee (Twitchell 2007). A similar church-as-retailer move is made with other merchandise, such as one2believe's toys, which will be more fully analyzed later: in much the same way that Oscar guests are given goody bags of new gadgets or *Oprah* studio audiences are given free books or CDs, churchgoers are sometimes given free toys before they are released in stores. These marketing strategies build a favorable impression of the film or toy, its manufacturer, and the church, who all become fun, entertaining, and godly at the same time. These are learned marketing behaviors, proven successful elsewhere and applied to the Christian niche market.

But why not just take already existing products and brand them as Christian or create specific ad campaigns targeted at this niche market? Because in our media saturated world, it is more important to brand Christianity, thereby merchandising the religious experience, trying at once to integrate Christianity seamlessly into popular culture (with movies and merchandising such as *VeggieTales*), yet simultaneously create an opportunity to further identify as Christian and rehearse the stories and values of Christianity in the toys and apparel in opposition to other elements of mainstream secular culture; and, importantly, to provide an opportunity to witness, evangelize, and spread the word as children share toys with one another, "wear[ing] their Christianity on their sleeve," quite literally, with some religious apparel. Bartow explains, "People feel called to live out a Christian lifestyle beyond going to church on Sunday. . . . They want to live it in their work, their ethics, their home and the way they treat everyone in their life" (Grossman 2006). It could be that in the fragmented postmodern world, with media saturation, people are looking for a way to unify and display their identities in a protectionist backlash stance. Especially with a conservative Christian identity, it becomes politically necessary to infuse every aspect of life with Christian ideology, in a second stance, one of evangelizing. Both stances have been used politically to normalize such policies as "abstinence-only" education, antiabortion laws, and antigay marriage rules.

Much Christian merchandise appears to be positioned as an alternative to mainstream culture. The products tend to be based on the assumption that there is something very wrong with the excesses of modern culture: too much sex, drugs, violence, and hedonism and not enough of the Ten Commandments. The marketing discourse attempts to distinguish these goods from mainstream culture by branding them as Christian. As this analysis will demonstrate, Christian branding seems to identify these toys/clothing as *wholesome*, sharing *values* and *lives of faith* that Christian parents want for their children and Christian adults cherish for themselves. Chastity, humility, piety, and the goal of salvation are encoded into the goods. For example, Christian product developers say, "Since 9/11, there's been a surge in faith-based products, says Bob Starnes, vice president of licensing at Big Idea, the firm behind *VeggieTales*. That's because most Americans have a 'faith perspective,' he says. Laurie Schacht, president of *The Toy Book*, a toy industry publication, says some parents also are dissatisfied with toys from conventional toymakers: 'There are a lot of wild things out there. Parents want to give kids wholesomeness'" (Horovitz 2007).

Despite a seeming agreement on some elements of encoding (minus different critical interpretations about the political implications of these encodings), there is dissension in the ranks regarding the decoding of these products. While some people rush to them, either as tools of identity promotion or of witnessing and salvation, others who identify as Christian distance themselves from the blasphemy and ridiculousness of the plastic Jesus. Non-Christians, or nonfundamentalists, tend to react with disbelief or in terms of kitsch. Notes will be made herein of moments of decoding.

Thus, what follows is first a thick description of several Christogimmicks: toys, jewelry, books, clothing, and websites. Items were selected based on their prevalence in the popular press regarding Christian toys and clothing. Branding is analyzed, and an attempt is made to determine what meanings the product produces about Christian life and what work this does in a cultural sense. A critical interpretation of each item will be provided in order to link the product to larger political and cultural discourses. Indication of audience reception is given in order to better understand the ways in which real people respond to the products' political and cultural essences, although a fuller reception study could be carried out at a later date.

"The Battle for the Toybox": Christian Action Figures from one2believe

one2believe is a success story in terms of the expansion of Christian consumer culture. The founder and CEO, David Socha, says, "The faith aspect is our No. 1 driver. It's all about Jesus" (Righton 2007). His reasoning continues, "Our goal is to give the faith-based community an alternative to Bratz dolls and Spider-Man" (Horovitz 2007). Socha approached over seven thousand churches and gave away the toys at them. Then, he gave four thousand free toys to the

Marines' toy drive. The Marines initially turned down the offer because Muslim and other non-Christian children and their parents would not want the Bible verses that appear with the toys. However, they eventually relented and accepted the donation (Righton 2007). The military often uses cultural products to propagandize American political goals. This includes media such as radio program Voice of America, as well as toys and candy dropped from bombers in the sky or tossed out to children from tanks, the same jets and tanks that are occupying their communities. The history of Christian missionaries is also rife with providing free books, clothing, and toys in order to present a positive, friendly image of the colonial project. The same strategy continues today with Christogimmicks.

When the company began to expand into mainstream retailers, especially Wal-Mart, one2believe launched a campaign titled "The Battle for the Toybox." The promotional material contains pictures of the toy lines, along with copy announcing the coup in being a leader in distributing Christian toys in a global store like Wal-Mart. The text reads, in part, "one2believe, a faith-based company, has been given the opportunity to spread the word of God to children throughout America" (one2believe.com 2007). Thus, they are attempting to brand themselves as "faith-based" (they don't say they're Christian per se, but we can understand "faith-based" as a euphemism for "Christian"). The evangelical thrust is apparent in their wanting to "spread the word," not just "sell toys." Then, they proclaim, "one2believe is in a battle for the toybox. Which side are you on?" By constructing a "battle" between faith-based/Christian toys and "other" (read "secular = heathen and unwholesome") toys, they are calling Christians to build a relationship with them based on defeating the "other," much in the same way that conversion and colonial missions work, in defeating the "heathen other" and converting people to Christianity. Here we have extended Christian colonialism to the toybox, building Christianity by buying one2believe's toys and protecting the toybox for God, from Satan.

The company has several product lines: P31 Dolls (to be addressed in a later section), Jesus Loves Me Bear (a plush toy that sings "Jesus Loves Me"), Spirit Warriors, Tales of Glory figurines, and Messengers of Faith talking dolls. The Messengers of Faith are dolls that speak Bible verses when squeezed. Each doll also comes with a book in which those Bible verses are printed. The line contains Jesus, Mary, Esther, Noah, Moses, David, Peter, and Paul, each for $19.99. The Jesus figure says, for example, "John, 3:16. God loved the world so much, that he sent his only son to pay for sin, so that whoever believes in him, may not be punished, but have everlasting life." This is a very different childhood experience than that of the kid squeezing the Teenage Mutant Ninja Turtles doll that yells, "Cowabunga, dude!" or playing with Bob the Builder, who quips, "Can we fix it? Yes, we can!" or the talking Bratz line that gives advice about boys, fashion, and friends when you push the button.

Tales of Glory are small, three-inch, plastic figurines. There are eleven sets, each with a biblical character and his sidekick. Examples include Jonah and the Big Fish, David and Goliath with five stones, Moses and the Ten Plagues (comes with Moses, Pharaoh, tablets and staffs, and a bush covered in locusts), and Jesus Walks on Water (Jesus, Peter, and a boat). Each set comes with a storybook that tells the Bible story, along with several quotes from the Bible. Tales of Glory boxes come with Bible points that can be collected and redeemed for gifts.

Finally, the Spirit Warrior set contains large plastic dolls of Samson and Goliath. Each resemble World Wrestling Entertainment wrestlers, with flashy costumes, bulging muscles, and an anticipatory fighting look on their faces. Each comes with a storybook. A play mat is also available, for $5.99, which contains different settings for "imaginative play" with the Messengers of Faith and the Tales of Glory dolls. Each doll's product description, in each toy line, ends with "children can make this story come to life with" whichever doll is being described. A similar claim is made by the popular press about another line of Jesus action figures: "Kids will have fun acting out the great epic stories through religious action figures" (Shiflett 2007, 75). The idea of "imaginative" play is pushed, with the play mat offering the perfect setting. How imaginative is it, though, to reenact an already existing story? The same critique has been made of Disney Princess dolls and toys, where the story is already written, and children's imaginative play is already structured to mimic, in some sense, the film that the toy is tied into (*Mickey Mouse Monopoly* 2001). Here, the Bible is the main feature, and the toys are the merchandise tie-ins sold as ancillary products. Play is structured through the biblical story of the character, who already has a name and a story and even comes with a small storybook to remind kids of the story and a few actual Bible verses in order to teach memorization of scripture beyond the general understanding of the story. In this way, the toys are meant to teach the Bible in order to craft identity, as well as to prepare kids for memorizing scripture, in order to evangelize and help convert others to Christianity and, for some, to infuse Christianity into public policy.

What of the argument, again made with Disney and with Barbie, that the encoded and intended uses are not always the ways in which the toy is used by children? Erica Rand, in her book *Barbie's Queer Accessories* (1995), ethnographically discusses the subversive ways that gay and lesbian children use Barbie to play out queer narratives and to imagine and perform queer identity. So, while some children play Barbie dress up and Barbie and Ken make out, other kids play Barbie dresses in Ken's clothes or Ken and Steven kiss. Does each kid play Moses brings the tablets down from the hill or Jesus walks on water? Or do kids put Jesus into the GI Joe Jeep to go plant landmines or play Mary and Moses make out? Or Samson and Goliath, are they a little gay as they writhe around on the Tales of Glory play mat? Certainly, this is not what the toy company or Christian parents intend for children's play, but if we are truly allowing "imaginative" play, then these are possibilities that arise and should be encouraged. This is not to say that there are no politics to the toys—there are. But it is important to allow for some agency and some slippage in meaning making in the minds of the kids who use them. It is harder to subvert something, though, that has a long history and rigid structuring, as kids always know how it is "supposed" to be. Barbie's "story" is not as rigidly set or even as well known as Mary's.

"Ordinary Girls, Extraordinary Faith": A Life of Faith Dolls

Some Christian toys are essentially a Christian-branded version of their secular counterparts. Take, for instance, stuffed animals, the Prayer Circle Friends. These plush toys mimic the Build-A-Bear line where children can choose their own parts, clothes, and accessories. Prayer Circle Friends distinguish themselves with their "prayer chip," on which children can record their own prayers before stuffing it into the doll. The result is a toy that prays along with the child (Family Christian Stores 2008). This product development strategy basically positions the toy as what I refer to as a "Christian-value-added" alternative.

Similarly Christian-value-added toys include the A Life of Faith Dolls (ALOF), a direct response to the American Girl Dolls line of toys, books, movies, and more. Learning from the success of American Girls, ALOF dolls attempt to shave off a portion of the American Girl market—the Christian portion. This is confirmed by the industry experts: Bartow, president of Family Christian Stores, sees these as being "for parents who want to offer their daughters the American Girl doll experience in a Christian fashion" (Grossman 2006).

Visiting the website, one sees that the Web developers have mimicked other tween/girl websites. Purples, pinks, hearts galore, fresh lines, and "real" pictures of "real" girls are found, as are invitations to chat and participate in the ALOF world. The line is anchored on the $99.99 dolls, modeled after American Girl Dolls, doll clothes and accessories, accessories for girls, and the ALOF Girls Club. The dolls, referred to as "heroines," like the American Girls, are supposed to have lived in the 1800s and are happy to share with you their experiences from a different world. The main dolls/characters include Elsie, a wealthy Southern Belle in 1840s; Millie Keith, a pioneer girl; Violet Travilla, a wealthy Victorian artistic girl living in 1877 (who happens to be Elsie's daughter, a generation later); Laylie Colbert, a plantation slave girl in the 1830s; and Kathleen McKenzie, a "gifted and spunky redheaded girl growing up in Fort Wayne with her parents and younger brother at the perilous dawn of the 1930s" (Life of Faith 2008b).

On the homepage, the visitor is greeted by a cute picture of seven girls dressed in the frilly dress-up ("historical") clothing and accessories, each holding a matching doll. The six girls in the front are white, the one girl in the back, peeking over another girl's hat, is African American (and appears to be holding the "slave girl" doll). Girls are called to click on the following links: "Embrace the vision," "Meet the heroines," "Live the faith," "Join the club," and, alas, "Shop the boutique."

When consumers shop the boutique, product pictures and descriptions are provided. The product description for Millie reads as follows:

> *Based on the classic Christian literature* by Martha Finley, this 18 3/4" *faith-based,* all-vinyl play doll was sculpted and costumed by award-winning designers. Millie Keith is fully-jointed so she can sit, stand, and be posed in many positions. *She can even put her hands together to pray!* Millie comes dressed in historical clothing true to the time period and setting of her story. Her purple frock is highlighted with lace and embroidered trim, and the tucked bodice has unique square buttons. She also comes with her lace-trimmed petticoat and pantalettes, purple Mary Jane shoes and white stockings, and her *miniature black Bible.* Her blue eyes twinkle with life, beautifully complementing her long blonde tresses. Her hair is made of Kanekalon, the finest wig fiber in the world,

> and her eyes have "real" lashes. Also available in the Millie Keith doll line: Over 20 different outfits and accessories that are unique to the historical setting and life experiences of Millie Keith as found in the A Life of Faith: Millie Keith book series from Mission City Press. (Life of Faith 2008b, emphasis added)

Branding the doll as "faith-based," the only difference we see here is that the doll comes with a Bible and can move her hands into prayer position (which is documented in one of the website's photos). The key is also the Christian literature upon which the doll is based, which you can also purchase.

A new addition to the collection from Mission City Press is the next book in the series of Violet Travilla books for $12.99:

> Open the pages of this book and step inside a lush, fragrant garden blooming with growth lessons, fruitful encouragement, and vital gardening tools that beautifully illustrate how you can enjoy a flourishing faith in God. Inspired by the life experiences of Violet Travilla (the charming Christian heroine from the A Life of Faith: Violet Travilla series) and formatted in thirty in-depth Bible lessons, this creative study guide takes you on a journey from cultivating intimacy with God in the garden of your heart to partnering with Him in the great harvest of souls. (Life of Faith 2008k)

Girls are encouraged here to enjoy faith in God, and the book is so centrally tied to Bible study that an oppositional or negotiated interpretation would be difficult. The language of gardening ("growth," "fruitful," "gardening tools," "flourishing," "cultivating," "garden," "harvest") paints a very robust, yet intense, model of a relationship with God. The gendered nature of the description is also not lost—the theme of hearts arises in product descriptions as well as in visual imagery on the website, using this design as a branding tool, as a way of saying, "Hey girls, God's cool, cuz God likes hearts J."

The book series also features, for $7.99, a journal for girls to write in:

> Violet's Daily Diary: A Personal Growth Journal for Girls is a unique "garden" journal designed to help girls chart the climate, growth, and progress of their heart's "garden" as they nurture their faith. This jour-

> nal features a guided, interactive format and a topical Scripture reference page. It is also a great companion product to the in-depth study guide, Violet's Life Lessons: Growing Toward God (Cultivating Your Life of Faith). (Life of Faith 2008j)

The garden and heart theme continues in the journal, although the "journal" is more like a workbook, where girls are not given free reign and blank pages but a highly structured and instructive environment in which the goal is not self-exploration, creative and angst-filled poetry, or silly drawings, but rather "charting . . . progress" in their "faith." Scriptures are integral, again. This is reminiscent of the WWJD journal, which supplies answers to the question "What would Jesus do?" and provides advice and scripture, along with pages upon which to journal. "He would avoid empty chatter," "He would choose his friends wisely," "He would obey his parents . . . obedience is the 'virtue-making virtue'" (Courrege 1991). It is unlikely that a young person would write about sexual exploration or masturbation on the page reading, "He would stand firm." Or, maybe she or he would . . . Outfits for real girls are also available, just as they are for American Girl Dolls.

At this point, the website very quickly moves us from the Christian-value-added model to the hard-core Christian consumer model. The space that the actual dolls and books take up is minimal compared to the indoctrination pages, which begin with the lure of a free gift. However, if you click on the link "God's free gift to you," you will not be sent a free accessory for your doll or a coupon for a free lip gloss. Instead, you will find this message:

> Did you know that you can become a Christian and have a personal relationship with God?!
>
> God is the God of the whole universe. He is the One who created heaven and earth and everything in them, and He created YOU! He made you just the way you are, and He loves you so much that His love cannot be fully expressed in words.
>
> Would you like to hear more? If so, click on the following links.
>
> *THE GIFT OF SALVATION*
> *WHAT DO I DO NEXT*
> *A HELPFUL REMINDER*
> (Life of Faith 2008f)

The free gift is . . . salvation, the punch line reminiscent of Ralphie in the classic *A Christmas Story*, who uses his decoder ring to find that the intriguing secret message he's been anticipating is to drink more Ovaltine—"a crummy commercial" (*A Christmas Story* 2003). In the embedded link to the Gift of Salvation, the coding is also "girl." Note how Jesus is in your "heart," as well as the use of "best friend" and "your very closest Forever Friend": Girls are told, "God wants to be your very, very best friend—closer to you than any human friend could ever be. In fact, God wants to be so close to you that He is willing to come and live inside of you—right inside your heart" (Life of Faith 2008e). This is where the free gift comes in: "God offers you a free gift—the gift of forgiveness of your sins and eternal life with Him." And then girls are instructed how to accept Jesus and the Holy Spirit. A prayer is provided, along with a promise that the girl will be born again and will protect herself from "the penalty of death and eternal separation from God" (Life of Faith 2008e). After girls have made their commitment, the "What to do next" link explains how to begin to tell others about the conversion, preferably Christians, but also non-Christians, as well as how to talk to God in prayer, buy a Bible, find a church where they teach the Bible and attend regularly, get baptized, seek out other Christians and befriend them, and then begin to tell others about God. Finally, the site admonishes, "Enjoy your relationship with Jesus—your very closest Forever Friend!" (Life of Faith 2008l).

If girls are looking for more ideas on "what to do," there are suggestions for *old-fashioned fun at home* (Life of Faith 2008g). Links to further-divided activities illustrate a heavy emphasis on integrating Christianity into every moment of a girl's life, from arts and crafts, to baking cookies, to parties with friends. If the Club Libby Lu's and spa parties for girls have become popular, one might see a reaction and co-optation of the trend, toward the Christian brand:

Fun activities: These include "A Life of Faith" game—write a story about a girl you know who lives a life of faith; "Old-fashioned Bible Study!"—where you make up invitations and invite friends over to study the Bible (submitted by Samantha S., age ten); "Faith Binders"—where you get a notebook, print out some Bible verses, and make a collage and use it for devotions every morning (Life of Faith 2008c).

Prayer projects: "Prayer with the Father is also exciting! The God who created the whole universe wants to spend time with you! Now that's pretty awesome!"—so write a song for God, write a prayer, have a prayer party, make a picture prayer journal where you put pictures of your family and write a prayer for them, and don't forget to include "our nation's leaders, too!" (Life of Faith 2008h).

Crafts: These include Bible verses trading cards, and Patriotism pins (because "Many times in history has a country been brought together by difficult and hard times. During those times courage and strength is found in God and in the encouragement of neighbors and countrymen. One way to show your support for your country is to make a 'Pin Flag'") (Life of Faith 2008d).

Recipes: These include Empty Tomb Muffins submitted by Abby D., age thirteen (Life of Faith 2008i).

To reiterate, these activities have little to nothing to do with the dolls and books; yet they are more generally focused on taking girl culture away from feminism and inscribing it with Christianity. Many online environments for girls contain a chat room or other messaging system. In the "Girl Talk" section of ALOF, I expected to see a chat room but instead found a topical index of questions written by girls, answered in Dear Abby fashion by the main doll character, Elsie. One entry, "Addictions," contained a letter by a twelve-year-old who was afraid she was addicted to reading. She was instructed that she was, indeed, unhealthy in her pursuit of reading and needed to invite the Holy Spirit to help her gain control of her addiction. Another thirteen-year-old girl wrote in, believing she was too proud of herself, and asked for scripture verses that would help her "get rid of pride." The entry for "witnessing" contained an entry from a scared fourteen-year-old girl, who wrote, "My best friend is unsaved. She doesn't go to church and believes in a totally different religion than me. I was just wondering if it is right to hang out with her." The response begins, "First, I would be somewhat concerned if she were truly your best friend. Since she is not a believer, how could you share and enjoy with her the most important thing in your life—Jesus?" and continues to advise the girl to distance herself from the friend. Girls can also start a club with their friends and receive a club packet of scripture and activities (Life of Faith 2008a).

A Life of Faith's slogan is "Ordinary girls. Extraordinary faith." The "ordinary girls" found on the webpage can be seen in the picture, and in traces of the write-ins. Testimony from a few girls is found on the portal entry, with their letters uncannily echoing the marketing discourse:

- "Your books have made my relationship with Christ deeper!"—Olivia, age ten (Life of Faith 2008a).

- "The books helped me get deeper in my faith, and helped me deal with everyday problems. I feel if I didn't have the books, I wouldn't be half as close to God."—Kelly, age eleven (Life of Faith 2008a) (Note: all *i*'s are dotted with hearts.)

This is not an interactive community of girls chatting about being girls but rather one of girls being told by adults how to be proper Christian girls, in a girl-friendly and fun way.

Are You a P31 Girl?

A Life of Faith is not the only popular Christian doll. one2believe has its own line of dolls—P31 dolls. The P31 doll line has only three different dolls, which are eighteen inches tall, have silky hair and sweet faces, and are dressed in trendy outfits (as opposed to ALOF's historical costumes). Each doll comes with a cookie cutter and some cards with recipes and ideas for games, crafts, and how to be a P31 girl, which will be defined momentarily. Favorable reviews of the dolls abound. Christian News Wire compares them to Bratz/Barbie dolls. The Bratz dolls, with their bare midriffs, gaudy makeup, and overtly sexualized forms, are often cited as the vulgar, undesirable toys that prompted the Christian response for a return to a *wholesome* and *traditional* girlhood: "Compassionate, charitable, tastefully dressed, physically fit, and caring are traits we all want our children to grow up possessing. However with all the negative images and damaging messages our society bombards our children with, you may be wondering how it can be done? A great way is to provide toys, which through play, teach young children these desired character traits" (Christian News Wire 2008). There is a genuine concern to protect girls and treat them respectfully, to teach girls to have self-respect and a sense of worth. The sentiment is also publicized by the CEO: "David Socha, one2believe's founder says 'girls today are influenced by their surroundings, and when a girl spends a lot of time with a doll that looks like she belongs in a brothel . . . we have problems. In creating the P31 dolls, our goal is to give young girls positive, contemporary dolls that instill values that girls will carry with them their entire lives. P31 dolls are high quality, fashion forward and with the included activity fun to play with'" (Christian News Wire 2008).

But what makes this doll such an "alternative"? What are these "desired character traits" and "values"? These are the values of P31, or Proverbs 31, a part of the Bible that describes the ultimate Christian woman. Proverbs 31:10–31 teaches about a woman's character as a wife, devotion as a homemaker, generosity as a neighbor, influence as a teacher, effectiveness as a mother, and excellence as a person (Proverbs 31 Woman 2008). one2believe's founder and CEO David Socha writes in his corporate biography that he has a "Proverbs 31 woman" at home, and dozens of websites exist devoted to the P31 woman. What does it mean to be a P31 girl today? And how is the use of the concept of the "P31 girl" and "P31 woman" used to brand Christian culture and Christian consumer culture?

The interpretation of these characteristics is that the traditional homemaker, as wife and mother tending house and submitting to her husband, is the ideal role for a woman. One verse from Proverbs 31 is emblazoned across the top of the P31 doll's box: "She extends her hands to the poor; yes, she reaches out her hands to the needy" (Proverbs 31:20). On the surface, P31 is meant to represent giving and selfless acts, as quoted in the verse on the box, but remember that the P31 woman, according to the entire reading, is not simply helping the poor but submitting to patriarchy. The doll's suggested activities include making a homemade card for an elderly neighbor, baking cookies for a homeless shelter or convalescent home (or her relatives), and donating some old toys to a church, Salvation Army, or orphanage. One card included with the doll is for the parents, who are encouraged to help their daughter bond with the doll so that the P31 principles become more engrained. Parental activities range from discussing the P31 principles (traditional gender roles) with their daughter to "involv[ing] [her] doll in as many activities as possible. Whether it is mealtime or a trip to the grocery store, allow your daughter to bring her doll along as a companion" (P31 Cards 2008).

At face value, this doll seems somewhat innocuous, if not somewhat socially responsible, with the attention given to helping the poor—especially in contrast to Bratz and their obsession with gossip, makeup, and primping. When we start to deconstruct the P31 doll culturally, however, we see thicker layers of meaning. If we look at the parents' card first, we start to see some interesting items. First, how many parents help "facilitate a bond" with a toy? Most parents are interested in facilitating bonds with friends and family members, rather than "bonding" with a plastic toy. A second look also notes that the activities in which the parents are encouraged to include the doll are stereotypical "female," such as meals and grocery shopping. Rather than suggesting taking the doll to a monster truck rally, karate lesson, or art class, the gendered spaces mentioned help code the doll as traditionally female, a traditional girl/woman. Parents are implicated in teaching the scripture, as well as in solidifying the identity of "P31."

The P31 identity is further complicated when we attempt to unravel the good-works aspect of the doll. The cards say of the P31 girl, "She works to make sure that everyone around her has all that they need" (P31 Cards 2008) and, as noted, suggests activities to help others. However, all the actions are highly individualized. There is no discussion of community, of joining or starting an organization, but rather of making an individual effort to donate or contribute toys or cookies. There is no call to join Habitat for Humanity and help build homes or to volunteer at an orphanage and "bond" with kids who have no parents. There is no discussion of trying to structurally alleviate homelessness, elder abuse or elderly loneliness, or other social problems that are implicated in the suggested activities. Of course, these dolls are aimed at small girls, who cannot really build houses. But there could be a fuller discussion of issues and other potential points of intervention.

Second, does the P31 cross the line between teaching about being a good friend and neighbor to teaching little girls to ignore their own needs and to serve others instead, to put themselves last and if there's anything left for them, only then can they partake? It is a fine line, indeed, trying to balance a sense of self-love and respect with contributions to social justice programs and the community. There is nothing wrong with being a kind person and helping the poor (who are obviously not the market for the doll—the dolls, while cheaper than ALOF at $40, are still expensive and are meant to serve at least a middle-class audience). These are commendable traits for a person to exhibit. Too often, however, girls will learn the "martyr complex" when the "serving" aspect is not kept in check with reminders that that they too matter, that they can do things for themselves—instead of being told that they will be punished for being proud and loving to read, as found on the ALOF advice pages. The P31 card reads, "She is nice and always looking for good deeds that she could do to help everyone around her. . . . She works hard to make sure everyone around her has all they need . . . yes, even her brothers and sisters!" Again, her job is to be *good*, to be *nice*, and to make sure *everyone else* has *all* they need. Social expectations dictate that "good girls" don't make mistakes, "good girls" and "nice girls" don't speak out, "good girls" don't play rough, "nice girls" don't hurt others' feelings, even if they are telling the truth. The labeling of girls in this manner puts a lot of pressure on them as they are constructing their identity to value being "good" and "nice" above being "strong," "powerful," "smart," "loving," and "unique."

Both ALOF and P31 dolls work to construct a traditional girlhood of crafts and baking. The words "traditional" and "old-fashioned" are used in the toys' marketing. This is not to suggest that, in and of themselves, there's anything problematic about crafts or baking, or mealtime, or grocery shopping. However, when these traditionally stereotyped "feminine" activities are continuously offered, accepted, and rehearsed without other alternatives, the toys send a broader message to girls about what girlhood should be about and what it means to be a good girl, or a real girl—the P31 girl. Girls who fall outside of these expectations run the risk of having poor self-esteem or being viewed as problem children by other children and adults who value these characteristics. Girls who are curious about their own sexuality, girls who identify as lesbian, girls who like to ride bikes and climb trees, girls who like blue and black instead of pink and purple, girls who would rather play with trucks instead of dolls, girls who want professional careers, and girls who are not interested in having babies one day are, in this discursive construction, not ideal.

Christofashion: From Witness Wear to Wait Wear

In both ALOF and P31, doll clothes and matching kids' outfits are emphasized in the marketing, either as historical and fun to play dress up with (for ALOF) or as trendy/tasteful, distancing them from more sexualized mainstream clothes (in the case of P31). As in any youth subculture, fashion and style play a large part in visually displaying a Christian identity, and an entire cottage industry of Christian apparel and accessories has taken off. T-shirts, pajamas, hats, socks, bracelets, watches, pins, backpacks, onesies, and even thong underwear can be donned as "armor" defending and promoting a Christian identity. Hundreds of online vendors specialize in these items, with many mainstream secular stores carrying several items as well, such as PutOnFaith, C28 (for Colossians 2:8), JesusBranded, and others. The clothes at issue here are used to boast identity, as suggested on a Christian apparel website: "Proclaim your Christian faith by wearing Christian clothing! Wearing Christian t shirts or Christian apparel and topping it off with a matching cap or beanie from Kerusso Christian products announces to the world your faith in Jesus Christ our Savior" (PutOnFaith 2008). This is a direct response to T-shirts such as "Future MILF" (mother I'd like to fuck), "Princess," and the suggestive branding of "Juicy" and "Pink" across a girl's bottom.

Christofashion can also be used as witnessing and conversion tools. The product description of a T-shirt reading, "May I pray for you?" comes with witnessing directions:

> May I pray for you is designed to motivate you. Imagine this:
> Person: "What's it say on your shirt?"
> You: "May I pray for you?"
> Person: "Sure."
> They say 80% of people will agree to prayer. Prayer moves mountains, we encourage you to play the odds. (JesusBranded 2008)

For the wee ones, mom and dad can buy a Pro Life onesie, simply stating, "I'm pro life," or the edgier, "Satan says vote pro choice" (ChristianShirts.net 2008). For preschoolers or kindergarteners, the Disney Princess theme is Christofied—little pink T-shirts for young girls read, "Yes, I am a princess. My father is the king of kings!" Parents can purchase Armor of God PJs—pajama top with large red cross, pants, large hat, and stuffed shield, reading "faith" on the shield, "salvation" on the cap, "righteousness" across the cross, and "truth" at the bottom of the cross along the edge of the shirt (Armor of God PJs 2008). The idea behind these clothes is that if kids are literally wearing the armor of god to bed, they will feel safe and secure and actually be protected from harm. They cost $40; activity coloring book sold separately.

Many Christian clothes exist for teens and adults and are invested in promoting Christian identity as protection, as well as for evangelizing. Take Witness Wear—wear the word.

> We chose the name Witness Wear because we find that when we wear items that suggest to people that we are Christians, it gets them asking questions and thinking . . . perfect opportunity to witness to people. In the name we have a cross symbol between the two words, this is here because as a company, we are Christ-centred and focused. Jesus is in the middle of both of our lives, so its only natural that He is in the middle of our business also. Wear is the second part of our name because we

> create items that people wear (such as clothes, bags, jewellery etc). (Witness Wear 2008a)

Some of their T-shirts read, "Hell is for wimps, guts is for God," and FISH (Found in Savior's Hands), or "I was dead once . . . I didn't like it." The product description reads, "Before we enter a relationship with Christ, we are all dead. If you are a Christian, you have been born into a living child of God. . . . Praise GOD! This is a perfect way to witness to your friends and family, its almost certain that people will ask you what you mean by wearing it!!!" (WitnessWear 2008b).

Taking a slightly different route is Wait Wear abstinence apparel. Founded by Yvette Thomas, a single mother of three who says that she wants to provide a good example for her children as to the importance of waiting until marriage before having sex, which she did not do and now regrets, the company's slogan is, "Wait wear. Where purity, power & passion meet phashion!" Its profile states, "Wait Wear is a young contemporary clothing line that boldly promotes chastity until marriage in all of its apparel" (Wait Wear 2008). Wait Wear has its own MySpace page that features a short video of the company's products being featured on *The Tyra Banks Show* in 2007; the company has also been featured on *The View* and *Good Morning America*. Their girls' shirts read, "Virginity rules," "Generation pure," "Wait is good," "Chaste girl," "New millennium girl, with vintage virtues," and "No overnite parking," and men's T-shirts read, "Don't believe the hype, by True Gentleman." A very elaborate T-shirt is designed like a highway road sign: "Abstinence Ave. Exit when married" with the interstate symbol changed to interstate marriage, with two wedding rings. The company sells undergarments, including thongs, which have slogans proclaiming the wearer's desire to wait until marriage before having sex. Wait Wear has 96 friends, including Miley Cyrus, recently in the news for her sexualized photo shoot. The company brings to light the contradictions of sex in our society. Thongs, very sexual undergarments, proclaim abstinence. A CEO who has had three children out of wedlock proclaims the virtues of waiting until marriage. The reception of the company's products has ranged from journalistic ambivalence on *The Tyra Banks Show*, to positive comments on their MySpace comment wall: 3131theory said, "This is great. Abstinence humor while aming [sic] a fashion statement" (February 5, 2008). Samack wrote, "Love your stuff! I would join your fan club if you had one!" (February 5, 2008).

Another genre of Christofashion directly links Christianity to hip hop culture. Two T-shirts attempt to suture Jesus to rap and hip hop in an apparent move both to capitalize on the popularity of hip hop and to recuperate what some have perceived to be the pimpification of rap and hip hop culture (which is, of course, an overgeneralization). JesusBranded manufactures a shirt, "JC on the MC," with a hip picture of a beatnik-looking Jesus, reading, "When Jesus had ended these sayings the people were astonished at his doctrine. For He taught as one having authority and not as the scribes. Jesus Christ, Master of Ceremonies" (JesusBranded 2008).

If Jesus is on the mic, then it is not a far cry to claim, "Jesus is my homeboy." This popular T-shirt was designed by Teenage Millionaire clothing company, which also makes a "Mary is my homegirl" shirt. Celebrities such as Ashton Kutcher, Madonna, Brad Pitt, and Pamela Anderson have been photographed in the clothes. Chris Hoy, designer and founder of Teenage Millionaire, says, "The Christians like it, the hipsters like it. . . . We had no idea it was going to be this big" (Donaldson-Evans 2004). The designer says, "We wanted an ethnic-looking Jesus—not the white, blue-eyed Jesus," which attempts to play into an Afrocentric politics and the critique that the typical image of Jesus is too fair in color to be accurate. Rather than being on sale at a specialty Christian store, the shirt sells very well at hipster mecca Urban Outfitters. "Hoy and Williams give credit to celebrities wearing them; their images plastered in magazines create buzz for the garment among hipsters," says the *Los Angeles Times* (Quintanilla 2003). On the E! Network, the shirts were called "kitschy" and "playful" (Donaldson-Evans 2004).

The hipster shirt has received some flack from the Christian community:

> Jesus isn't my Homeboy, he is my Savior and the King of Glory. . . . I am seeing a disturbing trend in Christendom today where we are trying to be so relevant and hip that we are actually becoming irrelevant. It doesn't disturb me as much that Madonna, and Ashton Kutcher wear blasphemous t-shirts, what does disturb me is that Christians love them too. (Jackson 2005)

In this statement, Christian NewsWithViews blogger Nicholas Jackson is okay if the T-shirt is kitsch, but he bemoans Christians becoming hip. As he sees it, the entertainment factor in Christian culture should be kept in check, and the focus should be on the serious pursuit of religious life, rather than on the frivolous and sacrilegious uses of Jesus in popular culture. Others critique the lack of "authenticity" of people donning the shirt. "'It's everywhere. It's at all the stores,' said Craig Gross, founder of XXXchurch.com. 'This is the latest thing. A lot of people are wearing them not because they want to display their relationship with God, but because it's the cool thing to do'" (Quintanilla 2003).

In Eugene, Oregon, a vendor at the infamous Saturday Market sells handmade plug-in nightlights of Jesus, Mary, and Joseph, like Bowling Jesus: this is kitsch. These toys are meant as a critique of both religion and popular consumer culture. The difference between these collectables and Christogimmicks is in the whole nature of the artifact—Christogimmicks are serious, for seriously religious people. They are not meant to critique either consumer culture or Christianity. One might see "Jesus is my homeboy," and have to stop and think, is this serious, or is this kitsch? It was the same with "What would Jesus bomb" T-shirts that appeared in the bodegas of New York City shortly after the Iraq War started in 2003. The culture-jamming element, the parodying of culture and social issues, is a difficult thing to interpret these days. A student of mine, several years ago, made a culture-jam project for class: The Jesus Enema. Packaged in a cardboard box and for sale at a drug store near you, the Jesus Enema was a critique of the hyper-Christianization of culture through this student's eyes. I had to wonder whether, if a Christian toy or pharmaceutical company had created such a product, it might have been successful. In the interpretive moment, the consumer/audience does become key, but so does the manufacturer and his or her politics and power.

CONCLUSION

Christian clothing and toys are everywhere: from Wal-Mart to Melrose Ave., Jesus is my homeboy and F.R.O.G. bracelets, to Abstinence Ave., P31 Dolls, and Army of God toys. Apparently the separation between consumer culture and Christian culture is very thin, and the ideology of conspicuous consumption is not at odds with conservative evangelical Christian life, even though Christogimmicks are positioned as wholesome alternatives to mainstream toys. A rollerblading Jesus, which once, in the not-so-distant past, would have clearly been seen as a blasphemous toy, is now marketed as Christian cool. Even adolescent coming-of-age and tween culture has inspired Christian commodities—perhaps in order to allow them to have one foot in and one foot out of such teenage rituals as journaling, costume jewelry, and dating, in order to enable Christian parents and leaders to allow their kids some of the "pleasures" of secular culture while keeping them under the protection of Christian politics.

Both Einstein (2008) and Twitchell (2007) have demonstrated a clear unity in enterprising religion and marketing. Perhaps this is because evangelizing and evangelical practice share some ethos and tactics with marketing—is conversion in religious affiliation any different from conversion in brand loyalty? Is piety and religious fellowship any different from brand tribes and brand faith? What do we make of this Bible scripture, which a friend supplied to me when we discussed my research:

> Jesus entered the temple area and drove out all who were buying and selling there. He overturned the tables of the money changers and the benches of those selling doves. "It is written," he said to them, "'My house will be called a house of prayer,' but you are making it a 'den of robbers.'" —Matthew 21:13–16 (New International Version)

From my research, it appears that most Christian companies and consumers believe that it's okay to be a rampant consumer—as long as you're consuming Jesus. The inscribed meanings for P31 *are* different from a Bratz doll. "Jesus is my homeboy" tells the world something different than "Future MILF." The ideological goal of most Christogimmicks is protection, identity display, and salvation. Protection: buying Christian toys, jewelry, and clothes will "protect" the consumer, especially the Christian child or youth, from anti-Christian forces, such as the overly sexualized Bratz dolls, the sex and drugs of rap, rock, and punk, or even the pagan witchcraft of Harry Potter. Salvation: do some Christian consumers take the protection stance one degree further and create a model of consuming one's salvation? If T-shirts are worn to prove devotion and witness others to salvation, then salvation itself becomes an act of consumption.

Perhaps we are entering the age of "religitainment"—much like the title of this book, *Christotainment*—which entails more than the artifacts themselves but rather a new way of experiencing religion or living a Christian life. It is through consumption that one experiences religion, not simply through attending services. In Christian consumer culture, the individual consumer becomes the central feature of the religious experience, rather than the institution, the church, the pastor, or the fellowship. Much like the consumer who thinks, "If I just purchase this Jenny Craig plan, I can lose those 30 pounds," "If I just buy enough books, I will be smarter," "If I wear these Juicy sweats, I will be couture," or "If I buy these Manolo Blahniks, I will have sex in the city," the Christian consumer might think, "If I buy Christian toys, wear Christian clothes and jewelry, I will be a better Christian and I will be saved"—a concept that I will call "consumer saviorism." Oddly enough, one of the things this consumption is supposed to save the person from is a hedonistic, ungodly, unholy, earthly consumer culture.

Making money that supports Christian companies and churches can leverage political power. In other organizations, it's crass capitalism with a secular company starting a new line, in which case, profit is the sole goal. In either case, discursively normalizing the images, words, and beliefs of Christianity has serious implications for secular culture, for people of other religions, and for the political projects of the far-right Pentecostal Christians. As this rhetoric/witnessing becomes public and reified through toys and normalized in the mainstream, the political projects of this group are made easier. Cultural goods and entertainment are not simply fun and entertaining but can impact political life and the possibilities one has in society in a globalizing world. Using T-shirts to convert, sending toys to Iraq to teach Bible stories and program Muslim children to accept imperialistic U.S. foreign policy, manufacturing dolls to teach girls to stay home and bake cookies, and selling figurines to rehearse scripture all imprint culture in a conservative way. Beyond the ideology of consumer culture lies the ideology of conservative Christian consumer culture: consume your Salvation.

ACKNOWLEDGMENTS

The author would like to thank Jeffrey Reale for the bible verse and for conversations regarding the issues in this chapter.

References

Armor of God PJs. 2008. www.armorofgodpjs.com (accessed July 18, 2008).

Bagdikian, Ben. 2000. *The media monopoly*. 6th ed. Boston: Beacon.

Baudrillard, Jean. 1999. Consumer society. In *Consumer society in American history: A reader*, ed. Lawrence B. Glickman, 33–56. Ithaca, NY: Cornell University Press.

Berger, Arthur Asa. 2007. *Ads, fads, and consumer culture*. Lanham, MD: Rowman & Littlefield.

Christian News Wire. 2008. P31 dolls teach young girls attributes of a true American girl. Christian News Wire, www.christiannewswire.com/news/281032011.html (accessed July 18, 2008).

ChristianShirts.net. 2008. www.christianshirts.net/products.php?id=4117 (accessed July 18, 2008).

Christmas Story, A. 1983. Directed by Bob Clark. Los Angeles: MGM.

Courrege, Beverly. 1991. *Answers to WWJD?* Tulsa, OK: Honor Books.

Donaldson-Evans, Catherine. 2004. Jesus chic is latest fashion trend. FoxNews.com, May 10, www.foxnews.com/story/0,2933,119408,00.html (accessed July 16, 2008).

Einstein, Mara. 2008. *Brands of faith: Marketing religion in a commercial age*. New York: Routledge.

Ewan, Stewart. 1976. *Captains of consciousness: Advertising and the roots of consumer culture*. New York: McGraw-Hill.

Family Christian Stores. 2008. Prayer circle friends. Family Christian Stores, www.familychristian.com/shop/product.asp?prodID=45774 (accessed July 15, 2008).

Frontline. 2001. Merchants of cool. First broadcast on February 27 by PBS. Directed by Barak Goodman.

Giroux, Henry. 2000. *Stealing innocence: Corporate culture's war on children*. New York: Palgrave.

Glickman, Lawrence B. 1999. *Consumer society in American history: A reader*. Ithaca, NY: Cornell University Press.

Grossman, Cathy. 2006. "Faith's purchasing power." *USA Today*, December 13, www.usatoday.com/news/religion/2006-12-12-faiths-purchasing-power_x.htm (accessed June 16, 2008).

Horovitz, Bruce. 2007. "Retailer Wal-Mart gets religious—toys, that is." *USA Today*, June 16, www.usatoday.com/money/industries/retail/2007-07-15-walmart-religion-toys_N.htm (accessed June 16, 2008).

Jackson, Nicholas. 2005. "Jesus is my homeboy," NewsWithViews.com, July 24, http://www.newswithviews.com/Jackson/nicholas4.htm (accessed July 18, 2008).

JesusBranded. 2008. I am JesusBranded. About.com, http://christianity.about.com/gi/dynamic/offsite.htm?zi=1/XJ/Ya&sdn=christianity&cdn=religion&tm=62

&f=10&tt=14&bt=0&bts=1&zu=http%3A//www.jesusbranded.com (accessed July 18, 2008).

Kilbourne, Jean. 1999. *Killing us softly*. New York: Henry Holt.

Klein, Naomi. 1999. *No logo: Taking aim at the brand bullies*. New York: Picador.

Life of Faith, A. 2008a. http://alof.com (accessed July 30, 2008).

_______. 2008b. Books, dolls, and accessories. A Life of Faith, www.lifeoffaith.com/shop/catalog/category_4_Dolls.html (accessed July 15, 2008).

_______. 2008c. Fun activities. A Life of Faith, www.alof.com/fun_activities.html (accessed July 19, 2008).

_______. 2008d. Fun crafts. A Life of Faith, www.alof.com/fun_crafts.html (accessed July 19, 2008).

_______. 2008e. The gift of salvation. A Life of Faith, www.alof.com/the_gift_of_salvation.html (accessed July 19, 2008).

_______. 2008f. God's free gift to you. A Life of Faith, www.alof.com/god_free_gift_to_you.html (accessed July 19, 2008).

_______. 2008g. Homemade fun. A Life of Faith, www.alof.com/homemade_fun.html (accessed July 19, 2008).

_______. 2008h. Prayer projects. A Life of Faith, www.alof.com/prayer_projects.html (accessed July 19, 2008).

_______. 2008i. Recipes. A Life of Faith, www.alof.com/recipes.html (accessed July 19, 2008).

_______. 2008j. Violet's daily diary. A Life of Faith, www.lifeoffaith.com/shop/catalog/product_223_Violets_Daily_Diary_cat_162.html (accessed July 19, 2008).

_______. 2008k. Violet's life lessons. A Life of Faith, www.lifeoffaith.com/shop/catalog/product_206_Violets_Life_Lessons_Growing_Toward_God_Cultivating_Your_Life_of_Faith_cat_162.html (accessed July 19, 2008).

_______. 2008l. What do I do next. A Life of Faith, www.alof.com/what_do_i_do_next.html (accessed July 19, 2008).

Linn, Susan. 2004. *Consuming kids: The hostile takeover of childhood*. New York: The New Press.

Marx, Karl. 1992. *Capital*. Vol. 1, *A critique of political economy*. New York: Penguin Classics.

Mickey Mouse Monopoly: Disney, Childhood and Corporate Power. 2001. Directed by Miguel Picker. Northampton, MA: Media Education Foundation.

Mitchell, Claudia, and Jacqueline Reid-Walsh. 2005. *Seven going on seventeen: Tween studies in the culture of girlhood*. New York: Peter Lang.

Newsweek. 1986. Pro-life and Christian toys. *Newsweek*, November 3.

one2believe.com. 2007. Will you join. one2believe, www.one2believe.com/battlefly.bmp (accessed July 15, 2008).

P31 Cards. 2008. One2believe.

Peterson, Karyn. 2007. Divine inspiration: Religious toys find their calling at retail. *Playthings* 105, no. 7 (July): 8.

Proverbs 31 Woman. 2008. http://solochristo.net/proverbs31woman (accessed July 15, 2008).

PutOnFaith. 2008. http://putonfaith.com/index.cfm/PutOnFaith_Home (accessed July 18, 2008).

Quintanilla, Michael. 2003. Of culture and commodity. *Los Angeles Times*, June 4, http://articles.latimes.com/2003/jun/04/entertainment/et-quintanilla4 (accessed July 16, 2008).

Rand, Erica. 1995. *Barbie's queer accessories*. Durham, NC: Duke University Press.

Reed, Tucker. 2002. "Religion." *Fortune*, October 14, 56.

Righton, Barbara. 2007. "What a friend Wal-Mart has in Jesus." *Maclean's*, August 6, 46.

Schor, Juliet. 2004. *Born to buy: The commercialized child and the new consumer culture*. New York: Scribner.

Shiflett, Dave. 2007. "God made flesh, then plastic." *Wall Street Journal* (Eastern edition), September 28, W11.

Steinberg, Shirley, and Joe Kincheloe, eds. 2004. *Kinderculture: The corporate construction of childhood*. 2nd ed. Boulder, CO: Westview Press.

Twitchell, James B. 2007. *Shopping for God: How Christianity went from in your heart to in your face*. New York: Simon & Schuster

Wait Wear. 2008. www.waitwear.com (accessed July 18, 2008).

Witness Wear. 2008a. www.witnesswear.com (accessed July 18, 2008).

_______. 2008b. I was dead once. 2008. www.witnesswear.com.au/cgcs__i_was_dead_once.php (accessed July 19, 2008).

VIII

Faith Talking Toys and Other Youth Purity Makers

LISA M. TRIMBLE

One of my favorite poems ever written is "Ode to Things" by Pablo Neruda (1994) in which he describes the joy and appeal various things have for him. Some things he loves because they tease and delight his senses, drawing his attention to the brilliance of the object's "deep-sea color" and "velvet feel." Other things warm him with the meanings and memories they are infused within his psyche, such as a thing that reminds him of the "softness of a woman's hip." Neruda's poem beautifully illustrates not only how our relationship with "things" is a complex and multilayered conversation with different ways of knowing and experiencing the world but how individual this process of meaning mapping is. For evangelical Christians, the preacher's directive to the congregation to be "in this world, but not of it" introduces an important spiritual dimension to the believer's cognitive and affective filtering. Being separate from the world necessitates creating ways to show both membership with evangelical culture and resistance to the influence of other communities. Anthropologically speaking, being human also means communicating the ways we have constructed our identities to others through signifiers, words, and actions. In doing so, some things become *purity markers* through a meaning-making process that differentiates them from similar secular items. Meaning colors "things" as being distinct and, for evangelicals, represents a powerful way of marking out metaphorical maps of spaces of consumer and spiritual purity. Understanding faith signifiers means deconstructing the dialogic relationship between material objects as text and the evangelical lifestyle as the context that surrounds, informs, and defines their meaning. As R. Harré has observed, "Material things have magic powers only in the contexts of the narratives in which they are embedded" (2002, 25). In this chapter I will look at some of the magic and contexts embedded in (usually adult-generated) narratives around the materials and experiences generated within evangelical youth culture. Culture is an optimal site for ideological colonization; we are constantly drawn into conversation with the text, subtext, and context of culture. We breathe it in as easily, instinctively (and often uncritically) as we do air, making it a convenient space to cultivate and affirm our sense of self and community.

UNDERSTANDING IDEOLOGY

Before we can meaningfully discuss the impact of ideology as it infuses material culture with meaning, we need to have a working definition of what ideology is. Daniel Bell articulated one of the clearest and most cogent discussions on ideology, in my opinion, in his important 1965 essay "Ideology and Soviet Politics." Bell acknowledges the "many ambiguous meanings and emotional colorations" associated with the term, as well as the power of ideologies to "somehow catch up one's passions and move people to action" (1965, 591). One of the ways to understand why ideology plays a significant role in our lives is to look at how it functions "as justification which represents some specific set of interests" (1965, 592) and how it serves to establish and maintain collective membership. "Each society," Bell writes, "needs some creed, intellectually coherent and rationally defensible, both to justify itself and to meet the challenges of—or to challenge—other creeds" (1965, 595). Infusing cultural objects with ideological meaning is an effective way of performing and communicating purity and distinction from others who do not ascribe to the same set of doctrinal principles. The power of ideology comes not just from the intellectual formation of an idea but also, as Antonio Gramsci (1971) would argue, from the enormous affective impact that *beliefs* generate in us when we engage with those ideas to the extent that they become part of our identity essence and inform how we move through the world (Fulton 1987; Billings 1990). In other words, the power and energy of a particular ideology to engage with and influence culture is directly informed by how deeply *internalized* it is within the ontology of believers and how large the community is that subscribes to that set of beliefs. We experience a sense of inner coherence and personal integrity when the ways we think, act, and feel are aligned. Purchasing with conscious intent that reaffirms what is important and valuable to us can be an emotionally rewarding and identity-confirming experience, and selling to the values market can be a highly profitable venture for retailers who can appeal to the worldview of this segment of consumers.

SHAPING AND PROTECTING YOUNG CHRISTIAN IDENTITY

Children represent a particular problem in fundamentalist Christian purity discourse as they are considered especially in need of guidance and spiritual protection from the corruptive influence of the secular world. Particularly in light of the advice of Christian parenting experts like Dr. James Dobson, evangelical parents feel an urgent duty to protect their children from being informed by worldly attitudes. When we consider that almost sixty-three million evangelical Christian adults in the United States say they had committed their lives to Christ *before* their eighteenth birthday (Sandler 2006), we can start to understand the vitally important role youth culture plays in recruiting and retaining young members of the faith. Lauren Sandler argues that the new and rapidly growing evangelical youth movement, which she terms the "disciple generation" (2006, 5), shares a passion for Christ balanced with an equally fierce and intense engagement with culture in a way that is "at once political, emotional, deeply anti-intellectual, and more galvanized" (2006, 5) than most of us could ever realize. The seeds that are intended to bear the fruit of passionate, committed, and Christ-centered youth are planted early by adults, who tend to them carefully and often. Dobson and other psychologists with evangelical leanings contend that children must be completely enveloped in Christian culture in order to develop the necessary spiritual tools to negotiate an upstanding moral and devout Christian youth identity (Hendershot 2004). Although this is partly a gatekeeping strategy of identity formation, it echoes how Pierre Bourdieu (1984) imagined into theory his notion of habitus. Bourdieu described how cultural attitudes and community perceptions midwife a lifelong (and often unconscious) relationship to our ways of knowing and being in the world. Put another way, inscribed on our psyche and bodies are remnants of the stories we have been told by our cultures, our families of origin, our communities, and our social contexts. Habitus is therefore the ground in which identity develops and takes shape. Educational philosopher Parker Palmer introduces a similar flavor of thought in his definition of identity when he states,

> By *identity* I mean an evolving nexus where all the forces that constitute my life converge in the mystery of self; my genetic makeup, the nature of the man and woman who gave me life, the culture in which I was raised, people who have sustained me and people who have done me harm, the good and ill I have done to others and myself, the experience of love and suffering—and much, much more. In the midst of that complex field, identity is a moving intersection of the inner and outer forces that make me who I am, converging in the irreducible mystery of being human. (1998, 13, emphasis in the original)

For many evangelicals, nurturing the inner spiritual identity of a child means ensuring, as much as possible, that the outer forces a child is exposed to both validate and affirm the beliefs of his or her religious community. Retailers have been quick to align themselves with these principles and to recognize that considerable opportunities for profit lend themselves to meeting the toy demands of Christian consumers. One of the ways to control the ideological wildcards that children encounter in their play is to offer Christian alternatives to secular toys. Toys in the evangelical sphere make a fascinating cultural study of some of the ways believers use their faith to frame and generate meaning. Market researchers Hampton & Ball refer to this phenomenon as speaking to consumers with a "doctrine-centered orientation" who will buy a product because it resonates positively with their values (Stein Wellner 2005, 72). Many of these playthings seem to serve a range of different purposes for the Christian consumer. Painting with broad strokes, I would suggest that some of the reasons born-again parents choose these products for their children's play would be because they (1) *affirm* their religious values and beliefs, (2) offer a *Christian alternative* to popular secular toys, or (3) incorporate an *evangelical message* or lesson into play. Some toys may move along various places on this spectrum depending on who is engaging with them, or playthings can simultaneously serve multiple purposes and have multiple meanings. In addition to the usual function of toys to be fun and/or educational, these toys have a perceived added dimension of protecting and shaping the child's spiritual ways of knowing and being.

An example of affirming consumerism for this market would include those who purchase toys that speak to specific constructions of gender identity aligning with traditionalist conservative values, such as those listed in the *All-American Boy's Adventure Catalogue*. Published by the Texas-based evangelical organization Vision Forum Ministries, this collection of toys is marketed to promote a specific construct of "traditional" boyhood culture (i.e., boys as active heroes with girls portrayed as passive and in need of rescue), particularly "in classed, gendered, raced and sexualized terms, attempting to pull in or sell to a particular class fraction of upwardly mobile consumers, most with allegiances to neoconservatism" (Weaver-Hightower 2008, 279).

The *All-American Boys Adventure Catalogue* promotes a specific construct of masculinity it terms "courageous boyhood," a fascinating blend of patriotism, militarism, piety, and virtue with a substantial dose of Daniel Boone thrown in for good measure. In the company's literature describing this notion of courageous boyhood, each idea is illustrated with a boy dressed in the costumes of masculinities of long-ago eras: pilgrims, pioneers, and WWII army troops. The ideological intent of shaping young masculinity this way, the website states, is as follows: "Every toy, tool, and book has been carefully selected to fit the overall concept designed to inspire and *motivate boys to dream big dreams for the glory of God*" (Phillips 2008a, emphasis added).

Perhaps not surprisingly, the Vision Forum has an entirely different understanding of what constitutes a righteous path for girls to follow. The complementary catalogue for girls, called the *Beautiful Girlhood Collection*, contends that their "glorious and beautiful vision" for girlhood "is a vision for *purity and contentment*, for faith and fortitude, for *enthusiasm and industry*, for heritage and home, and for joy and friendship" (Phillips 2008b, emphasis added).

Appropriate playthings for girls, in this highly regulated, gendered construct, include colonial-style dresses, crocheted white gloves, prairie bonnets, "modesty slips," and high-priced infant dolls to care for and nurture. In the boyocracy of Vision Forums Ministries, the thirst for adventure and capacity for daring is clearly in limited supply and should not be wasted on girls, as it might interfere with their "enthusiasm," weaken their desire to commit themselves to "industry," and challenge their overall "contentment" within the confines imposed by gender.

Not all Christian retailing is as overt about ideological branding as the subsidiaries of Vision Forums, however. Another illustration of affirming consumerism with a more subtle marketing strategy would be those Christians who engage in a kind of consumer activism by supporting companies with their purchases, which they believe will continue to support Christian values. Even if their products are not immediately identifiable as religious (such as generic sand pails and beach balls manufactured or distributed by companies that have publicly identified as sharing the same ethos as the consumer), buying from these companies validates Christian identity. Important in this action is not so much that overt Christianity is being propagated but rather that their purchases are *not* supporting or profiting secular organizations. Drawing on Apple's (1995) analysis of "the dual nature of culture both lived and as a commodity" (Weaver-Hightower 2008, 279), it's not a huge leap in logic to make the argument that buying Christian toys is, for some, a means of stockpiling ideological collateral and trying to preserve traditional social mores.

SUPERHERO CAPES AND MIGHTY SWORDS MEET CHRISTIAN CAMP

Our fascination and wonder with stories of magic and realms of godlike creatures with superpowers have played out in our collective imaginations since the advent of language. Most of our folklore allows good to triumph over evil, justice to prevail over tyranny, and righteousness to be the clear winner over those who would seek to do wrong. Catholics, with their collective of saints at the helm ready to heal and bless any believers who ask, are less concerned with the problem of magical creatures than their evangelical Protestant counterparts. For fundamentalist Christians, magic (and its twisted sister, witchcraft) has vaguely satanic affiliations, making stories like the cultural phenomenon of Harry Potter, which are so rooted in the paranormal and mystic, particularly threatening to their belief system. Still, the allure of magic, the fun of tying on a cape and pretending to fly while conquering the bad guys, is a powerful draw for imaginative and energetic children. Problematic for evangelicals are not so much the superheroic flying, mighty strength, or other marvels but the *source* of the power from which these extrahuman abilities are drawn. If the source of these paranormal gifts can be clearly assigned as God-given (as opposed to being ambiguously defined or, worse, affiliated with sorcery), these stories of fantasy and myth can be made acceptable to born-again parents, and there is considerable profit to be made in offering a Christian alternative to secular favorite toys.

A recent newcomer and good example of popular culture being sanitized for Christian consumption is *Bibleman,* an extremely popular set of children's videos produced by Pamplin Entertainment, with slick promotion that includes live tours of stage shows, as well as spin-off marketing of books, toys, costumes, and videogames. This show is to the *Mighty Morphin' Power Rangers* what Jimmy Swaggart was to Jerry Lee Lewis: a colorful and "saved" version of its more rock 'n' roll cousin. *Bibleman* gets his strength from God and can often vanquish his foes simply by reciting Bible verses. On those occasions when he must fight, he is protected by the "Shoes of Peace, Waistbelt of Truth, Shield of Faith, Breastplate of Righteousness, and Helmet of Salvation." He brandishes a light saber–like "Sword of the Spirit" (see International Superheroes 2008). Like all superheroes, *Bibleman* is supported by a few evil-fighting sidekicks (Cypher and Biblegirl) and regularly confronts his share of villainous foes. Perhaps one of his most intriguing enemies is the unusually named Wacky Protestor. Some of the more inventive weaponry this character utilizes includes the "Wacksonic Cloud of Darkness," which chemically inspires a strong need to be alone, and an elaborate transporter with which he nefariously plans to trap Sunday school students in an alternate dimension (International Superheroes 2008). The show includes the same campy sets as secular versions of similar shows (i.e., *Teenage Mutant Ninja Turtles* and *Transformers*), as well as similar outrageous costumes and storylines that detail the glorious fights (and inevitable victories) of the heroes.

As they cannot live an existence completely separate from the rest of the world, believers' response of offering alternate culture for their faith community is not a new phenomenon; religions often develop their own texts in response to (and in dialogue with) the secular cultural contexts surrounding them. Foods become blessed and edible through complex rituals of preparation and serving; particular clothing identifies members of a religious community; music becomes holy not through an arrangement of notes but through words carefully chosen to resonate with praise and worship. We use signifiers of language, appearance, and ritual to distinguish between that which is holy and that which is either prohibited or a mundane part of daily living. Evangelical Christians often apply the same strategies to selecting toys for their children. A Bible verse painted on the side transforms a remote control monster truck into a "Victory Truck." A My Little Pony look-alike becomes suitable for little Christian girls when it is called a "Praise Pony." Praise Ponies come with ten accessories similar to those that come with their My Little Pony cousin, such as combs, brushes, and elastics for their long pink hair, and the toys are somewhat ambiguously named for "positive traits from the Bible"(Christian Dollar Store 2008). Although it is difficult for some of us to grasp the spiritual component of brushing cotton candy–colored hair on an magical pink horse, the Praise Pony does manage to make the toy palatable to Christian parents. The packaging also contains a "positive message" supposedly directly from the pony for the young girl who will eventually play with it as a way of "building spiritual and moral values." Other cultural clones include a trio of ethnically diverse girl dolls marketed as P31,[1] which bear a striking resemblance to Bratz dolls, albeit more modestly attired ones (Meachem 2008). Hoping to cash in on the $4.6 billion industry that Christian products represent in the U.S. market alone (Birke 2008), the Bible Princess line of dolls makes the unusual pairing of a Bratz aesthetic with female characters from the Bible, complete with a wardrobe appropriate to Middle Eastern women of the time and accompanied by conspicuously cute, Disney-like animal friends.

WHAT DOES JESUS SAY?

In the fall of 2007, Christian toy manufacturer and distributor one2believe landed the holy grail of retail contracts: over four hundred Wal-Mart stores would carry their line of faith-based toys as a pilot project over the holiday season to test consumer response. The toys were also picked up by the online retail division of Target. The products being tested included biblical action figures (Tales of Glory), and the Messengers of Faith line of twelve-inch-tall talking dolls representing famous biblical characters. Some of the famous figures immortalized in the Messengers of Faith collection included Jesus, Mary, Joseph, Peter, Paul, Esther, and Noah. Jesus reads John 3:16 in a soothing voice, and all the characters narrate their personal stories and quote biblical text. Before going to market, one2believe formed alliances with over seven thousand churches in the United States, testing their products, building consumer relationships, and conducting market research. Relationship building is an integral part of successful Christian marketing, and it paid off handsomely in preholiday sales; many stores sold completely out of the dolls long before the holiday shopping season was over (Boyles 2007). The figures have been so successful that several more talking characters are in development, and the company plans to release a Spanish-speaking Jesus within the year.

Despite the high sales, the dolls are not without their critics. The children's charity Toys for Tots declined a donation of four thousand of the talking Jesus dolls for their 2006 toy drive, expressing concern that the evangelizing dolls would not be appropriate for non-Christian families, who might take offense at their sermonizing. Shortly thereafter, however, the charity did accept the toys, stating that they had found "appropriate places for these items" (Asma 2007). Others wonder what the benefits are for children to play with a toy that clearly puts so many limits on the possibilities of imagination with such clearly defined roles and manners of speech. Toy-industry analyst Sean McGowan of Needham and Company in New York suspects that not all the devout are delighted to see a representation of their savior keeping company with He Man, Captain Picard, and Mr. T., and he wonders how stores will come to terms with leftover stock when sales eventually fall off. "No one wants to mark down Jesus," he observed (Mintz 2007).

The Spirit Warrior line is produced by the same company and features thirteen-inch reproductions of the brawny behemoths Samson and Goliath as muscle-bound goons who look like they would be quite at home with any of the Conan the Barbarian toys. According to biblical lore, Samson was a brutal man with little regard for human life, who killed frequently for sport and in anger. He reportedly murdered a thousand Philistines with the jawbone of an ass before being betrayed by Delilah into revealing the secret of his strength. Captured and bound in the temple of his enemies, so the narrative goes, he once again regained his strength and pushed down the pillars, killing an additional three thousand people. Little is known about Goliath other than his immense stature, the considerable fear he put into the hearts of the Israelites, and his gruesome death by decapitation as orchestrated by David. Most bewildering about these dolls is that, to date, they are the only two in this line (although more are in development). At the moment, they are signifiers floating in a folklore sphere without being attached to the referents that give them meaning; there is no David to slay Goliath, no Philistine to enrage Samson.

There is, however, significant discursive meaning anchored in the name Spirit Warrior that will be recognizable to most contemporary adult fundamentalist Christians.

In the wake of several new age masculinity movements that have emerged on the cultural landscape in North America over the past few decades, a Christian version has established a strong foothold with some segments of evangelicals. Based on the writings of John Eldredge in his book *Wild at Heart: Discovering the Secret of a Man's Soul* (2001) and with the premise loosely adapted by some evangelical men's groups, such as the Promise Keepers, Christian men are often exhorted by their leaders to be "spiritual warriors," strong men who are willing to fight for (and protect) their families, their values, and the cause of righteousness. Eldredge's book resonated powerfully with fundamentalist Christians who, in this time of feminist and queer backlash, worry about a perceived impending crisis involving the emasculation of the Christian male; within three years of publishing, it had sold 1.5 million copies in English and was translated into sixteen other languages. Eldredge's ministry inspired thousands of men to participate in "weekend warrior boot camps" (and amassed considerable profits doing so), which teach Christian males how to be men living with a sense of adventure, unafraid of risk taking, and chivalrous in their relationships with women (Elsworth 2005). The metaphorical warrior is an important concept in the discourse around what it means to be a Christian man and in the construction of masculinities in boys. Despite their mythic narratives, however, Samson and Goliath remain curious choices to link with a metaphor of godly masculinity. Interestingly, the *language* they are marketed with signifies them as toys suitable for Christian children, placing considerably more importance on the phrase "Spirit Warrior" than the stories attached to the characters, who might in other circumstances not be considered the best role models for manhood.

It is interesting to consider questions of how unstable and shifting meaning can be when attached to representations, especially when we contrast the way meanings are intended (by adults) with the inevitable fluidity of youthful interpretation. Talking Jesus dolls are meant to be both an educational device for teaching Bible stories and verses and a tool for kidvangelism, but in a child's imagination, the action figure could morph into a superhero, a bank robber, or even (as my son used to do with Barbies) a convenient and effective ramp for his toy trucks to climb. My intention is not to be glib about the sacred meaning of these representations of Jesus or other faith-based toys but rather to show that once sacred objects are introduced into the secular sphere, the boundaries of *sacred* become permeable and shifting. Adults should recognize that the meanings we assign are never fixed; as noble as our intentions may be about the educational or performative aspects of a toy, ultimately its meaning will rest with the child.

WWJD BRACELETS, WITNESS WEAR, CHRISTIAN TATTOOS, AND OTHER PURITY MARKERS

Social cognitive theorists argue that people for whom religious beliefs are very important often use heuristics to make quick and efficient assessments of how to make sense of a situation and develop an appropriate response (Carone and Barone 2001). One such heuristic ended up having substantially more staying power than even its author could have imagined when he posed the question, "What would Jesus do?" over a century ago. Positioned as the crux at the heart of the Christian socialist parable *In His Steps* (1956), Charles Sheldon asked the question to inspire social action and challenge the complacency he felt many Christians suffered from when it came to advocating for better living conditions for the poor. In 1989, a Michigan youth group leader thought the youth in her church could benefit from a tangible reminder of the moral compass question, "What would Jesus do?" (WWJD) and had inexpensive nylon bracelets printed with the acronym (Borden 2006). The trend caught on quickly with evangelical adolescents and inspired an industry producing a range of other witnessing wearables, including bracelets inscribed with FROG (Fully Rely on God), GOLF (God Offers Love and Forgiveness), and PUSH (Pray Until Something Happens). Bracelets such as these and the other ideological branding devices act as purity markers, outwardly displaying to the world that the individual wearing them ascribes to a particular set of beliefs that make him or her distinct from nonbelievers.

At first consideration, heuristic tools like the WWJD bracelet appear to occupy a liminal psychological and cognitive space, poised on the threshold of being fully and fallibly human while connected to the (literal and metaphorical) thread of expectations of the divine. Presented with a problem, the item we have chosen to signify and communicate our beliefs inspires an emotional reaction as we consider the moral consequences and outcomes of our choices.

As J. R. Averill suggests, believers know they are part of a faith tradition "when they experience the emotions considered appropriate to that religion" (1996, 90), and purity markers are a tangible reminder of the connection between the beliefs they hold to be true and the way one should act to affirm those beliefs. Once again, however, the problem of meaning is a complex one. For example, with the rise of the abstinence movement in the United States, bracelets with the slogans "True Love Waits" and "Worth Waiting For" became popular forms of ideological branding. Youth wear the jewelry often as reminders of chastity pledges they've made, promising to maintain their virginity until they are married. The rings and bracelets are marketed at Christian bookstores as good gifts for adults to give to the adolescents in their lives. One of the problems with branding, however, is that although someone wears the product, he or she does not necessarily ascribe to the ethos promoted by the brand; by wearing Nike, one does not automatically become an athlete. Some people will wear the running shoe because they like the aesthetic of it or it makes them feel like they are part of a desirable group. The same is true of WWJD bracelets and abstinence wear; although they appear to be an heuristic tool to assist with moral decision making, they may also function just as things that are pleasing simply because of their look or because they are trendy and popular with other youth.

Another intriguing cultural mirror is not a literal one of shiny glass but rather a poly-cotton blend festooned with slogans and popular-cultural icons: the T-shirt. "Witness wear," as it is sometimes called in Christian circles, is clothing (usually a T-shirt) that identifies the wearer as aligning with Christian-centric values. The art of a good T-shirt slogan lies in its ability to deliver a punchy or provocative line or image and to inspire thought, a laugh, or further conversation. For evangelicals, this can double as a purity marker that indicates the wearer is part of a religious community and as a social tool that opens up opportunities to witness and share beliefs with others (Uncle Makk's Christian T-shirt Shop 2008). Messages may be clever references to popular-cultural symbols with a Christian twist (i.e., Jesus died for MySpace in heaven), or they may have multilayered meanings, such as the one currently popular with the emergent skate movement of young evangelicals: "Body piercing saved my life" (referencing both their alternative look and the crucifixion of Christ).

Piercings and tattooing, for many young Christians, is part of an important ritual of "self-branding" that, in some ways, is a modern parallel to the suffering endured on the cross, as well as a reflection of the "intense tribal mentality of Christian youth" that author Lauren Sandler has observed as being increasingly on the rise (2006, 54). The Christian Tattoo Association (CTA) offers a MySpace page for inked believers to share their latest tats for inspiration and encouragement, and it includes images of everything from a tame and minimalist fish symbol on the back of a woman's neck to one man's extreme scarification of the word "JESUS" carved in two inch letters covering his entire forearm (CTA 2008).

Alternative and hipster youth culture is so infused into young Christianity that it becomes almost impossible to imagine a successful youth ministry that *doesn't* incorporate pop culture into its evangelical strategy. Recognizing broad and sweeping sociocultural shifts, some youth pastors are realizing that this generation, the Millennials (or Generation Y, as they are sometimes called) respond very well to messages that sympathize with and help make sense of the fragmented human condition of these times (Murray 1997; Oblinger 2003). Brian D. McLaren, currently enjoying tenure as a highly influential youth pastor who has been key to shaping this brand of Millennial Christianity, understands that delivering this message effectively to young people means doing so through a matrix of affect, culture, and postmodernity. He notes, "If you were a missionary going to Spain, you'd have to learn to think and speak Spanish. If you are a missionary going to any educated culture on earth today, I think you need to learn to think and speak postmodern" (Sandler 2006, 49).

WHAT HAPPENS AT HARD AS NAILS STAYS AT HARD AS NAILS

Another intriguing cultural reference that has woven its way into the narrative landscape of this generation (and subsequently flavors youth evangelism in fascinating and disturbing ways) is Chuck Palahniuk's classic nihilist, anticonsumerist, postmodern warrior angst story, *Fight Club* (1996). In Palahniuk's narrative, the protagonist is disillusioned with what he feels is the diminishing construct of masculinity in a society in which the measure of manhood is how successful a man is at being a corporate viking, metaphorically raping and pillaging consumers for his own gain. In response, he establishes a violent, militaristic cult of personality that offers men an opportunity to rediscover the warrior within by rejecting capitalism and fighting one another in strictly regulated environments. The 1999 film adaptation by director David Fincher inspired similar fight clubs across North America and retains its iconoclastic cult status today. Not surprisingly, in this latest generation of Christianity, aggressive, emotive, and in-your-face teen ministries are beginning to emerge in response to many of the cultural mores of Western adolescence. One of the most controversial of these is that of self-described "non-ordained Catholic minister" Justin Fatica and his Hard as Nails ministry. Offering a hardcore physical and emotive experience, Fatica verbally flagellates his thousands of young followers, ties them to crosses, and sells his brand of Christ's unconditional love and acceptance that comes with an intense adrenaline rush. In 2007, HBO produced a documentary on his unusual and controversial ministry, setting off alarms within both the secular and devout populations. *Newsweek* described Fatica's stunning and outrageous theatrics as "drill-sergeant-like assaults" and referred to a provocative segment of the film (*Hard as Nails* 2007) that has many critics worrying about the emotional and physical abuse he inflicts on his disciples:

> "If you sin, you better have the courage to bash Jesus' face in!" Fatica screams at one cherubic girl, pushing her to the verge of tears. "Have you sinned in the last 24 hours? Have ya?! HAVE YA?!" Fatica wants his disciples to feel the pain that Christ suffered for their sins. At one session, a kid picks up a metal folding chair and whacks Fatica—at his direction—on the back, as the minister repeatedly screams to another supplicant, "Jesus took all this pain for you!" He re-creates Calvary, ordering teens to carry heavy crosses up a hill, or asking them to stand, arms extended against the wood, while their peers pound the cross with a hammer and scream insults. (Ali 2007)

Methods utilized by Hard as Nails are not usually condoned by more mainstream youth ministries, and its critics contend that this over-the-top, intense emotional experience is exploiting a well-known fact of adolescent development: the frontal cortex of the adolescent brain is not fully developed until adulthood, making youth particularly susceptible to affective manipulation. Teenagers feel emotions such as exhilaration, joy, fear, and despair acutely and often guide their decisions based on their intense emotive experiences (Dahl 2004). Despite the widespread critique of Fatica's evangelical scare tactics, however, other ministries emulate the model in less overt but equally successful ways. The warrior metaphor informs how "soldiers" in the Lord's army should act in these times of culture wars, where good and evil routinely battle for the souls of the world.

The Lord's Boot Camp, an affiliate of Teen Missions International (based in Merritt Island, Florida), was possibly a tamed-down inspiration for the Hard as Nails model and was the subject of a 2008 documentary shown on the popular news program *48 Hours* (*48 Hours* 2008). Teen Missions was founded in 1970 as a venue for adolescents who were interested in contributing their time and talents to overseas missions. Youth involved with the project have the option of either working on a construction-oriented team (building schools, airstrips, and other structures) or on an evangelical team, on which they will preach, witness, stage puppet shows, and sing their message of the need of the world to accept Christ as its personal savior. Enjoying longstanding ties with evangelical churches throughout North America, the organization sends approximately forty-eight teams a year to over thirty countries worldwide. Combining elements of "Scared Straight" boot camps for delinquent youth, it is popular not only with Christian youth, but as a moral and disciplinary vehicle for judges and parents who send wayward youth there in hopes of straightening them out. It would not be uncommon for a youth convicted of robbing a liquor store to be on the same team as one who is the president of her high school Youth for Christ chapter. Before embarking on their international mission, teens participate in a two-week "boot camp," situated thick in the heart of the swampy and humid Florida everglades. The Lord's Boot Camp takes very seriously the strategies employed by the military in creating troops who can work effectively as a team and incorporates similar methodologies into training the young evangelicals it will unleash on the world.

Participants are subjected to rigorous and relentless physical tests of endurance and tenacity. Awakened at five A.M., they collectively run the "OC" (obstacle course) immediately thereafter. Half-asleep, they swing across the "Slough of Despond" (a stagnant and fetid pool of water), climb "Mount Sinai" (a tire mountain), and navigate other obstacles, at the end of which each member of the team must scale a twelve-foot wall with only the assistance of other team members. Teams who do not complete the course in the required fifteen minutes are assigned SBs, or "Special Blessings," which involve menial manual labor, such as digging a hole or filling in one that another team dug while being disciplined for its failures.

Katrina[2] is an alumna of the 1987 Gibraltar evangelical team of Teen Missions and is now an adult without a particular religious affiliation. I interviewed her about her experiences and how she reflects on them now, twenty years later, with a nonevangelical worldview.

> The whole process was physically and emotionally exhausting. We were consistently pushed beyond our limits, and allowed very little in the way of unstructured, free time. There were about 3,500 young people who were going on missions that year. We would go from nonstop physical activities, with a few breaks to pray or read the Bible, to highly charged and emotional rallies in the evening. There would be preaching, singing, and we were encouraged to burn off steam by chanting, stamping and yelling. It was a powerful and intoxicating mix. You really started to feel swept up in the incredible velocity and emotional momentum that can be generated in a crowd of thousands of teenagers screaming and shouting. Reflecting on it now, it seems like classic cult or military-style programming techniques of isolation from family and friends in a secluded location, allowing little time for independent thought or space and rallying with rowdy shouting and crowdthink as the sun went down on a hot and tiring day. (Trimble, forthcoming)

Ironically, for Katrina, participating in this summer mission eventually shifted her entire religious perspective and, ultimately, made her question her faith and leave the church.

> Many of the people living in Gibraltar were either Spanish or Muslims from nearby Algeria. We were taught songs and puppet skits in Spanish, and I preached French sermons in the town square, which were directed at the Muslims. Several Muslims took up our invitation to be born again and receive Jesus as their savior. We would usually have to pray with them in the secluded and private back room of one of the local Catholic churches, however. Our translator nervously informed us that by becoming Christians publicly, it was entirely possible they would be killed by their families when they returned to Algeria to renew their work permits and that we needed to take this very seriously.

> Suddenly, it didn't seem like such an adventure when people's lives were at stake. I had not been prepared for that possibility, or what the life changing implications could be for others after I returned home to my safe little existence in Canada. Others I encountered were incredulous at my cultural arrogance. "Have you read the Qur'an?" they would ask. "Do you know anything about Islam? You can't speak even one word of Arabic, and yet you come here and tell us we're going to hell?!" I was humbled by my own arrogance and that of my faith. I couldn't continue to be part of it on my return, something that annoyed and troubled my congregation when I refused to speak about my experiences after I came back. (Trimble, forthcoming)

CONCLUSION: THE DIALOGIC SELF, CULTURE, AND MEANING MAKING

Infusing an object or experience with meaning involves a complex epistemological and ontological process that is in constant dialogue with our sense of self and the world around us. For people who do not live their lives within the evangelical sphere, the idea of engaging with and checking in with God as a sort of moral and cultural barometer that informs consumer purchases, selection of toys, and expressions of faith on clothes or (more radically) carved into one's body may seem outside of the scope of understanding. We might marvel at people who would subject themselves to intensely regimented and exhausting physical or emotional stress in the name of Jesus and wonder what their motivation could possibly be. Our own meaning-making processes seem so different that it becomes difficult to fathom the affective dimension that faith can play in shaping the way believers experience the world. However, as Hubert Hermans, Harry Kempen, and Rens van Loon remind us, perhaps we are not so different from many of the evangelicals in the ways we move through and interpret the world:

> Nevertheless, imaginal dialogues play a central role in our daily lives: They exist alongside actual dialogues with real others and, interwoven with actual interactions, they constitute an essential part of our narrative construction of the world. Even when we are outwardly silent, for example, we find ourselves communicating with our critics, our parents, our consciences, our gods, our reflection in the mirror, the photography

> of someone we miss, a figure from a movie or a dream, our babies or our pets. (1992, 28)

Our understanding and interpretation of meaning flows from the conversations we have, consciously or not, with our sense of self and the many dimensions of possible human perspective and experience. For some who identify as born-again Christians, the desire to locate and segregate meaning-making filters almost exclusively through a religious matrix is a powerful one, particularly as a means of ensuring that children and youth make life choices considered appropriate to, and in synergy with, their communities of faith.

Notes

1. This is a reference to the Bible verse Proverbs 31:20, "she extends her hands to the poor and stretches out her hands to the needy." Each doll comes packaged with two cookie cutters, a cookie recipe, Bible lessons, and a list of activities that suggest ways the girl can "work to make sure that everyone around her has all they need."
2. This is a pseudonym.

References

48 Hours. 2008. The lord's boot camp. First broadcast on April 12 by CBS. Produced by S. Reiner. Directed and written by Heidi Ewing and Rachel Grady.

Ali, Lorraine. 2007. For the love of Christ: Jason Fatica yells, threatens and humiliates teens into finding Jesus. You got a problem with that? *Newsweek*, December 15, www.newsweek.com/id/78181 (accessed July 15, 2008).

Asma, Stephen T. 2007. Holy toyland: The mega toy retailer Wal-Mart is now selling biblical toys like the talking Jesus. *In These Times*. http://inthesetimes.com/article/3319/holy_toyland (accessed May 21, 2008).

Averill, James R. 1996. Emotion: Here and now, then and there. *International Journal for the Psychology of Religion* 6, no. 2: 89–94.

Bell, Daniel. 1965. Ideology and Soviet politics. *Slavic Review* 24, no. 4: 591–605.

Billings, Dwight. B. 1990. Religion as opposition: A Gramscian analysis. *American Journal of Sociology* 96, no. 1: 1–31.

Birke, Sarah. 2008. The toy David. *New Statesman*, January 28, 20.

Borden, A. L. 2006. *Making money saving souls: The Christian bookstore field in the United States*. Unpublished PhD diss., Emory University.

Bourdieu, Pierre. 1984. *Distinction: A social critique of the judgment of taste.* Cambridge, MA: Harvard University Press.

Boyles, Crystal. 2007. It's Samson v. G.I. Joe for Christian toymaker. *Anderson (South Carolina) Independent Mail,* October 26, www.andersonindependent.com/news/2007/oct/26/its-samson-v-gi-joe-christian-toymaker (accessed May 28, 2008).

Carone, Dominic A., and David F. Barone. 2001. A social cognitive perspective on religious beliefs: Their functions and impact on coping and psychotherapy. *Clinical Psychology Review* 21, no. 7: 989–1003.

Christian Dollar Store. 2008. Christian toys and games. Christian Dollar Store, www.christiandollarstore.com/toys.html (accessed July 15, 2008).

Christian Tattoo Association. 2008. http://groups.myspace.com/index.cfm?fuseaction=groups.groupProfile&groupID=106060782&MyToken=62c063ca-1d1b-4185-b1be-c9e5c873d0e2 (accessed July 15, 2008).

Dahl, Ronald E. 2004. Adolescent brain development: A period of vulnerabilities and opportunities. *Annals of the New York Academy of Sciences* 1021: 1–22.

Eldredge, John. 2001. *Wild at heart: Discovering the secret of a man's soul.* Nashville, TN: Thomas Nelson.

Elsworth, Catherine. 2005. Christian warriors battle to rediscover God in boot camps. *Telegraph,* January 24, www.telegraph.co.uk/news/worldnews/northamerica/usa/1481904/Christian-warriors-battle-to-rediscover-God-in-boot-camps.html (accessed May 28, 2008).

Fight Club. 1999. Directed by D. Fincher. Hollywood, CA: Art Linson Productions, 20th Century Fox.

Fulton, John. 1987. Religion and politics in Gramsci: An introduction. *Sociological Analysis* 48, no. 3: 197–216.

Gramsci, Antonio. 1971. *Selections from the prison notebooks,* ed. and trans. Quintin Hoare and Geoffrey Nowell-Smith. London: Lawrence and Wishart.

Halkias, Maria. 2007. Talking Jesus nearly vanishes. *Dallas News,* December 9, www.dallasnews.com/sharedcontent/dws/bus/casual/stories/DN-p2Jesusdoll_09bus.ART.State.Edition1.2a568d4.html (accessed May 28, 2008).

Hard as Nails. 2007. Directed by D. Holbrooke. New York: HBO.

Harré, Rom. 2002. Material objects in social worlds. *Theory, Culture & Society* 19, no. 5–6: 23–33.

Hendershot, Heather. 2004. *Shaking the world for Jesus: Media and conservative evangelical culture.* Chicago: University of Chicago Press.

Hermans, Hubert. J. M., Harry. J. G. Kempen, and Rens J. P. van Loon. 1992. The dialogical self: Beyond individualism and rationalism. *American Psychologist* 47, no. 1: 23–33.

Hill, Peter. C. 1999. Giving religion away: What the study of religion offers psychology. *International Journal for the Psychology of Religion* 9, no. 4: 229–249.

International Superheroes. 2008. Bibleman. International Superheroes, www.internationalhero.co.uk/b/bibleman.htm (accessed May 30, 2008).

Johnson, Mark. 1987. *The body in the mind: The bodily basis of meaning, imagination and reason.* Chicago: University of Chicago Press.

Meachem, Karla. 2008. Christian toys for girls and boys, www.christiantoysforgirlsandboys.com (accessed July 15, 2008).

Mintz, Jenni. 2007. What can Jesus say? Push the button. *Ventura County Star,* December 6, www.venturacountystar.com/news/2007/dec/06/what-can-jesus-say-push-the-button (accessed May 28, 2008).

Murray, Neil. D. 1997. Welcome to the future: The Millennial generation. *Journal of Career Planning and Employment* 57, no. 3: 36–42.

Neruda, Pablo. 1994. *Ode to common things.* New York: Bellfinch Press.

Oblinger, Diana. 2003. Boomers, Gen Xers and Millennials: Understanding the "new students." *Educause Review* 38, no. 4: 36–45.

Palahniuk, Chuck. 1996. *Fight Club.* New York: W.W. Norton and Company.

Palmer, Parker. J. 1998. *The courage to teach: Exploring the inner landscape of a teacher's life.* San Francisco: Jossey-Bass.

Phillips, Doug. 2008a. The all-American boys adventure catalogue. The Vision Forum, www.visionforum.com/boysadventure (accessed July 15, 2008).

_______. 2008b. Beautiful girlhood collection. The Vision Forum, www.visionforum.com/beautifulgirlhood (accessed July 15, 2008).

Sandler, Lauren. 2006. *Righteous: Dispatches from the evangelical youth movement.* New York: Viking.

Sheldon, Charles. M. 1956. *In his steps: "What would Jesus do?"* Chicago: Moody Press.

Stein Wellner, Alison. 2005. The morality play. *Inc. Magazine*, February, 72–77.

Trimble, L. M. Forthcoming. "I thought I was saving souls": Adult accounts of their experiences as adolescent evangelical Christian missionaries in Jesus boot camps.

Uncle Makk's Christian T-shirt Shop. 2008. Cool Christian T-shirts by Kerusso, www.christiantshirtshop.com/cool-christian-tshirts.html (accessed July 15, 2008).

Weaver-Hightower, Marcus B. 2008. Inventing the "all-American boy": A case study of the capture of boys' issues by conservative groups. *Men and Masculinities* 10, no. 3: 267–295.

IX

The Stillborn Twin

The Christian Lifestyle Beats with the Heart of Rock 'n' Roll

PHILIP M. ANDERSON

Rock music seeks release through liberation from the personality and its responsibility. . . . [It is] among the anarchic ideas of freedom which today predominate more openly in the West than in the East. But that is precisely why rock music is so completely antithetical to the Christian concept of redemption and freedom, indeed its exact opposite. Hence music of this type must be excluded from the Church on principle, and not merely for aesthetic reasons, or because of restorative crankiness or historical inflexibility.

—Joseph Ratzinger, prefect of the Congregation for the Doctrine of the Faith, later Pope Benedict XVI, address to the XVIII International Church Music Congress in Rome, November 17, 1985

It's time to remove the blinders—guard yourself and those you love from one of Satan's most powerful tools!

—Fight the Good Fight Ministries website ad text for *They Sold Their Souls for Rock 'n' Roll,* a ten-hour documentary hosted by former child television star Kirk Cameron

> *Do you remember when everyone began analyzing Beatle songs—I don't think I ever understood what some of them were supposed to be about.*
>
> —Ringo Starr, *The Beatles Illustrated Lyrics*

The connection between rock 'n' roll and Christian rock is right there in the name: Christian rock is a subcategory of rock, just like heavy metal and all the other subgenres and variants. The fact that most evangelicals, those who don't condemn all "beat" music outright, see Christian rock as an alterative to rock does not change the fact that the structure, even the DNA, is essentially the same.

The line between sacred and secular in music is a fine one in any case, even in families. Infamous rocker Jerry Lee Lewis and infamous evangelist Jimmy Swaggart are first cousins (along with not so infamous Mickie Gilley, the country singer). Early rock 'n' roller Clyde McPhatter's brother was the pianist in the Abyssinian Baptist Church, known for its Columbia Records gospel recordings supervised by John Hammond. Producer Jerry Wexler, in his autobiographical *Rhythm and the Blues,* argues that soul music, exemplified by Aretha Franklin (a minister's daughter), is simply a secularization of the gospel. And, certainly, had Elvis's stillborn twin brother Jesse lived, we know he would have been a preacher of the gospel.

Rockers themselves drift toward the sacred: Jerry Lee and Elvis, among many others, made gospel records. Little Richard embraced evangelical Christianity as early as 1957. Other Christian converts include Cliff Richard, Richie Furay, Bob Dylan (for a short time), and Mark Farner, and the list goes on and on. Jim Morrison of The Doors made sacred records, even if they weren't necessarily Christian. Moreover, there is always the question of whether there is any difference between Van Morrison shouting out "Gloria" to a relentless beat or medieval monks chanting "Gloria" a cappella. Given Morrison's later duet with Cliff Richard, the two "Glorias" might have been one and the same. "Inspirational" pop music is usually nothing more than sacred sentiments that have been secularized or given a secular twist, such as the pop anthem "From a Distance/God Is Watching Us," and so forth.

But Christian rock is neither sacred nor secular but only a wolf in sheep's clothing. On second thought, and to use proper Christian metaphors, Christian rock is actually a sheep in wolf's clothing. Christian rock is part of the plan to convert the heathens (or save the saved), a message in a whiskey bottle (empty, of course), a channel for lost souls to be rounded up and put on the train to Jordan, rather than the downtown train. Christian rock is the "word" driving a freshly washed Coupe de Ville within the speed limit; it's Jesus as a cool guy (not a hippie—that's secular); it is a communion wafer inside the corned beef sandwich. Christian rock is the lure to bring kids to salvation.

I do not plan to list, sort, or critique individual Christian rock bands. The Wikipedia entry on Christian rock presents an excellent overview. I also recommend a visit to Larry Norman's website. Larry Norman is the "father of Christian rock," formerly the "father of Jesus rock," who recorded the first Christian rock album in 1970. A description of his recent farewell concert on Christianity today.com provides a revealing look at the direction sophisticated Christian rock has traveled (Sanford 2005). Another place to witness the cultural range of Christian music is ClassicGod.com, a site for CDs, history, T-shirts, and other artifacts of the Christian rock culture.

I also do not want to venture into the territory of discussing the "sincerity" of various Christian musicians. Read any of the number of books on Christian rock and its controversies that appear when you type "Christian rock" into the Amazon.com book search. As with all musical genres, there is a question of who is "authentic." Are some in Christian music because they failed in the secular arena? There are also critiques of Christian superstars, such as Amy Grant, who crossover into popular culture (some with accompanying scandal) and lose some of their "cred" in the evangelical world. All I am interested in here is the culture that produces the phenomenon of Christian music, as represented in its "popular" rock (and, by analogy, its soul, country, and folk forms), and how that phenomenon appears to function in its cultural context. In other words, how come there is such a thing as Christian rock at all? How can the devil's music be a path to righteousness?

When one considers the history of evangelical Christianity and rock 'n' roll, the immediate images that come to mind are of Southern teenagers burning Beatles records in response to John Lennon's brilliantly ironic, and totally self-deprecating, 1966 statement about the group being bigger than Jesus. One of the defining features of fundamentalist Christians appears to be a lack of a sense of humor (remember how sacrilegious the "smiling Jesus" illustration was?). In old newsreel footage, one can see the denunciations of the "devil's music," but that has quieted somewhat with the growth of Christian popular culture and marketing during the 1990s. But no thoughtful person could miss the fact that most of the early attacks on rock were in the South, where the music's decidedly "jungle" element was problematic. Later, it became a problem that the Beatles were "foreigners" who were replacing the white southern rockers like Elvis in the hearts and minds of America's youth.

I do not mean to stereotype citizens of the former Confederacy; I merely wish to point out their "rebel-ness." Herein lies the heart of the contradiction I would like to explore between rock and evangelical Christianity. Evangelism is a rebel cause, the Southern states were rebellious (and still are), and rock 'n' roll represents rebellion. It is no coincidence that Brando's character Johnny is standing by the jukebox when he gives his famous answer to the question "What are you rebelling against?" (*The Wild One* 1953). Evangelical Christianity is a rebel cause against humanism, against the secularization of government and culture, and even against organized religion. The immortal question, put to a righteous evangelical, gets the same answer as Brando's existentialist biker's: "What have you got?" On the other hand, we must remember that Satan's downfall, his loss of grace, resulted from his rebellion against God.

My late wife's parents were evangelicals, though Northerners and on the educated, almost intellectual, side of the evangelical culture. My contacts with their religious culture were fleeting and surface, I admit, but the common theme in their worldview (their testimony, as it were) was a complaint about everything and everybody who didn't subscribe to their Christian worldview. They were rebels against society, waiting for the Truth and the Way to arrive in the form of the Second Coming. Succumbing to worldly ways was a sure ticket to hell, which waited for all the secularites. They paid their taxes, but they paid a serious tithe to their church as well (Caesar and God, as it were). They worked in the secular world, but it was clear to me that they, as teachers, taught moral and ethical behavior as a primary goal. They were decidedly anti-institutional and, in that way, more than a little antigovernment.

My former in-laws were wonderful singers and loved music deeply. But the biggest continuing fight they had for years with their daughter was over listening to rock music. The argument, as I understood it, was pretty simple: rock 'n' rollers were secular types promoting sinful behavior by their actions, appearance, and message of sex, drugs, and roll 'n' roll. Who can argue with that notion—it was the 1960s after all—or blame any parent for that particular stance? The answer for the Christian community was to find music that was Christian in its attitudes and message but had enough of the new beat and instrumentation of the popular music revolution to satisfy the kids.

I remember my wife's leftover records from her teenage years were recorded by groups I had never heard of, but they were apparently part of a vast secret network of Christian pop stars who were quite successful. As a teenager, she listened to regular rock at a girlfriend's house, but she developed a real connection with Christian rock. In the late 1970s, we attended a performance of a brother and sisters Crosby, Stills, and Nash–style band called The Second Chapter of Acts. The performance was in a huge church and not much different from many rock shows we had been to, except for the lack of smoke (very unusual in those days, if not so any more). The only other difference was the themes in song lyrics. It was regular folk rock with a Christian message.

Most of these Christian bands didn't get much press in the 1970s or early 1980s. The press about Christian rock (then called "Jesus music") during those early years was usually when something like Bob Dylan's short-lived conversion to Christianity affected his recordings, or *Time* or *Newsweek* ran a cover story on "Jesus freaks." The public press reporting on Christian music really heightened with the emergence of Christian heavy metal bands, actually post-metal hair bands exemplified by the still-rockin' Stryper (Isaiah 53:5, "by his stripes we are healed"), whose first album sold over sold five hundred thousand copies and remained on the Billboard 200 for forty weeks in the 1980s.

The news angle here was that Christian heavy metal appeared after the evangelical Right had tagged heavy metal as the devil's music. Heavy metal heroes such as Ozzy Osbourne, lately of the ominously named Black Sabbath, and his ilk were not only condemned but threatened with real political and legal force. Both Osbourne and the members of Judas Priest found themselves in courtrooms defending themselves against charges that they had caused the suicides of different young men through subliminal messages in their records. Songs such as Osbourne's "Suicide Solution," a song warning against alcoholism, was presented as evidence that heavy metal was encouraging "normal" teenagers to commit suicide.

The Parents Music Resource Center (PMRC) appeared in 1985 to focus its attack on heavy metal in particular, with Tipper Gore as the head witch hunter. Their political drive against heavy metal, despite brilliant testimony before Congress by, among others, Frank Zappa, resulted in the now ubiquitous

Parental Advisory sticker. Significantly, K-Mart and Sears, among others, pulled targeted records from their stores. One supposes that would make more room for "good" music.

And here is the clue to the heart of Christian music and its supporters. The tactic used in the PMRC congressional hearings was to read the lyrics of the songs out loud, stripping them of their musical context. The only time the record was played in any of these public spectacles was to attempt to ferret out alleged subliminal messages in the recordings, another tactic guaranteed to strip the music of its context. Reading the lyrics without the music not only privileges the lyrics (a tenet of good Christian song writing) but is an exercise guaranteed to trivialize the artistry of the musician.

Tellingly, the reading of lyrics stripped of their musical context is also a comedic device. Most famously, on the original *Tonight Show* in the 1950s, Steve Allen used to get huge laughs by reading rock 'n' roll lyrics (e.g., "Tutti Frutti") straight-faced, with dramatic pauses and emphases. Not insignificantly, Allen also featured performances by Elvis Presley and Jerry Lee Lewis on his show. Presley, embarrassingly, was required to sing "Hound Dog" to a real basset hound, and Lewis's knocked-over-and-kicked-away piano stool was thrown across the stage by an off-camera Allen to comic effect. Allen later milked the lyric-reading routine with Beatle songs like "Hello Goodbye."

One is also reminded of the ridiculous cultural controversy in the mid-1960s over the rumored "obscenity" in the Kingsmen's recording of Richard Berry's "Louie Louie." That tempest in a teapot involved the FBI agents listening to the record hundreds of times. The published lyrics were clearly not obscene, so the evidence resided in the recording itself. No charges were filed in the end, when law-enforcement officials concluded that the words, as sung, were simply incomprehensible. The absurdity of this drama is heightened when one considers that the U.S. legal system was trying to find obscenity, a significant legal and cultural concept, in what some have dubbed the dumbest song ever written.

So Christian rock is really about changing the message but keeping the beat. Even churches have drummers these days, though the lack of a "rhythm section" is one of the things that used to set sacred music apart from the secular. The beat of the music brings the listener to the message. If you can't fight them, if you can't outmarket them, then join them, seems to be the message. The largest hypocrisy in this whole enterprise shows in the attempts by the Christian Right to condemn secular music be quoting only the lyrics, then selling the sacred message though contextualized melody, harmony, and rhythm. Even more troubling in this scenario is the fact that most people can't recite the lyrics to the songs they love in any case. Any number of comedic books reporting misheard song lyrics demonstrate that the message of music is not just, or only, in the words. Read *'Scuse Me While I Kiss This Guy*, a compilation of hilarious reports of what people think they are hearing on famous recordings as an example (Edwards 1995). The title is a reference to what many people apparently think Jimi Hendrix sings in "Purple Haze," rather than "'Scuse me while I kiss the sky." In other words, the medium is the message. People listen to music for the joy first and the words second. The Christian rock movement attempts to use the joy of music (and the throbbing beat) to sell the message of evangelicalism merely by changing the words.

The phenomenon and tactic of co-option are not unique to the Christian lifestyle mavens and their associated hucksters. Sam Phillips of Sun Records was always accused of selling Elvis as a white boy who sounded black. Pat Boone covered Little Richard's "Tutti Frutti" for the wholesome white teenager crowd. Jerry Wexler's comment about soul and the secularization of gospel also has co-opting elements. But the most outrageous example of attempts at co-opting was John J. Miller's article in *National Review* listing the "top fifty conservative rock songs of all time" (Sisario 2006). Unbelievably, the number one "conservative" song was "Won't Get Fooled Again" by The Who, the original guitar-destroying, self-destructive, working-class protopunk band.

In response, the *New York Times* quoted Dave Marsh, "longtime rock critic and avowed lefty," on this twisted argument that rock 'n' roll is really conservative in its "message." Marsh saw the list as "a desperate effort by the right to co-opt popular culture." He then went on to make one of the key points I want to make here:

> What happened was, my side won the culture war, in the sense that rock and related music is the dominant musical form, not only in the U.S. but around the world. . . . Once you lose that battle, you lose the war, and then a different kind of battle begins: the battle over meaning. (Sisario 2006)

As I will demonstrate later, you can do one of two things to co-opt rock music for the Christian lifestyle movement: you can attack the secular side of rock 'n' roll by labeling its message satanic or you can substitute a Christian message.

Christian rock's sheep-in-wolf's-clothing tactic for the conversion and maintenance of souls is not unique to its music. In recent years, the Hell House phenomenon, designed to counteract the devil's holiday of Halloween, has gained a nationwide following. Evangelical pastor Keenan Roberts has developed a haunted-house kit that is based on "Christian" themes, including souls being tormented by the fires of hell (instead of zombies and monsters) as scary tableaux aimed at bringing souls to salvation through "Scared Straight" methods. Masquerading as a typical haunted house, the experience attempts to "trick" the youthful participants into seeking salvation. Featured on the October 3, 2005, segment of *CNN News Night with Paula Zahn*, Pastor Roberts talks of Hell House as "creatively packag[ing] the message of the gospels." He wants to "make it palatable" to Christian youth and potential converts.

The marketing tactic is really Jesus in a Freddy Krueger mask, aimed to provide an alternative to secularized Halloween. Most troubling for many social commentators is the prejudice played out in the Hell House scenes, including a gay man dying of AIDS, a lesbian committing suicide in despair over her sexuality, and a young rape victim dying during an abortion procedure. CNN dubbed the segment "Scared into Salvation," a clear reference to the "Scared Straight" juvenile justice program that has been institutionalized in many states. The connection with "Scared Straight," the infamous prison-based reform movement for young offenders, in which prisoners serving life sentences are allowed to threaten young adults under the supervision of law enforcement and with the court's sanction, is important. In its behavior theory, it is the fear of ending up like these prisoners that scares the juvenile straight, but it is more likely fear of ending up in jail with these men that scares the kid into righteousness.

Much of the message of evangelical Christianity—not the new Joel Osteen brand of "Dr. Phil with financial advice" but the tradition that traces itself back to Jonathon Edwards' "Sinners in the Hands of an Angry God"—is about fear: fear of the world, fear of losing salvation, fear of being "tricked" by the devil into going to hell. Western culture is full of stories of the trickster, Old Scratch, working to steal souls. In the secular versions, "The Devil and Daniel Webster" in story or "The Devil Went Down to Georgia" in song, the hero outsmarts or outplays the devil, a very humanist and rationalist moral. In the sacred versions, the souls are dragged by the devil into hell if the protagonist doesn't follow Jesus. There is no rational way out of the devil's grasp; only the power of faith can save.

I think the devil-as-trickster notion explains why evangelicals are so obsessed with subliminal messages in records and coded messages in literature (or images of Jesus on the bathroom door, though that appears to be a big deal with Roman Catholics). The worry is that kids will be seduced, unknowingly, by the dark side (George Lucas reference intended) and their immortal souls will be tricked into Hades. The parents' job is keep the children from the lures that Satan has set, to help them renounce worldly things and ideas, to avoid the start of a slide that leads to secularization and eventual damnation. The message in rock 'n' roll is a humanist message of love and fun and excitement, all taking place at the roadhouse by the crossroads. Rock 'n' roll is about a woman dressed for Sunday even though it's Saturday night. Redemption comes on Sunday morning, but it might be better if we all stayed home on Saturday night, just in case, so we are up early for church.

So, the argument that no one really understands the words, or mishears them in most cases, or that they are just syllables that fit the rhythm and rhyme of the song doesn't carry weight with the evangelical "subliminal" crowd. The words themselves are not even the message because the message is hidden. Irony rears its ugly head again here, when the evangelical movement attacks literature by reading texts literally rather than metaphorically, thereby missing the "hidden" meaning entirely. The same is true of the treatment of decontextualized song lyrics that are then given a literal reading rather than being treated as poetic language.

Evangelicals remain tied to the "literal" word of God, the words of the Bible and Jesus, even though the leading evangelical Bible is the only "translation" that has very little to do with the ancient texts. This is a cake-and-eat-it-too situation that, undeniably, fits very well with the other contradictions in evangelical practice. That's why Christian rock continues to be tolerated: it may be the devil's music, but at least clean-cut white boys and girls play it to proclaim a Christian message. And the money it generates feeds the soul of the church and its attendant "Christian-based" businesses.

The most recent development, and an especially pertinent one here, is the growth of the Christian rock festival during the 1990s. A story of one franchise, "youth minister" Ron Luce's Teen Mania, appeared on the front page of the *New York Times* on October 6, 2006 (Goodstein 2006). Luce, who holds an MBA from Harvard, claims to have "reached" two million teenagers over the past fifteen years through his Teen Mania stadium events. He was hosting forty events on the 2006 schedule, managing with an unpaid "road crew" of seven hundred teenagers who were interning for a year at Teen Mania's Honor Academy in Garden Valley, Texas.

The two-day event, according to the reporter, begins with an entire day of Christian music, with attendant "pogo-ing" and "hundreds stream[ing] down the aisles for the altar call and kneel[ing] in front of the stage, some weeping openly as they prayed to give their lives to God" (Goodstein 2006). On the morning of the second day, Luce distributed scraps of paper on which the adolescents wrote "all the negative cultural influences, brand names, products and television shows that they planned to excise from their lives" (Goodstein 2006). The participants then "streamed down the aisles, this time to throw away the 'cultural garbage'" (Goodstein 2006).

The key word in the above description is "excise," the transitive verb form of "excision" (i.e., surgical removal). Much of the Christian lifestyle is a rejection of the secular culture. Any one engaged in a good faith discussion of American culture should be deeply concerned that the Christian lifestyle considers the secular humanist elements in U.S. culture to be mere "garbage." Teaching this sort of intolerance for the views of others, dare I say it, seems more than a little un-Christian. The naming of names, as in product names, also has a whiff of boycott and censorship to it. In any case, one can see that these events are not about expanding one's horizons, but more like shutting the windows and pulling down the shades. The evangelical *message* of these organized "mania" events rides the waves of rock music onto a spiritual shore that happens to be overrun with Christian lifeguards.

This separation of form and content represents a fundamental breakdown in the understanding of popular music and culture at the heart of Christian rock. That misunderstanding is that music and words can be separated when the words were written for, or to, music. The great hymn writers of the nineteenth century, following the great church-sponsored composers of the seventeenth and eighteenth centuries, understood that the Christian message was best conveyed through the joy of music. At the least, church was more uplifting with music than without; or, people were more likely to attend church services that were entertaining. In recent years, that impulse has been turned on its head by complaints about religious music (e.g., "O Come, All Ye Faithful") being played around the various winter holidays. These songs are great music, which is why they remain. The objection for some is that they carry a Christian message. In this situation, evangelicals get a taste of their own medicine.

In many ways, the use of music defines evangelical worship. Even the most sophisticated of the big-time television preachers uses music as a required element in the service. Increasingly, these performances, while hardly rock 'n' roll, mimic exactly the popular music one finds on television variety shows and in entertainment centers from Las Vegas to Disney World. Music is the sound track of the mediated, televised world and cannot be ignored as some sort of worldly frill. Music is central to marketing a vision in this multimedia world. The old-time gospel and tent-show traditions are simply reinvented as theme and background music and, primarily, musical performance. Even Christians cannot avoid facing the music. In this deal with the devil, the evangelicals have signed on the bottom line of the entertainment contract.

But, to get back to my point about the relationship of words to music for a moment: secular rock criticism (rock critics are the secular equivalent of evangelical preachers—think about it) has failed rock music as well. These critics also split form and content, focusing on the words of the song to the exclusion of the music. Most rock critics are not musicians but writers, so they tend to focus on the words. There has even developed an idea over the years that rock/folk/blues music is so simple that it doesn't matter anyway: it's the same three chords with a message. Many new rock movements, especially those championed by rock critics, return to a simple music with a new message. Witness punk rock or rap music. The secular rock world invites the decontextualization of music that its critics use so effectively.

I repeat: the music is the message, not the words. I can demonstrate this with a single anecdote. In 1984, Ronald Reagan's campaign managers starting playing Bruce Springsteen's recording of "Born in the USA" at campaign events. Reagan himself praised Springsteen in a speech in New Jersey, citing his message of hope. Anyone who had read the lyrics to the song knew it was a message of anger and betrayal, a cry of despair against an uncaring government and society by an unemployed Vietnam veteran. But Reagan's people, who were genius propagandists, knew that no one could understand a word Bruce Springsteen sings in the song except the repeated refrain, "Born in the USA, I was born in USA." In that context the song sounded like virile, jingoistic shouting. Bruce, no innocent himself, didn't help interpretive matters by flaunting his denim-clad, manly, but perky, ass on the cover of the album using the red and white stripes of the American flag as wallpaper. He was wearing blue jeans and a white T-shirt and had a red hat emerging out of his back pocket, in case the enormous flag didn't make the point. I believe the photograph was part of the "message," since those were Springsteen's buff years when he also made his first video.

When the words become the message, it is almost always to the detriment of the music. A majority of music lovers object mightily to the exploitation of music to provide political and other social-control messages. Music is more than a marketing tool to most people. There was a time when a song by The Who wouldn't have been used for a television theme. Led Zeppelin wouldn't have been a sound track for Cadillac advertisements. There was a time when rock 'n' roll would not be used to sell Jesus. That is the triumph of marketing, of the brave new world we now inhabit, where "results" is the mantra, and "results" means money. Music becomes a tool, whether a tool of the devil or of Madison Avenue or of commerce. How could any good Christian buy into music as a tool?

I wonder sometimes whether my new favorite band is called Tool for the sexual innuendo, the mechanistic metaphor, or as a brilliant postmodern, or postironic, comment on its own commercial situation. The drummer, Danny Carey, is into the occult, an interest that has nothing to do with why I listen to him play. And, yet, on his website one finds criticism from people who cannot listen to him because of the "message" (FAQ, www.dannycarey.org). He also has, according to his website, an obsession with vintage analog synthesizers: does that mean that listening to Tool will make me reject the digital age?

You see, I do not believe Christian kids, born-agains or evangelicals or Episcopalians for that matter, love music only for its words. That's why people love *poetry*. People love music because it is music—they like the feeling they get from hearing it. Calling it jazz or blues or heavy metal or Christian rock does not make music something other than music. Music is music is music, to paraphrase Gertrude Stein. Music is the message. Only the devil would try to use music to change the way people behave. Ozzy Osbourne's biting the head off a pigeon is a triumph of marketing and publicity, but no one would buy his records if they did not enjoy the music. Nobody I know, except maybe the same fraternity brothers who used to swallow live gold fish, would bite the head off a pigeon as the *result* of listening to Osbourne sing.

Jazz, blues, and heavy metal are all genres of music (like orchestral and opera and brass band) and involve differences in the way it is performed. Christian rock is only about the words and the lifestyle of its players. One clear criticism of Christian rock is that it is not a type of music at all. Christian folk/rock/pop, says the more astute critic, is simply a grafting of Christian lyrics onto popular music forms. Interestingly enough, most truly fundamentalist Christians object to Christian rock on that basis: that it is merely a grafting of sacred words onto unacceptable secular forms. Ric Llewellyn's astute *Christian? Rock* (2007), an online tract of the Fundamental Evangelistic Association, treats all of these theological and musical points, as does polymath Rick Meisel on his Biblical Discernment Ministries website (1999).

Christian rock is part of a conflicted, materialistic "Christian" lifestyle. Christian rock is in the same category as the *Left Behind* series of books that are science fiction/fantasy titles employing apocalyptic evangelical themes (first volume published in 1995). With as many as 50 percent of the U.S. population claiming born-again or Christian status, that's a big market (at least sixty-two million books sold, in fact). The Christian lifestyle is big business, including networks of "Christian" businessmen, homeschooling packages, multimedia, coffee mugs, and concerts. The current rage, apparently, is a T-shirt that reads, "Body Piercing Saved My Life" on the front and, on the back, shows a picture of Jesus on the cross, stigmata emphasized.

One is reminded of the alternative music revolution after Nirvana and the Seattle grunge breakthrough in the early 1990s. Grunge was a lifestyle (flannel shirts and those short pants, if I remember). I also remember that, very shortly afterward, all of the mainstream radio stations were playing "alternative" music, and the Top 40 charts overflowed with "alternative" music. Given the obvious, that alternative was an alternative to the Top 40, how could alternative be the mainstream? These are the same 1990s that fertilized the flourishing of the new Christian lifestyle and the recent growth of Christian music. Christian music even has its own marketing acronym: CCM, for contemporary Christian music. I can tune to CCM stations on my XM satellite radio. A Christian lifestyle is easily available to everyone. I have to wonder if the new bans on smoking, for instance, are so easily accepted not because of the public health cost but because of the new, cleaner living demanded by the growing influence of the Christian lifestyle.

The "marketing" of the Christian lifestyle has also entered the mainstream. The May 22, 2006 *New Yorker* includes a piece on marketing *The Da Vinci Code* to both "Christian" and "secular" audiences, following on Mel Gibson's *The Passion of The Christ* and the role the Christian market played in its blockbuster success (Boyer 2006). A 2005 *New York Times* story chronicles the Walt Disney Company's marketing of the big-budget film *The Chronicles of Narnia: The Lion, the Witch, and the Wardrobe.* In this case, the company was drumming up interest in the film by releasing music from the film to radio stations: "Disney's tricky marketing strategy for Narnia—which includes aggressively courting Christian fans who can relate to the story's biblical allegory while trying not to disaffect secular fans—is particularly tricky when it comes to music" (Leeds 2005, E1, E7).

Disney planned to offer both a "Christian" and a "secular" sound track CD. It's all about the marketing apparently. The growing Christian film and music market has spun off Christian software and Christian video games, a market that now includes "about 100 active game developers" (Bosman 2006).

The Christian lifestyle movement even has its own born-again stand-up comedian. Brad Stine, a conservative Christian, has found a niche for born-again humor, riffing on creative design versus evolutionary theory, gay marriage, judicial activism, and other surefire comic topics (Leland 2005). While most of this marketing is about lifestyle, it has other intended and unintended consequences. Stine makes a very good living working churches, Christian retreats, and "Promise Keeper" events. He also works many corporate events, an arrangement that undoubtedly involves a captive audience, including many nonevangelicals. Disturbingly, Stine entertained the Republican House and Senate Retreat (Greenbrier Estate, West Virginia, 2005), "trading banter with House majority leader, Tom DeLay, and having his photograph taken with Katherine Harris, Dennis Hastert and Rudolph Giuliani" (Leland 2005, B7).

Maybe the former President Bush's proclaiming born-again status has something to do with all this change as well. I don't have access to the contents of his iPod to see if he currently listens to CCM. However, a 2005 story on the former president's iPod does tell us something about his music. In a CNN.com story, George W. Bush's media advisor, after revealing the songs placed on the president's iPod for listening to while he was mountain biking, says, "No one should psychoanalyze the song selection. It's music to get over the next hill." On the other hand, Caitlin Moran of the *London Times* noted, "No black artists, no gay artists, no world music, only one woman, no genre less than 25 years old, and no Beatles" are on the list (Wilkinson 2005).

I need a moment to defend the ex-president's music choices from both charges: first, that the music is only to "get over the next hill," and second, that the music somehow reflects a lack of sensitivity to race, class, and gender. The first is a typical functionalist response to music by Philistines of every stripe who argue that music doesn't mean something all by itself to the listener. Bush listens to music that speaks to him. That's his business—unless, of course, there is a subliminal Communist message undetected by the FBI in those George Jones songs or in "My Sharona" by The Knack.

I also object mightily to the assertion by the *London Times* reporter that the lack of diversity in the artists represented on the iPod reflects on the then-president's attitudes. The president was listening to music from his youth, not really a very liberal time as I remember it for all the revolution. But it was his youth, a time, cognitive scientists say, of strong impressions on cognitive functioning that account for the strong imprinting of music we hear during that period of our lives.

This *London Times* reporter's line of reasoning, that our musical tastes are deterministic expressions of our current politics rather than our youthful experience, is a bit of vulgar Marxist twaddle. The next thing you know, she will be arguing that blue men can't sing the whites (a personal nod to Vivian Stanshall), or that white people should buy jazz records but only black people should play jazz (a personal nod to Wynton Marsalis). And, certainly, that sort of categorizing and legitimating is what the evangelicals say about Christian music: only Christian musicians are allowed to play but every heathen should buy it, for their own soul's good, as well as the financial health of the Christian lifestyle industry. This sort of blather is all about marketing and cultural power for the purpose of enriching the enfranchised. I cannot imagine how many businessmen have become "Christians" to benefit from that status in the new economy. I cannot imagine how many new bands are emulating U2's cultural politics when one sees how piety and power produce monetary results.

I would love to see what a new Christian music would sound like. The old Christian music, the English and American hymn and psalm, has been co-opted by black churches. Maybe ending segregation of the races in the churches might bring Christian music full circle. But the new Christian lifestyle looks white to me. It is not tolerant of the religious music of other "cultures." It is not really looking to assimilate into the culture at large. It is a rebellion that hopes to win, in Vice President Dick Cheney's own words, the "culture war." If we take that threat to its extreme, then Christian rock is a movement to replace rock 'n' roll, to put a different face on the boogie man and to use it, exploit it, for everybody's own good. If Christian rock wins the "culture war," all music will be much less for it. This insight certainly colors all government attempts to tag any sort of popular music as obscene since market forces, cultural supremacy, and space in the CD racks at Wal-Mart are involved.

As for me, and I assume for many other folks, I personally do not want to be "sold" on Jesus. I do not want to be told to "listen to the message." I do not want my love of music to be turned into something that is "good for me." I especially do not want to be lulled into a state of complacency so that I can be "tricked" into salvation. The real heathens are those who exploit the joy of music for propagandistic purposes or for personal gain. Elvis wasn't the devil, but Col. Parker is certainly in the race. Jimmy Page may have dabbled in the black arts, but manager Peter Grant has a smell of sulfur about him. Ozzy Osbourne is not Beelzebub, but manager Sharon Osbourne could audition for the role. Bruce Springsteen is not an evil force, but manager Jon Landau could sell Satan on a stick (with an American flag dangling off his tail). We shouldn't confuse the rock 'n' roll lifestyle with rock 'n' roll music; we shouldn't confuse Christian lifestyle music with Christianity. Please don't confuse Jerry Falwell or Pat Robertson with Jesus. And, for God's sake, don't make Ozzy Osbourne your personal savior.

Rock 'n' roll does have a message. Pope Benedict, merely an ambitious cardinal when he spoke, had it right in the quote at the beginning of this chapter. Rock 'n' roll is about liberation. Like Neil Young says, it's "rockin' in the free world." At least Pope Benedict has the courage of his convictions. I don't want him messing with my music in any case, so I thank him for rejecting it outright. It is the evangelical Christians, the Puritans, whom I resent for trying to use the freedom of rock 'n' roll to trap people into living in a self-imposed prison of self-denial and antihumanist sentiment. It's the fundamentalists who want to prevent me from hearing the music of my choosing that are the biggest threat to freedom.

But here's the rub: Christian rock, as its most conservative critics claim, is definitely opening the door for Christian kids to the larger world of experience and to liberation from sectarian views. The late British sociologist Raymond Williams once wrote about nineteenth-century attempts to introduce a "controlled" literacy into the English working classes. As he wryly observed, there is no way to teach a man to read the Bible that won't allow him to read the radical press (Williams 1974). There is no way to listen to Christian music that won't make the listener more likely to accept other *musical* experience. Maybe that's one of the reasons why the board of the National Association of Evangelicals, "an umbrella group representing 60 denominations and dozens of ministries, passed a resolution deploring 'the epidemic of young people leaving the evangelical church'" (Goodstein 2006).

So, Christian rock is a problematic marketing tool, a slippery slope for the Christian lifestyle. If kids are going to listen to rock music anyway, the Christian pastor says, then they are better off listening to praises of God than stories of sexual conquest, or drug experiences, or the joy of racing down the highway with your girl by your side. That's the devil talking, brothers and sisters. The message is in the beat, in the tension and release of the rhythm, in the pure ecstatic joy of the human voice in harmony. The words don't mean a thing—your kids are in the moment of ecstasy. Ain't no going back after that.

But, that's religious experience: pure ecstasy. God gave rock 'n' roll to you (Russ Ballard of Argent wrote that; Kiss made it an anthem). The words we sing are all from humans. We need to listen to God and not to the inarticulate ramblings of humans. Almost postironically, the song "Cum on Feel the Noize," written by the clownish Noddy Holder and covered on recordings by three of the most incomprehensible, incoherent, and inarticulate bands in the history of popular music (i.e., Slade, Quiet Riot, and Oasis), says it all for rock music. And, well beyond any irony, Gene Simmons says that "Noize's" classic vision inspired Kiss's sine qua non, "Rock and Roll All Nite." The Lord works in mysterious ways.

The beauty of the above songs is the sheer joy of their "antimessage": have fun and be happy, or, in other words, shut up and dance. Maybe that is evil to some people. Under those rules, the "message" of Christian rock is as evil as any other message that seeks to use the power of music to control behavior. Rock 'n' roll never forgets, even the cognitive scientists agree. Not experiencing music can affect cognitive development and probably social development. Anyone who has ever met someone who doesn't enjoy music knows that from experience anyway.

I have nothing against God or Jesus or Allah or any other object of worship. I am, to quote Albert Einstein, a "deeply religious non-believer." I just cannot believe that some half-educated popular preacher or musician is my path to salvation. On second thought, that probably makes me a Roman Catholic. I also have no problem with musicians singing about God. I don't think Van

Morrison wants to trick me into being a Christian anymore than he wants to trick me into being Irish. The same goes for U2. I also don't think that guy who used to be Cat Stevens wants to trick me into being a Muslim either. When he first became a Muslim, he quit music because of its role as the tool of the devil; he must have realized how foolish that was and is now back recording.

I admire people who make music, and I love people who love music. Music changes people, but nobody has any control over that, as both Pope Benedict XVI and cognitive science agree. And truthfully, having sat through the reality show about the Osbournes, can anyone believe that Osbourne has any plans for mind control or that the devil would be in cahoots with a man who can barely manage to get from the kitchen to the bedroom without stepping in dog poo?

But I am impressed with Osbourne because of his unrelenting joy in making music. I am impressed as well with his dominant-culture, media-created doppelganger, George W. Bush, a born-again leader of a great empire and a recovered alcoholic and drug abuser, who pretends to be a simple man of the people. Bush enjoys music while he is exercising (and maybe at other times), which says something important about him. It doesn't matter who sings the songs or if the music is from old recordings. It doesn't matter that he allowed his spokespeople to present his music dismissively as merely something functional to get over the next hill. At least he listens to music.

Metaphorically speaking, music *is* a way to get over the next hill. Everyday, music gets us over the next hill. When former President Bush is listening to his iPod, riding his mountain bike, you know he's in touch with the Almighty. He may hear country legend George Jones "sangin'" about the difficulties of life, a small tear shed for the greater glory that awaits. But George Jones's words disappear into a sad wailing, a cool wind of loneliness and fear deeply imbedded in traditional country music. And he knows, as Jesus said, "The Kingdom of God is within you." The message is all there in the music.

References

Bosman, Julie. 2006. "Christian message, secular messengers." *New York Times*, April 26, C13.

Boyer, Peter. 2006. "Hollywood heresy." *New Yorker*, May 22, 34–39.

Edwards, Gavin. 1995. *'Scuse me while I kiss this guy*. Palmer, AK: Fireside Books.

Goodstein, Laurie. 2006. "Fearing the loss of teenagers, evangelicals turn up the fire." *New York Times*, October 6, A1, A20.

Leeds, Jeff. 2005. "Marketing of 'Narnia' presents challenge." *New York Times*, October 12, E1, E7.

Leland, John. 2005. "An evangelical comic provokes holy laughter." *New York Times*, September 17, B7, B13.

Llewellyn, Ric. 2007. *Christian? Rock.* Fundamental Evangelistic Association, www.feasite.org/Tracts/fbccrock.htm (accessed September 5, 2008).

Meisel, Rick. 1999. "Christian" rock music. Biblical Discernment Ministries, www.rapidnet.com/~jbeard/bdm/Psychology/rockm/satanic.htm (accessed September 5, 2008).

Norman, Larry. 2008. www.larrynorman.com (accessed September 5, 2008).

Prial, Dunstan. 2006. *The producer: John Hammond and the soul of American music.* New York: Farrar, Straus, and Giroux.

Sanford, David. 2005. "Farewell, Larry Norman." *Christianity Today*, www.christianitytoday.com/music/news/2005/larrynorman.html (accessed September 5, 2008).

Sisario, Ben. 2006. "Listening to rock and hearing sounds of conservatism." *New York Times*, May 25, E3.

Wexler, Jerry, and David Ritz. 1994. *Rhythm and the blues: A life in American music.* New York: St. Martin's.

Wild One, The. 1953. Directed by Laszlo Benedek. Culver City, CA: Stanley Kramer Productions.

Wilkinson, Peter. 2005. "Bush bares soul with 'iPod One.'" CNN.com, April 13, www.cnn.com/2005/SHOWBIZ/Music/04/12/bush.ipod (accessed September 5, 2008).

Williams, Raymond. 1974. *The long revolution.* New York: Greenwood Press Reprint.

X

Crossover Christian Rock and the Music Industry

Tendencies, Discourses, and Limitations

SILVIA GIAGNONI

In February 2006, I had an interview with John Styll, former editor in chief and founder of *CCM* magazine and now president of the Gospel Music Association. Styll received me in his office in Nashville, surrounded by a plethora of platinum and golden discs hanging there to show the achievements of the Contemporary Christian Music (CCM) that today the organization chaired by Styll represents.

In the interview we discussed the current status of the Christian rock industry with specific attention to the subject matter of my research, the phenomenon of crossover. It was my opinion then (and it is even more so now) that the increased number of crossover Christian hits in the mainstream charts signaled an important change in the industry and in society at large. *Nothing Is Sound*, 2005's Columbia album by alternative crossover Christian rock act Switchfoot, peaked at number five on the Billboard 200 chart,[1] and a single from *The Beautiful Letdown*, "Meant to Live," scored a number eighteen the year before, hitting good positions with singles on the Modern Rock or Mainstream Rock charts. Later that year, Metalcore band Underoath released *Define the Great Line* (June 20, 2006), which debuted on the Billboard 200 chart at number two. The album sold ninety-eight thousand copies in its first week and was certified gold by the Recording Industry Association of America (RIAA). After over thirty years of existence in a separate market, today Christian rock is able to compete with other genres in the mainstream market. During our conversation, John Styll succinctly, yet aptly, explained this phenomenon as follows: "the system is now wired for success" (personal communication, February 16, 2006).

Furthermore, since September 11, there has been a resurgence of spirituality and religion in popular culture geared to meet the needs of a shocked nation in search of reassurance and answers, and there has been a more favorable political climate with a born-again president in the White House who has supported an augmented presence of religion and, specifically, a brand of Christianity that better supports neoliberalism (conservative evangelicalism) in the public sphere.

Another reason for increased crossover incursions into the mainstream charts is related to the general, recent, and dramatic demise in album sales that has occurred in the music industry. As Jeff Leeds reports in the *New York Times* online, "In the shift from CDs to digital music, buyers can now pick the individual songs they like without having to pay upward of $10 for an album. . . . Sales of albums, in either disc or digital form, have dropped more than 16 percent so far this year." Indeed, Christian rock has been favored by this business conjuncture as it has a strong, solid fan base that goes to buy the album in the first week the record comes out, thus pushing it up in the charts.

In attempting to show how Christian bands have been able to cross over successfully, I investigate the systematic market fragmentation in the music industry and its use of cross-media marketing strategies that allow crossover Christian bands to succeed in both the Christian and the secular arenas, the role of the Christian-oriented label Tooth and Nail, and the longtime role of the Cornerstone Festival in creating an alternative scene for Christian rock artists. I conclude by pointing to both the present and inherent limits that contain the expansion of this ideological genre.

To begin with, the phenomenon of relatively small Christian labels owned by corporate majors is not a new one; it actually dates back to the 1970s. Myrrh had a joint agreement with A&M and Sparrow Records with MCA. In fact, as Keith Negus illustrates in *Music Genres and Corporate Cultures,*

> The absorption of independent labels has been a feature of the music business throughout the twentieth century and has become increasingly

> institutionalized through a series of joint ventures, production, licensing, marketing and distribution deals which have led to the blurring of the "indie"/"major" organizational distinctions and belief systems. (1999, 35)

And there is more. Sparrow Records, one of the major Christian music labels, was founded by Billy Ray Hearn in 1976 after he left Word. In 1992, EMI bought Sparrow and, soon after, Star Sound Records[2] and Forefront Records, and later other Christian sublabels such as Re:think and Credential Records. Before retiring, Hearn helped create EMI Christian Music Group (EMI CMG), which was established in 1994.[3] As we read on the website, the manifest scope of this division is to "impact popular culture and resource the church with music and related content and services with a biblical world view." In 1997, Charlie Peacock's Re:think was bought by Sparrow Records and became part of EMI CMG. With a widespread formula that comprises the needs of both the artists and the industry, the group is now responsible for the label's artistic development, sales, and marketing activities, whereas the label (Re:think) concentrates on the talent side of management. "With this type of deal," Chris York, artists and repertoire specialist for EMI CMG, told me, "alternative Christian albums make it into mainstream outlets—Wal-Marts, Targets, and Best Buy" (personal communication, April 22, 2006). Columbia Records,[4] a recording label now owned by the corporate group Sony BMG, signed Switchfoot to Red Ink in 2003 from Re:think (EMI CMG). Word Records, which sells primarily in the CCM market with worship and Christian acts, was distributed in the general market by A&M Records from 1984 until 1990, then switched to Epic Records until 2002 when Word Entertainment Group, then part of Gaylord Entertainment, was sold off to Time Warner. Word Records and its sublabels are now part of the Warner Music Group. Therefore, the majors have control today over most of the Christian rock industry; thus, they are interested in pushing this genre as well.

However, the type of marketing deployed to promote these Christian rock acts is not always accepted by these bands. Case in point is indie rock group Mute Math.[5] Mute Math released their debut album *Reset EP* in September 2004 for the band's own label, Teleprompt Records. Mute Math, a successful crossover Christian rock band, had been featured in *PopStar* and *Spin* magazines and had already made live appearances on MTV and ABC (*Jimmy Kimmel Live*). In early 2006, Teleprompt sued Warner Brothers Records for breach of contract and negligent misrepresentation in the promotion of the band. The major's misdeed? Warner had promoted Mute Math as a Christian act. The lawsuit was settled out of court along with a new contract with Warner Music Group. Negus aptly illustrates the functioning of the music industry:

> Whatever decision is made *generically* . . . will have a determining influence on everything that happens to the performer or record thereafter . . . and once signed, once labeled, musicians will thereafter be expected to play and look certain ways; decisions about recording sessions, promotional photos, record jackets, press interview, video styles, and so on, will all be taken with genre rules in mind. The marketing and packaging policies, in other words, that begin the moment an act is signed are themselves determined by genre theories, by accounts of how markets work and what people with tastes for music *like this* want from it. (1999, 176, emphasis added)

Alternative rock act Mute Math did not want to be pigeonholed and confined into the Christian market. This position is widespread among the majority of Christian rock bands today; to be labeled as Christian limits (or even nullifies) both their evangelizing endeavors (it does not make sense to preach to the choir) and their hopes for being appreciated and succeeding *as rock bands* in the mainstream. However, Mute Math's reaction to Warner Brothers Records's marketing signals the often uneasy relationship between major and independent labels.

On the other hand, the market fragmentation allows the majors to better target these artists in the two markets (Christian and so-called secular), but it has also favored their crossover and, most importantly, the consequent blurring of the two scenes. One way this has occurred is through the presence of Christian rock songs in popular movies. Recording companies have widely deployed cross-media marketing strategies that have contributed to the crossover of Christian rock bands into the general market.[6] This move on the part of the industry suggests a serious investment in these bands. Indeed, as Andrew Leyshon and others point out, "The use of music within advertising or within motion picture or television soundtracks can be the signal for a significant increase in CD sales, often outstripping the sales of artists being promoted through conventional marketing channels" (2005, 183). The synergy between the movie and recording industries is common practice in today's integrated media markets.[7] If Sixpence None the Richer's "Kiss Me" was released by indie Christian label Squint Entertainment and represented a one-time crossover incursion—the song was then featured in a series of movies and TV shows (the first episode of *Grey's Anatomy* and movies like *She's All That* and *Be Cool*)—recent releases of crossover Christian acts have been accurately planned according to synergetic cross-media marketing. Let's take P.O.D. One of the best-selling artists for Atlantic Records, the band released "Sleeping Awake" on May 26, 2003, for Madonna's Maverick Records.[8] The track was included in the film *The Matrix Reloaded* by the Wachowski brothers, which opened the same month. The following November, *Payable on Death* was released for Atlantic Records and soon certified gold. Although "Sleeping Awake" was added to the album as a bonus track only for some European records, the long-awaited sequel of *The Matrix* undoubtedly helped the album's sales in the general market. On the other hand, the presence of P.O.D. further suggests Christian connotations for a movie that already presents messianic themes. Likewise, the song "Satellite [Oakenfold Remix]" was included in *The Tomb Raider: Cradle of Life* sound track that came out in July 2003. Most significantly, in August 2004, "Truly Amazing" was on the album *The Passion of The Christ: Songs*, a collection of songs inspired by the favorite evangelical blockbuster, which includes tracks by Christian artists such as former Creed vocalist Scott Stapp ("Relearn Love"), Kirk Franklin ("How Many Lashes"), MxPx ("Empire," featuring Mark Hoppus), Big Dismal ("Rainy Day," "Reason I Live"), and BeBe Winans and Angie Stone ("Miracle of Love"). *Daredevil*, released in February 2003, was another movie that had Nappy Roots featuring Marcos Curiel from P.O.D. in "Right Now" and Evanescence's hits "Bring Me to Life" and "My Immortal."

Another example of cross-media marketing is Christian rock songs featured in prime-time TV series, such as Kutless's song "All of the Words," which was heard on the NBC show *Scrubs*.[9] For crossover Christian rock artists, this represents a major achievement and assumes religious connotations as James Mead, guitarist for Kutless, excitedly told me:

> It [*All of the Words*] played for almost two minutes unedited, and the song is about just praising Jesus and worship. It's a complete and blunt song about worshipping the Lord, and it played in a really climatic part of the show where there wasn't any talking or dialogue. There was just our song playing. And totally unedited, that was what went over the air

> to eight million people. So it's very cool to see the Lord opening doors for us. (Personal communication, May 13, 2006)

These cross-media practices enormously favor the mainstreaming of Christian rock insofar as they open up new venues for the bands and new listening possibilities for mainstream audiences. Thus, as Christian rock (both its sonic and discursive components) gets disseminated through the mass media, audiences are likely to assign content to the music that was unforeseen by producers.

Furthermore, as a result of these new business paradigms, new "Christian-oriented"[10] recording labels have emerged. The most successful example is surely Tooth and Nail Records, which was founded in 1993 by Brandon Ebel and soon after incorporated by EMI CMG. Tooth and Nail records are mainly distributed outside Christian outlets. If you go to Barnes & Noble or Best Buy, you will most likely find CDs by Norma Jean[11] or Anberlin[12] (two of the bands on Tooth and Nail's roster) in the rock or subgeneric section and *not* in the Christian/gospel one. However, a personal anecdote can shed light on the still undetermined generic status of these records. I was in Chicago in November 2005, and while taking a look around a general-market music store, I came across a sign reading, "Relient K is located in the Christian section," which was placed by the letter K in the rock section. Somebody, probably the store manager, must have thought he had to direct disoriented costumers.

Tooth and Nail is an example of a record label that has bet on the winning strategy of *diversification*. The Seattle-based company contains multiple sublabels, each catering to a different genre of music: Solid State Records distributes noise, metal, and hardcore bands; BEC Recordings sells to the CCM market and includes the Utah-based Uprok Records dedicated to Christian hip hop; Christian-oriented Takehold Records, which features everything from emo rock to metal, was also acquired by Tooth and Nail in 2002. In the past, other Christian artists gravitated around Tooth and Nail; for instance, the electronic, pop-oriented Plastiq Musiq, created by Ronnie Martin of Joy Electric in 1997, partnered with the label in 1998 and 1999. Although Tooth and Nail has today gained the respect of the indie music industry, its Christian orientation has defined, for good and for bad, the label's identity since the beginning. The sublabels generally license most of their titles to Tooth and Nail Records for marketing and distribution. The label's founder, Brandon Ebel, has understood that the music industry is not merely a site of production:

"genre provides a way of linking the question of music (what does it sound like?) to the question of its market (who will buy it?)" (Beaujon 2006, 73). The diversification strategy of Tooth and Nail has provided "a way of viewing the company's labels, genres, and artists by dividing them into discrete units (strategic business units) . . . spreading its risks across various musical genres and potential sources of income" (Negus 1999, 47).

A very different outcome befell Squint Entertainment, the indie label founded by alternative Christian rock artist Steve Taylor and financed by Word Records. After the booming success of Sixpence None the Richer, the label started to fall apart, creating problems for the band in the release of its second album. Word laid off Squint when Sixpence was still accruing a lot of consensus in the general market. Steve Taylor told his version of the story at a press conference at the Cornerstone Festival in 2003. Reportedly, the withdrawal of the financial support was due to a change in management at Word; a country executive took Roland Lundy's place and started asking Taylor questions about Squint's diversification strategies. At that time, the label was promoting Sixpence None the Richer along with the rock act Chevelle and hip hop act L.A. Symphony. Taylor was refused the autonomy in running the label previously granted to him by Lundy, who had now compromised with the new management. So, the label faced bankruptcy, thus threatening the rising career of Sixpence.

Today, the corporate music industry often argues that the Internet ruined the industry as an excuse for investing in a narrower roster of artists; this is an updated version of an argument that has circulated since the 1970s when cassette-recording technology came out (at the time the mantra in the industry was "home taping was killing the music"). The truth is, selections in the music industry are made according to commercial judgments and cultural assumptions, which are suppositions about audiences.

The music business is always on the lookout for new cultural trends in the industry and in society at large:

> Which artists will be successful and will they sustain their success? Which genres are worth investing in for the long term (or for a short period)? What are the up-coming future musical trends likely to be—and does the company have skills (artists, staff) and structures (distribution and promotional) to be able to deal with them? (Negus 1999, 32)

These are some of the questions people in the industry ask themselves before investing in the artists or in specific genres.

For Christian-oriented labels, following the commercial criterion also means understanding the generic boundaries as well as their inclination to shift. This scenario is defined by the massive crossover of Christian rock bands and the concurrent process of genre rearticulation. The music industry is changing in relation to the *cultural* assumptions about what rock represents in youth culture today and its concomitant role in CCM. Indeed, as Reebee Garofalo contends,

> Historically, the rock and rap axis of U.S. popular music has most often been associated with rebellion, defiance, an oppositional stance, and resistance toward authority. Post-9/11, this same music was also conscripted into the service of mourning, healing, patriotism, and nation building. At least since Elvis that was a new role for this music. (2005, 434)

Starting in the mid-1990s, alternative rock became a "cash cow" in the music industry, according to the terminology developed by the Boston Consulting Group.[13] A "cash cow" produces "sizeable profits, and with minor modifications and modest ongoing investment this category can bring in regular revenue and maintain the company's market share. Cash cows can be managed with a fairly straightforward administrative structure and standard promotional system" (Negus 1999, 48).

Most crossover Christian rock bands want to be (or present themselves as) apolitical and uncontroversial. Even when committed to humanitarian causes, they rarely question the social roots of global problems, such as poverty, hunger, or water scarcity. And they implicitly reinforce capitalistic values by failing to challenge the (religious) problem of corporations' lack of ethical responsibility.

Also, in order to cross over, Christian rock has to be "less blatantly Christian": for instance, there can't be too many references to Jesus Christ in the songs and videos or on the album covers targeting general audiences (sometimes there are different releases for the two markets). Hence, I argue that Christian rock is also becoming hegemonic to the extent that it reproduces both the mainstream imperative logic of ambiguity *and* promotes conservative cultural values.

Furthermore, having recently discovered the potential of a genre (rock) about which conservative Christian consumers have ever been suspicious, the CCM industry has made the conscious decision to invest massively in the market. Indeed, the longtime opposition to the musical form (rock as "the devil's music") is now residual within the evangelical community and confined to determined manifestations of rock that express negativity, drug abuse, and overt sexual promiscuity. Rock is to be rejected only to the extent that it is part of the "secular" character of popular culture that evangelicals are trying to transform. Rock music is today embraced and reinvented, and its central value of authenticity is reproduced, as Grossberg puts it, "in new forms, new places, in new alliances" (1992, 208–209). Otherwise, how else could we account for the growing number of churches that call on bands to play rock music inside their place of worship? Rock is used by both CCM and the mainstream industry to attract young crowds. Christian rock is no longer the bold idea of some "fundamentalist freaks," as it was in the early 1970s; now it is a widespread *practice.*

One of the reasons for such a change in strategy is that evangelicals have realized that today rock is no longer apt to accrue sentiments of protest and real opposition to the system—protest rock, for obvious reasons, is not supported by mainstream media.[14] In fact, alternative Christian rock bands have been around since the early 1970s (back then it was called Jesus rock) but have only blossomed from the mid-1990s on; in this sense, Tooth and Nail played a pivotal role in backing a lot of them and creating the indie Christian scene. Anberlin, mewithoutYou, Starflyer 59, and Underoath are just some of the bands that have had their songs played on rock radio, their albums listed on the modern rock and mainstream charts, and their videos aired on MTV and highly popular on YouTube.

If Tooth and Nail has been able to create the winning marketing strategies for crossover Christian rock acts, the Cornerstone Festival has definitely been the haven giving major crossover bands the opportunity to reach their first national audiences, P.O.D. being a case in point. The band played the New Band Stage as its first-time show out of San Diego.

Unable to perform in major "secular" venues and unsupported (if not mistreated) by traditional Christianity, a group of Christian rock musicians got together and decided to found their own festival in the attempt to create a space for these artists and their audiences. Like other Christian festivals born after Cornerstone that have attempted to recreate its successful formula, such as Sonshine (Willmar, Minnesota), Agape Music (Greenville, Illinois), Creation Festival (Northeast/Northwest), and Spirit West Coast (Monterey and Del Mar, California), Cornerstone is an "all-age" event. Entire families travel to the middle of the Illinois countryside (since 1991, the festival has been hosted by the Cornerstone Farm[15] in Bushnell, Illinois) for a week of rock music, community, and faith. No alcohol is sold at the festival, mainly "because it creates problems," as John Herrin, the festival's director, puts it; the use of illegal drugs is neither allowed nor promoted, there is no nudity, few people smoke cigarettes, and lyrics do not have explicit sexual content (personal communication, May 13, 2006). In 2006, eighteen thousand people attended the festival in Illinois, and forty-five hundred participated in the satellite event in Florida. Most significantly, as a national gathering for alternative independent Christian rock bands, the festival has become a showcase for emerging Christian rock groups and has helped create a progressive scene within CCM.[16] That's where artists-and-repertoire people go check out new acts.

Herrin explained to me that whereas about 50 percent of the bands are invited by the organization to play on the three main stages, the other 50 percent "are little bands who applied to little showcase stage, and really this is an opportunity for them to kind of show their stuff and play their music" (personal communication, May 13, 2006). For emerging Christian rock bands, to play Cornerstone means to gain what Sarah Thornton calls "subcultural capital," as it is a sort of recognition from the alternative Christian rock community: "it was like almost arriving," Scaterd Few's Allan Aguirre says in the video *Cornerstone Festival: Twenty Years and Counting.*

Cornerstone was born out of the Jesus People USA (JPUSA) experience of born-again Christians like John Herrin and Glenn Kaiser, who have worked for over thirty years in the inner city of Chicago. JPUSA supports homeless-shelter programs with low-income houses for poor families and owns a Christian school for kids from broken homes and a residence for seniors. The Jesus People community of Chicago adheres to the social gospel and the idea of doing good deeds in the community. Herrin likes to recall that Cornerstone is not just entertainment but "part of a growth process," as "at the core of what we do there's a passion to share our faith" (*Take it Back?* 2006). At Cornerstone, Christianity becomes the unifying, ideological principle not only for all the different musical subcultures but also for a variety of political and social approaches to religion: next to antiabortion group Rock for Life's booth, you can find the Revolution Church, led by Jay Bakker (son of famous televangelist James Bakker), who reaches out in pubs and bars to young social outcasts and speaks against the alliance of evangelicals with Republicans, or the booth of the Christian humanitarian organization World Vision, which is committed to helping children in need and to ending the water and food crisis. All these groups show quite different aspects of evangelical Christianity and what it means to be a Christian.

On the other hand, the dominant *weltanschauung* among young American Christians seems to combine humanitarianism with neoliberalism. An influential thinker in the Bush administration has been Roman Catholic theologian Michael Novak,[17] whose ideas of progress through neocapitalism have today become hegemonic. Novak, a strong opponent of liberation theology, also believes that poverty and social injustice in Latin America (and all over the world) can only be eliminated by expanding the neoliberal model. Today many evangelicals strive to reconcile popular culture, religion, and social change by deploying the culture of transformation par excellence (rock) to advance their version of the gospel. In light of this reformulation of Christianity, it comes as no a surprise that many Christian rock musicians seem to reconcile their humanitarian efforts with a deep belief in the capitalist system, the only one in which human creativity can truly develop, according to Novak.

As far as the music is concerned, the existence of Cornerstone further proves the vital importance of the margins to feed the mainstream. The question here is, what is the mainstream? For these musicians, more often than not, it is the Contemporary Christian Music industry, in which they will probably end up selling the majority of their records. Christian rock, indeed, has been a subculture within CCM since its establishment. In the process of mainstreaming a band (be it to the CCM or the "secular" market), Christian rock has to deal with its own generic status and its ideological boundaries. If it is crucial for evangelicals to spread the gospel and, thus, really cross over, musicians have to decide what type of compromises they are willing to make: whether or not they are going to downplay their outspokenness about Jesus and how they intend to articulate their Christianity. The case of crossover Christian rock shows the constitutive power of labeling and discourses on reality. Speaking of Christian rock uncovers the Pandora's box of what it means to be Christian in the United States, with all the attached meanings (and stereotypes) that these bands constantly struggle with.

Whether characterizing them as a big family or an endangered subculture, press treatment of Christian artists has been too soft, and rare examples of honest criticism are to be found in the evangelical press. Often sugarcoated with Christian rhetoric, the real effort has been to protect sales and maintain old-time fans of a band in a big, but segregated and ideologically defined, market. But these types of constraints—despite what Novak thinks—do not get along with the development of art and creative freedom. The difficulties experienced by musician-run labels like Re:think and Squint not only betray the usual indie/major conflicts but also signal the permanent lack of agreement about what Christian music should be, as Jay Howard and John Streck (1999) have already identified in their analysis of CCM.

Finally, new Christian journalism (*Relevant* magazine, *Risen*) today covers both Christian and non-Christian artists in the attempt to provide teenagers with *another version of popular culture,* so that they do not have to go "outside" to find it. As a matter of fact, *Relevant* produces alternative discourses around Christianity, but these discourses stem not only from a religiously grounded point of view but also from a historical and cultural context in which hegemonic definitions of Christianity are extremely conservative. Thus, its positions cannot be too progressive either. Also, as Cameron Strang, president and founder of Relevant Media Group, told me, the magazine's contributors are

> Music journalists, business leaders that we ask to ask to write about business issues, some are our age, some are not. Our average writer is probably in their upper twenties. They probably have another job and they write because it's their passion and they write about music on the side. That's probably most of our writers. Twenty-five percent of our writers are full time journalists and probably ten or fifteen percent of our writers are pastors or business leaders or people who are expert in a certain field, not about music, but about the other stuff we cover. (Personal communication, May 13, 2006)

Admittedly, the scarcity of professional expertise further demonstrates that music is primarily considered to be a tool (but doesn't the music business always consider music just a tool whose most important purpose is to make money?), a medium for reaching higher purposes (humanitarian causes, enhancement of personal and collective spirituality). *Relevant* is not just a music magazine; nor does it aspire to be. As Simon Frith reminds us, "Criticism not only produces a version of the music for the reader but also a version of the listener for the music" (1996, 68). Indeed, *Relevant* provides the Christian alternative to *Rolling Stone* or *Spin*, a filter of popular culture that also shapes audiences' expectations and attempts to fulfill their needs and desires.

However, new technologies can open up new possibilities for both audiences and artists. Indeed, some ideological limits are overcome by the emerging forms of consumption that have come to redefine the role played by traditional retailers (Christian bookstores) as gatekeepers. Howard and Streck point out,

> If an individual hopes to purchase, hear, or read about the latest album from Hawaiian Rail Company, Marty McCall, Burlap to Cashmere, Jaci Velasquez, Third Day, This Train, or any other two hundred plus artists and groups that constitute CCM, they had better head to the local Christian bookstore. Tune in to the local Christian radio station, or pick up a copy of *Contemporary Christian Music* or *True Tunes News* because they won't likely find what they're seeking on the shelves at Sam Goody or in the pages of *Rolling Stone*. (1999, 12)

Since 1999, when Howard and Streck wrote *Apostles of Rock*, a lot has changed in the music industry by virtue of the enormous advances in digital technology. This does not impinge upon Howard and Streck's more general argument, insofar as CCM is still a viable generic category and in a many ways still a subculture with countercultural aspirations. However, the Internet has created a multiplicity of venues for crossover Christian rock. It is a market in which any music fan can buy songs or records through retailers like iTunes or eMusic or directly from an unsigned band; it is a place to consume both music and video clips, at the same time that it is an interactive arena in which both artists and audiences can exchange opinions through forums, chats, and so forth via social-networking websites like MySpace.

In the digital arena, if a band is censored by Christian retailers and one is a fan of that band, one can always go to its website or MySpace page and check what the members of the band have to say on the matter, then decide whether to buy the record or not. However, the reduced power of gatekeeping seems to offer new possibilities for both Christian audiences and bands.

For homeschooled Christian kids, this truly represents a way out. Surfing the Internet looking for music they like represents a form of resistance for many Christian kids, who are thus able to escape parental control of their daily leisure activities. Most importantly, they are exposed to a variety of points of view, which incites free thinking. Homeschooling, after-school programs, Bible study groups, youth groups, and church-run organizations for "free time" can be seen as attempts to limit teenagers' moments of privacy. "Idle time is the devil's workshop," according to the youth assistant pastor (cited in Enroth et al. 1972, 97), hence the attempt to control kids and keep them out of "trouble" (drugs, alcohol, sex). The ideological underpinning that permeates these activities and defines their meanings is meant to reduce exposure to non-Christian—and, specifically, in evangelical terms, secular humanistic—views of the world. Consequently, in this new scenario, Christian bookstores no longer exercise the power they used to over the Christian rock band's artwork, lyrics, and behavior.

As Garofalo points out, the Internet also represents the "possibility of a business model that could link consumers directly with the artists and music of their choice, bypassing the record companies completely" (2005, 423). Indeed, in the corporate music business, majors profit from large sales on a few artists rather than smaller sales on larger numbers of artists. In business, the risk factor is what prevents most labels from investing a lot of money in bands on the rise when they are not sure whether they are going to fly. Like many others, St. Augustine–based experimental rock band Bernard sells its albums on the Internet and at the merchandising table at their live venues. For the record company (Floodgate Records), this represents a lower investment as the price for distribution is dramatically cut. For the fans, it results in a lower price.

Mute Math is another example of an indie rock band that has been able to hit the news by word of mouth. Mute Math uses MySpace.com and Purevolume.com as showcases for their explosive live performances. They videoblogged their single "Chaos." The band from New Orleans has sold over thirty thousand copies of *Reset*—ten thousand copies through Teleprompt's online store in the first month of its release—and have over one hundred thousand friends on MySpace.

New strategies and business models have emerged in the contemporary music industry to respond to the emergence of software formats and Internet distribution systems, as Andrew Leyshon and others illustrate (2005). Today indie bands are able to carve out their niche and record, tour, and create their music without needing a recording label. In this sense, the East Coast quintet Clap Your Hands Say Yeah is a living example that bands today can succeed even *without* the support of a record label.

However, discourses are still unquestionably important in directing audiences among the multiplicity of choices. As Roger Wallis reports in his study on the music industry in the digital era, The Internet does "provide an opportunity for suppliers of niche music genres to reach international audiences. The main challenge *concerns the choice of marketing strategies in a noisy information environment*" (2006, 304, my emphasis).

For crossover Christian bands, for instance, how to market themselves on the Web is a crucial issue. Eli Scott, songwriter and guitarist for The Awkward Romance, a band without a label that reportedly has over thirty-three thousand friends on MySpace, told me they have discussed whether to name themselves as a Christian band or not:

> We are labeled as a Christian band on MySpace and we did that with a purpose in mind. And we may change it. We have talked about it, because it does affect the way we are perceived by people. They see it's Christian, so it's just a block. They don't care about it, they won't listen to us.

Whereas Christian radio still seems to be quite conservative as it caters to an older audience (and Christian and "secular" radio stations remain separate),[18] online radio networks are flourishing as well. For instance, RadioU.com and TVUlive.com, part of the nonprofit Spirit Communications, are examples of these new trends. Finally, the tax-exempt status of churches, religious organizations, and some of these media groups (Cornerstone Communications, Spirit Communications) that support and promote Christian rock further acts to facilitate the genre's development.

In sum, I have shown how commercial, technological, and cultural changes are affecting the current discourses around Christianity and rock and thus contributing to the crossover of Christian rock bands. I have also illustrated how cross-media practices aid the process of crossing over for Christian rock as they open up new venues for both musicians and listeners. The practice of scoring movies and TV shows is contributing to further blurring the division between Christian and secular rock and facilitating the incorporation of Christian fragments into the mainstream culture. New technologies have favored new forms of distribution and consumption, and these have challenged the role of traditional gatekeepers. Even though crossover Christian rock still needs to deal with its own ideological boundaries, it seems destined to grow. As Styll said, "The system is now wired for success."

Notes

1. Whereas the Hot 100 chart is more heavily weighted to radio play than to sales, Billboard 2000 represents the mainstream album chart and reflects the bulk of sales (Garofalo, *Rockin'*, 453).

2. In 1994, Star Song was acquired by EMI. In 1998 the label was dedicated to reissuing reprints.

3. Starting from the early 1990s, under the direction of new CEO and president Jim Fifield, Thorn-EMI went through a process of restructuring. EMI Music purchased Chrysalis Records, SBK, and, most importantly, Virgin Records.

4. Columbia Records comprises Epic Records, Columbia Classical, Nashville Records, Legacy Recordings, and Sony Wonder.

5. Mute Math plays a mix of genres, which includes ambient, arena rock, indie and experimental, and electro rock.

6. "The perceived advantage of cross-selling music on the back of other cultural artifacts . . . was one of the main drivers behind the construction of the large media conglomerates, of which many of the leading record companies are now a part" (Leyshon et al., "On the Reproduction," 183).

7. Today, *Pop Stars, American Idol,* and other similar shows have proved how marketing comes even *before* production in the music business.

8. Before that, P.O.D. contributed to the sound track of the movie *Any Given Sunday* featuring Al Pacino with the songs "Bless Me Father," and "Whatever It Takes," also released on certain international versions of *Satellite* and *The Fundamental Elements of Southtown.*

9. As reported on CCM in May 2006, "The March 28 episode of NBC's *Scrubs* underscored an especially tear-jerking, touchy-feely moment with the decidedly evangelical track 'All of the Words' by Kutless. In fact, these lyrics just jumped right

out of the screen: 'By your grace you let me come talk to you / It's not that I'm worthy / I thank you Jesus for the love that you have shown.'"

10. Christian labels are different from Christian-oriented labels as the latter feature some non-Christian acts.

11. Norma Jean is a crossover Christian metal core group. The Georgia-based band was nominated for Best Recording Package at the 2006 Grammy Awards.

12. Anberlin is an alternative rock crossover Christian band from Orlando, Florida.

13. Negus observes, "Strategic calculation is built on a desire for stability, predictability and containment" (1999, 52).

14. For instance, the compilation album *Peace Not War* featuring Public Enemy, Midnight Oil, Ani DiFranco, Sleater Kinney, and Chumbawamba did not do well also for lack of airplay and appropriate promotion.

15. Jesus People USA (JPUSA) has recently purchased the land on which the festival takes place every summer.

16. Other similar events have been created recently as showcases for emerging Christian bands: Gospel Music Association's Music in the Rockies in Colorado and America's Christian Music Showcase (ACMS).

17. Novak has created a religious common ground for social conservatives, libertarians, and the Christian Right. After being awarded "Favorite Democrat of the Year" by the Republican Party in 1976, Novak became a supporter of Ronald Reagan and one of the most influential neocon political intellectuals of the last thirty years. Novak's work has been geared toward bringing religion into the public square. For instance, Novak helped found the Institute of Religion and Democracy. He is also a well-funded scholar with the American Enterprise Institute (AEI). This political and intellectual theologian's three decades of theoretical work have provided the moral, ethical, and theological justifications for American capitalist culture.

18. Some Christian rock artists are played on Christian radio (among these, Third Day, Switchfoot, and Reliant K), but emerging musicians often complain that Christian radio does not take risks and only plays "approved" and "safe" Christian acts. The Gospel Music Association has an important influence when it comes to determining the status of an artist within the industry.

References

Beaujon, Andrew. 2006. *Body piercing saved my life: Inside the phenomenon of Christian rock*. Cambridge, MA: Da Capo Press.

Brown, Steven, and Ulrik Volgsten, eds. 2006. *Music and manipulation: On the social uses and social control of music.* New York: Berghahn Books.

Enroth, Ronald M., Edward E. Ericson Jr., and C. Breckinridge Peters. 1972. *The Jesus people: Old-time religion in the Age of Aquarius.* Grand Rapids, MI: William B. Eerdmans Publishing Co.

Frith, Simon. 1996. *Performing rites: On the values of popular music.* Cambridge, MA: Harvard University Press.

Garofalo, Reebee. 2005. *Rockin' out: Popular music in the USA.* 3rd ed. Boston: Prentice Hall.

Grossberg, Lawrence. 1992. *We gotta get out of this place: Popular conservatism and postmodern culture.* New York: Routledge.

Howard, Jay R., and John M. Streck. 1999. *Apostles of rock: The splintered art world of contemporary Christian music.* Lexington: University Press of Kentucky.

Leeds, Jeff. 2007. The album, a commodity in disfavor. *New York Times,* March 26, www.nytimes.com/2007/03/26/business/media/26music.html?_r=1&oref=slogin.

Leyshon, Andrew, Peter Webb, Shaun French, Nigel Thrift, and Louise Crewe. 2005. On the reproduction of the musical economy after the Internet. *Media, Culture & Society* 27, no. 2: 177–209.

Negus, Keith. 1999. *Music genres and corporate cultures.* New York: Routledge.

Swartzendruber, Jay. 2006. State of the chart. *CCM* 6 (May).

Thornton, Sarah. 1996. *Club cultures: Music, media and subcultural capital.* Middletown, CT: Wesleyan University Press.

Wallis, Roger. 2006. The changing structure of the music industry: Threats to and opportunities for creativity. In *Music and manipulation: On the social uses and social control of music,* ed. Steven Brown and Ulrik Volgsten, 286–311. New York: Berghahn Books.

Albums

Mute Math. 2004. *Reset* (EP). Teleprompt/Warner Bros.

Sixpence None the Richer. 2003. *Kiss me.* Warner/Reprise.

Switchfoot. 2000. *Learning to breathe.* Re:think.

_______. 2003. *The beautiful letdown.* Red Ink/Columbia.

_______. 2005. *Nothing is sound.* Columbia Records.

Underoath. 2006. *Define the great line.* Solid State Records.

Various artists. 2003. *Daredevil: The album.* Wind-up Records.

_______. 2004. *The Passion of The Christ: Songs* (original songs inspired by the film). Lost Keyword.

Videos

Take it back? Evangelical Christianity & popular music. 2006. Directed by Silvia Giagnoni and Eleonora Orlandi. Italy/USA (available from Silvia Giagnoni, Auburn University, Montgomery, Department of Communication and Dramatic Arts, PO Box 2444023, Montgomery, AL 36124-4023).

The Cornerstone Festival: Twenty years and counting. 2004. Directed by Jeremy Gudauskas. United States: Generation One.

XI

Christotainment in Punk Rock

Complexities and Contradictions

CURRY STEPHENSON MALOTT

Religion is not simply a topic among topics but the driving force of American history. . . . [W]ithout close attention to Protestant Christianity it is impossible to make sense of our past. . . . The Protestant Passion, the insatiable desire to redeem mankind from sin and error . . . has been manifest in a variety of forms. . . . While the great majority of professing Christians belonged to particular sects or denominations . . . many were stoutly and sometimes stridently opposed to the churches. This was perhaps most strikingly the case with the abolitionists. . . . Generally speaking, however, their weight fell on the side of political and social conservatism. The theological emphasis was on personal piety, good works, and individual salvation. The tendency was to ratify the existing order and support, without qualification, the sanctity of private property.

—P. Smith (1984, 554–555)

As we engage in a study of Christotainment and what has proven to be its democratic *and* antidemocratic interventions in contemporary cultural contexts, it is worth noting that the Christianity brought to the Americas in the fifteenth and sixteenth centuries tended to be informed by a colonialist authoritarianism and the divine right to rule, which is an ancient European tradition whose current structures, in both its Catholic and Protestant manifestations, can be traced back to the hierarchal and "temporal organization" of the Roman Empire, the westernmost provinces of which extended into the heart of northern Europe (Diop 1987). In other words, Europeans brought to the Americas the basic idea that the king is the king and the world is his domain because God said so (Malott 2008). However, according to Donald A. Grinde in "Iroquois Political Theory and the Roots of American Democracy" (1992) many of the "founding fathers" of the United States, Benjamin Franklin most notably, rejected this European model, drawing instead on the brilliance of the Iroquois system of shared governance designed to ensure democracy and peace by putting power and decision making in the hands of the people united in a confederation of nations and not in the divine right of a ruler. Despite the eventual corruption of the United States and the forceful resurrection of the Columbian pedagogy of conquest and plunder, which, it can be argued, was never completely subverted (Malott 2008), many non–Native Americans, such as the abolitionists of the mid-nineteenth century among countless others, have continued to hold on to the indigenous ideals of democracy, freedom, and liberty (Grinde 1992; Smith 1984).

The content of the present chapter underscores one incredibly complex location at which this antagonistic relationship between democracy (counterhegemony) and authoritarianism (hegemony) has manifested itself—that is, in the culture war between conservatives and progressive to radical artists in the underground punk rock music scene. In what follows, I examine various manifestations of counterhegemonic Christotainment in punk rock. As argued below, Christotainment is defined broadly here as including all songs that are Christian-centered, even if they are anti-Christian. From this interpretive framework, we can say that there exists a dual continuum within Christotainment. On one hand there exists a continuum from radical to conservative. At the same time, there exists a continuum of time spent engaged in the terrain of Christotainment. For example, at one extreme are artists whose whole identity is situated within Christotainment and at the other are artists who rarely flirt with Christotainment, perhaps recording one song that deals with the subject matter. Above all else, this analysis demonstrates the complex and contradictory nature of social production and reproduction and the multiple challenges for counterhegemonic movement (Malott and Peña 2004).

As alluded to in the above quote, P. Smith (1984) locates the primary difference between competing approaches to American Christianity in the way the nature of sin is articulated, which demonstrates the difference between a democratic perspective and one based on hierarchical mysticism. In other words, are those in poverty simply suffering the wrath of God by paying for their inherent weakness and bad habits, or are they "more sinned against than sinning" (Smith 1984, 562)? Following Smith, we begin with the recognition that religion has been put to use both as a tool of coercion and as a vehicle for justice. The interest here is in uncovering both the hegemonic and counterhegemonic tendencies within the contemporary manifestations of Christotainment in punk rock. Because leaders within the Christian Right began a holy culture war against that music most outside the control of corporate influence and regulation during the 1980s, this chapter briefly looks at the attempts to silence the spaces of underground, transgressive culture as the context in which independent punk rockers have developed their own underground, counterhegemonic versions of Christotainment—the primary emphasis here. First, however, I quickly outline the larger context that gave way to the current wave of fundamentalism.

THE LARGER CONTEXT

In her classic text *Religion: The Social Context* (1992), M. McGuire situates the emergence of the most recent surge of Christian fundamentalism in the United States as a direct response *by the bosses* to the "social and political turmoil of the 1960s and 1970s" (McGuire 1992, 218) that led to civil rights legislation and the desegregation of schools (Marsden 2006). As the bosses have consciously devised new methods of plundering the earth and extracting value from human labor power, an increasing number of the world's people have entered the ranks of the poor, the impoverished, and the pissed off. Scared of the swelling tides of discontent, the ruling class continues to draw on whatever tactics it has at its disposal to keep the masses in line, such as fear. What has proven especially effective in keeping people scared and in line? Religion. The war launched by Tipper Gore and continued by Joe Lieberman and Lynne Cheney, for example, against underground cultures not only reflects how scared elites are of their own populations but the extent to which fundamentalism has influenced mainstream politics.

What is the ruling elites scared of? They fear what the billions of people around the world whom they use and abuse everyday have done and are doing to end their own suffering. Again, this is not a new fear. It is not a secret to the powers that be that people are not as stupid as they would have us believe we are. In the United States, the ruling class can only wish working people were as dumb as the schools are designed to make them, to paraphrase Jello Biafra (1991). Contextualizing the ruling class's cultural attack on the poor and oppressed in the United States, Biafra (1998) argues that, ultimately, this campaign, outlined below, is an attempt to silence the spokespersons of an increasingly disgruntled populous.

Before we proceed with our discussion on Christotainment, let us pause for a moment to consider how fundamentalism has been defined and characterized by leading scholars in the field of religious studies. According to George Marsden in *Understanding Fundamentalism and Evangelicalism,*

> An American fundamentalist is an evangelical who is militant in opposition to liberal theology in the churches or to changes in cultural values or mores, such as those associated with secular "humanism." Fundamentalists are a subtype of evangelicals and militancy is crucial to their outlook. Fundamentalists are not just religious conservatives, they are conservatives who are willing to take a stand and fight. (1991, 1)

Marsden puts special emphasis on the militancy of fundamentalists. It is precisely this militancy, what we might call right-wing activism, that has made fundamentalism such a powerful tool for mobilizing against those proclaimed to be enemies of God. However, the relative success of the fundamentalists cannot be attributed solely to their militancy. Such militancy would be useless if it were not for the movement's anti-intellectualism, evidenced by such absurd propositions as blaming teen suicide and gang violence on rock 'n' roll and rap/hip hop music. Anti-intellectualism has been a defining characteristic of fundamentalism throughout its history. Marsden argues in his critically acclaimed *Fundamentalism and American Culture* (2006) that since at least the first half of the twentieth century, fundamentalists have been accused of being ignoramuses and bigots, who are against reason, overly emotional, and motivated by a desire to support, without question, the status quo.

As a result, the right-wing fundamentalist religious movement has been widely critiqued as nothing more than a ruse to foster civil obedience among an increasingly impoverished, miseducated, alienated, and disgruntled citizenry. Commenting on the irony of this use of Christianity, Mumia Abu-Jamal, himself a victim of severe state censorship, comments,

> Isn't it odd that Christendom—that huge body of humankind that claims spiritual descent from the Jewish carpenter of Nazareth—claims to pray to and adore a being who was a prisoner of Roman power, an inmate on the empire's death row? That the one it considers the personification of the Creator of the Universe was tortured, humiliated, beaten, and crucified on a barren scrap of land on the imperial periphery, at Golgatha, the place of the skull? That the majority of its adherents strenuously support the state's execution of thousands of imprisoned citizens? That the overwhelming majority of its judges, prosecutors, and lawyers—those who condemn, prosecute, and sell out the condemned—claim to be followers of the fettered, spat-upon, naked God? (1997, 39)

Is it not also odd that an increasing number of American Christian leaders, most notably televangelist fundamentalists like Billy Graham, Jerry Falwell, and Pat Robertson, support the use of their God not only to silence the condemned, as noted above, but to condemn those who deviate from their own set of beliefs? Perhaps this phenomenon is not so much "odd" as indicative of the tendency within contemporary right-wing Christian fundamentalism, according to the late prominent theologian Vine Deloria among many others, to remain uninformed about the "actual scholarly knowledge of Jesus and his times, the nature of the Roman world, and the movement of the early church" (1994, 231) and to hold firmly to the movement's own "traditional mythologies of American life" (1994, 226)—in a word, to its anti-intellectualism. Such mythologies tend to be informed by a version of the Protestant work ethic that explains the accumulation of wealth as God's reward for those who have been *good* Christians—and a good Christian in this context is one who uncritically works hard for the bosses and tolerates no ideas or values that differ from those held by the conservative Right. The absence of historical and scholarly knowledge and the perspective it offers has enabled today's leading fundamentalists to remain secure in their ideology "because it is the idealized, law-abiding, goody-goody projections of themselves, which they call Jesus, that forms the object of their devotion" (Deloria 1994, 231).

As alluded to above, distinguishing this contemporary fundamentalism from the movement of the 1920s "is its deep involvement in mainstream national politics," with adherents currently estimated to be in the hundreds of millions (Marsden 2006, 232). Most significantly signaling the political rise of fundamentalism in the contemporary era was Ronald Reagan's successful campaign for governor of California in 1966 made possible by the support of the religious Right (Marsden 2006). President Reagan thereafter ushered in a new wave of fundamentalist-elected presidents, and in so doing marked an era of national, militant anti-intellectualism that has remained very much alive and well to the present moment. As a primary influence of Tipper Gore's campaign against popular music—a campaign based on the laughable assumption that rock music is responsible for social problems such as teen suicide, teen pregnancy, and drug use—the Ronald Reagan/George H. W. Bush era had deep ramifications with long-lasting implications.

In her book *Raising PG Kids in an X-Rated Society,* Tipper Gore notes, "President Reagan, in announcing plans for a new national strategy against illegal drugs, pointed directly to the influence of rock music on drug use" (1987, 133). In making her case, Gore quotes Reagan, who has argued essentially that rock musicians have rendered drug use socially acceptable by making their own usage public and part of their personas, thereby contributing to the increase in teen consumption and, paradoxically, to both suicide and sex. Nowhere in this discourse of sin and temptation are structural factors mentioned, such as the alienating and exploitative nature of capitalist work and consumer society, for possible explanations as to why youth might find appealing the temporary relief from the daily reality of their lives offered by some mind-altering substances. The conservatives also deny any possible benefits, such as a critical perspective on material reality, offered by a temporary change in consciousness. Rather, it is the assumed *immoral* aspects of popular culture that supposedly account for what is considered to be the deviant behavior of an easily influenced youth. It therefore follows that popular culture must be regulated to protect the children. What could be better suited for this work in an American context than the anti-intellectualism and militancy of right-wing Christian fundamentalism?

Responding to critics who contend that the Parents Music Resource Center's (PMRC) movement against music violates artists' First Amendment rights, Gore argued that they did not advocate the banning "of even the most offensive" records but, rather, sought to inform consumers of the content of their musical purchases through a labeling system designed to "protect . . . children from explicit messages that they are not mature enough to understand or deal with" (1987, 26–27). The labels reading "Parental Advisory: Explicit Lyrics" that came out of this campaign have been dubbed "Tipper stickers" by proponents of the independent music scene. Gore has commented that the success of this labeling system has provided an invaluable tool to assist parents in "avoid[ing] the twisted tyranny of explicitness in the public domain" propagated by "a few warped artists [and] their brand of rock music [that] has become a Trojan Horse, rolling explicit sex and violence into our homes" (1987, 28–29). The result of this labeling system, as we will see below, has limited the ability of small independent record labels to get their albums into the large chain stores, keeping them out of the hands of the majority of Americans who live outside the large urban centers.

The view of the world endorsed by Christian fundamentalism, its axiology and ontology, for example, by definition, has made the movement personally responsible for eradicating all competing philosophical perspectives. In the realm of popular music, the fundamentalist axiology (concerning what is good and bad) is based on the assumption that Paul McCartney of the Beatles and Mike Love of the Beach Boys are *good* because they, like Tipper, are "disturbed by the entertainment industry's penchant for the violent and explicit"; the Dead Kennedys and Prince, on the other hand, are *bad* because they represent the "moral and artistic decline of American entertainment" (Gore 1987, 167). The ontological (concerning the nature of being and existence) perspective behind these axiological assumptions is that God is the center of the universe and the white, middle-class, puritanical culture of many fundamentalist leaders represents the highest level of moral development, rendering its adherents responsible for forcing it on the rest of humanity. However, this work of God has not proven too glamorous to be mediated by market mechanisms.

Not only have the fundamentalists gone after music and alternative culture through laws and legislation, but they continue to use media in an attempt to scare kids away from the evils of devil music, such as heavy metal, punk rock, and rap/hip hop. The roughly thirty-year-old "Hell House" phenomenon, popularized by Jerry Falwell, stands as a scary example of right-wing, fundamentalist Christotainment and illustrates how fundamentalists use scare tactics to foster adherence to strict dogma regarding behavior and belief. At hundreds of active Hell Houses in service during Halloween in North America, "audiences" are led through a number of scenes, acted out by real people right before their very eyes, designed to highlight the consequences (which always entail going to hell and suffering for eternity) of abortion, gay marriage, homosexuality in general, teaching evolution in school, and listening to rap, heavy metal, and punk music, for example. As we will see below, these outrageous fundamentalist claims have provided the underground punk music scene's *push back* with a seemingly unlimited supply of material for counterhegemonic Christotainment.

THE COUNTERHEGEMONIC PUSH BACK

Again, one of the unintended consequences of the censorship campaign spearheaded in the 1980s by Tipper Gore has been the manifestation of counterhegemonic Christotainment as an unofficial campaign informing the public about recent trends in Christian fundamentalism. For example, the publication of Biafra's first spoken word album marked the beginning of a new kind of punk record, the lecture/commentary, which effectively deepened the democratic impulses of Alternative Tentacles and the punk movement more generally. Milagros Peña and I document the development of these trends in our book *Punk Rockers' Revolution: A Pedagogy of Race, Class, and Gender* (2004), which analyzes message trends over time on three record labels, Alternative Tentacles, SST, and Epitaph. What follows is an updated summary of our findings, focusing on Alternative Tentacles, which underscores the contemporary relevance of punk as a counterhegemonic force.

Theoretically, our study rejected a commonly held belief among Frankfurt School theorists such as Theodor Adorno and Max Horkheimer who argued that popular culture is an embodiment of the ideas, values, and beliefs of the dominant culture and therefore has no redeeming qualities. We were equally dissatisfied with the romantic idea that subcultures like punk rock are not affected by the hegemony that permeates the dominant society and therefore manifest themselves as pure forms of counterhegemony. What drew our attention were more complex understandings of cultural reproduction and production in the theories of resistance found in the work of scholars like Paul Willis (1977) and his groundbreaking study of student resistance.

For me, Paulo Freire's many books provide the most comprehensive theoretical context for understanding the complex and contradictory nature of this phenomenon. Freire consistently argues that the goal of education in an authoritarian society (such as the United States) is to condition the minds of working people to accept their subordination as natural and inevitable. Such indoctrination is a direct attack on people's humanity, on their creativity. While these forms of manipulation are unquestionably destructive and limit the possibility for humanization, they can never be complete. In other words, while one's humanity can be limited, it can never be totally destroyed. That is, people have the capacity to become conscious of their own consciousness and therefore the potential to become revolutionaries. However, as men and women engage in the neverending process of reflection and action, their hegemonic conditioning (what they have inherited) inevitably gets in the way of what they strive to acquire, that is, counterhegemonic consciousness. When we study the consciously counterhegemonic spaces created by punk rockers, we therefore find elements of that which has been inherited, such as sexism, reemerging in that which they are attempting to acquire. The extent to which our practice is free of hegemony, generally speaking, depends on our willingness to reflect critically on ourselves and change our actions accordingly.

After scientifically analyzing message trends over time, I can say with confidence that Alternative Tentacles has become more counterhegemonic. While the amount of content coded as counterhegemonic remained relatively consistent between the 1980s and 1990s (around 80 percent), the message presenters became less white and less male. As a result of these findings, we began talking about punk rock not so much as defined by a particular musical style or aesthetic but as an increasingly democratized cultural space. As mentioned above, the spoken word record has opened up new possibilities within spaces created by punk rockers. Alternative Tentacles, in collaboration with AK Press, has published dozens of such records by revolutionaries from all walks of life, from Earth First! activist Judi Bari to former Black Panther Party and Community Party USA member Angela Davis. The list of spoken word titles offered by Alternative Tentacles/AK Press speaks for itself in terms of just one area in which the label has contributed to counterhegemonic struggle. While the following list is not comprehensive, it offers an instructive representative sample:

- Noam Chomsky: The Emerging Framework of World Power; Case Studies in Hypocrisy: U.S. Human Rights Policy: Rhetoric and

Practice; New War on Terrorism; Propaganda and Control of the Public Mind

- Ward Churchill: Monkeywrenching the New World Order; In a Pig's Eye: Reflections on the Police State, Repression, and Native America
- Angela Davis: The Prison Industrial Complex
- Greg Palast: Live from the Armed Madhouse
- Robert Fisk: War, Journalism, and the Middle East
- Judi Bari: Who Bombed Judi Bari?
- Michael Parenti: Rulers of the Planet
- Mumia Abu-Jamal: All Things Censored
- Jello Biafra: If Evolution is Outlawed, Only Outlaws Will Evolve; I Blow Minds for a Living; Beyond the Valley of the Gift Police; Become the Media; In the Grip of Official Treason
- Howard Zinn: A People's History of the United States
- Jim Hightower: The People Are Revolting! (in the very best sense of the word)

Because people who are into punk rock tend to follow closely what the labels are doing, publishing lectures by Noam Chomsky, Howard Zinn, Ward Churchill, and Michael Parenti, for example, has had the effect of exposing people to ideas that they would not otherwise have encountered. It is hoped that the influencing will go both ways, leading academics to an engagement with the subjugated knowledge of the increasingly diverse community of punk rockers. The spoken word phenomenon has been an important development for Alternative Tentacles, which Biafra himself has used to expose the new and old Tippers and their PMRCs in his many "Talks on Censorship" over the years, and in so doing, he has demonstrated the connection between the fundamentalists and the White House. We can understand Biafra's work here as an example of counterhegemonic Christotainment because it is a form of entertainment (or edutainment) that takes Christian fundamentalism as its primary subject matter. What follows is a look at some recent song lyrics by various bands that serve the same counterhegemonic function in the realm of Christotainment. These songs are written and performed by left-leaning punk rockers and are therefore relatively easy to understand. However, a new subgenre of punk is more firmly grounded in Christotainment as its practitioners present themselves as Christian radical punk rockers. Bands like The Knights of the New Crusade, discussed at length below, exemplify the practice of this perspective.

Sarcastically referring to the prominent Christian leader Billy Graham's questionable professional training and subsequent theological praxis, Deloria writes that "having never attended a seminary, he did not have the opportunity to study Christian history or doctrine and had no chance to be led astray by the facts" (1994, 226). Similarly, the recent sarcasm within the song "Leaving Jesusland" (2006), by legendary punk rock band NOFX (a left-leaning band that rarely operates in the terrain of Christotainment), can be contextualized within the preceding analysis offered by Deloria (1994). In his opening verse, "Fat Mike," NOFX lead vocalist and bass player, sings,

> *We call the heartland, not very smart land*
> *IQ's generally low and threat levels are high*
> *They got a mandate, they don't want man-dates*
> *They got so many hates and people to despise*

While the message transmitted though Jesusland is clear and, as we have seen above, relatively accurate, as critical educators we are compelled to mention, if only as a side note, that associating IQ with intelligence uncritically legitimizes the often racist biases built into the tests themselves. However, the anti-intellectualism within the fundamentalist movement is well documented (Marsden 2006), and NOFX's intended message and critique therefore remain relevant. Not only does the analysis offered by NOFX and other punk bands discussed below extend our understanding of fundamentalism, but it also demonstrates the widespread opposition to restrictive dogmas within organic, cultural spaces such as those created and recreated by punk rockers—the object of attack by prominent right-wing Christian fundamentalists, explored above. At its finer moments, punk rock therefore acts as a keeper of hope, an ontological human need (Freire 1992).

The most transgressive of the small independent labels, noted above, has arguably been Jello Biafra's Alternative Tentacles (Malott and Peña 2004). Since its inception, Alternative Tentacles has consistently supported and endorsed publications that firmly transgress the basic structures of power and challenge conservative values of intolerance (Malott and Peña 2004). What becomes apparent is that Biafra has spent a considerable amount of time challenging and rewriting the curriculum of Christotainment. However, Biafra's identity as an artist is not situated within the domain of Christotainment, but some of the artists on his label, highlighted below, are. In "Jesus Was a Terrorist" by Jello Biafra with Nomeansno (1991), Biafra, operating in the realm of Christotainment, echoes the irony that surrounds the fundamentalist movement:

Jesus was a terrorist
Enemy of the state . . .
Today bible-thumping cannibals
Reap money from his name

Again, such lyrics and examples of counterhegemonic Christotainment point to the hypocrisy of right-wing Christian fundamentalists who claim to be followers of the rebel-leader Jesus, while simultaneously persecuting contemporary revolutionaries; Biafra (1987, 1989, 1991, 2000) has consistently pointed out such hypocrisy through his spoken word performances. Echoing this sentiment in "Christian? Christ-like?" another Alternative Tentacles spoken word artist, Mumia Abu-Jamal, speaking from Pennsylvania's death row, notes that "Christianity became, in America, the faith of the slavemaster, the alleged belief of the rich, the protector of the propertied. For the slave, though, it was more farce than faith; in his eyes what was truly worshipped by all was wealth" (1997, 45).

Another relatively recent Alternative Tentacles release, *New Dark Age Parade* (2006) by one of Canada's most influential punk bands of the late 1970s and early 1980s, the Subhumans (not to be confused with the U.K. Subhumans), offers yet another voice critiquing Christian hypocrisy, focusing on their propensity for violence. Like NOFX, the Subhumans rarely engage the stage of Christotainment, but when they do, the spirit of counterhegemony always informs their approach. In their hard-hitting song "I Got Religion," the Subhumans sarcastically speak from the perspective of a "born again" shedding light onto fundamentalists' understanding of the mind of the converted under the influence of white supremacist, warmongering, fundamentalist doctrine. In the opening verse, musician and political activist Gerry Hannah writes, "I've been born again and now I'm lily-white. I want to prove my faith and get into a fight." Bringing the collective implications of this white, God-laden violence into clear focus, the song, reaching a crescendo, indignantly continues,

I want to start a war and show my master's wrath
I want to leave a bloody ruined aftermath
I'm always free from guilt whatever I may do
I can always tell them it was god who told me to

In another track, "Clash of the Intransigents," which again takes aim at the violence that often surrounds religious fundamentalism, in both Christian and Islamic manifestations, the Subhumans (2006) offer a faith-centered analysis of the U.S. invasion of the Middle East:

Killing a family won't get you to heaven
Saluting a flag won't make your country secure
It's time to say no to this unholy destruction . . .
I question your theology

Following this verse, the first two lines of the song's chorus—"Is an act divine when it's written in blood? Are a people free when they're dead in the mud?"—capture the essence of this genuinely old-school-sounding (harsh and aggressive with the harmonic smoothness of pop) punk album, *New Dark Age Parade*, as a whole. The record's artwork contributes significantly to the album's message. The cover displays an image embodying the signifiers of a white, nuclear, middle-class family taken from a 1950s magazine. The father, mother, and son (holding the family dog) stand arm in arm, all smiling with bright, rosy cheeks. This essentialist image of the white American family is situated in the context of a sky filled with the silhouettes of World War II U.S. fighter planes. The backdrop of these images is alternating bright and light yellow sunrays, contributing to the sense of uneasy happiness the cover art engenders. Adding a final layer of contrast, the header bears a bold black and white "Subhumans," and the accompanying footer similarly reads "New Dark Age Parade," leaving no doubt in viewers' minds as to what the title refers to.

While the Subhumans' record draws on the use of cleaver irony—a shallow, manufactured happiness in the context of the death and destruction of war, all cloaked in the essentialist anti-intellectualism of religious fundamentalism—Nausea, another Alternative Tentacles band, transmits similar messages but contributes to a slightly different tradition, or subgenre, within punk rock Christotainment. Nausea's identity as band is more firmly grounded within

Christotainment than is the case for the previously mentioned groups. That is, the imagery the band uses to identify itself, as argued below, is decidedly anti-Christian. One of Nausea's recent Alternative Tentacles reissues, *The Punk Terrorist Anthology, Vol. 1* (2006), rather than employing the clever sarcasm and irony of pop-punk bands like the Subhumans and NOFX, draws on the gritty and grimy harshness of hardcore punk rock in its images, lyrics, and sound.

The cover of *The Punk Terrorist Anthology, Vol. 1* makes no attempt at subtlety. The background displays a torn and tattered U.S. flag held together with safety pins. Placed on top of this stained and corroding symbol of patriotism is an upside-down, white, crucified, and bloodied Jesus figure. The record itself, as a form of commodity text, is firmly situated within the realm of Christotainment. "Nausea" is written across the top in a font we might aptly dub "electrocuted." Emblazoned along the bottom of the composition in a font that looks like jagged handwriting is the name of the album, *The Punk Terrorist Anthology, Vol. 1*. As a whole, this hardcore cover art would surely offend any patriotic Christian—clearly the intended effect. The song titles and lyrics, as we will see, are represented well by the record's artwork. Of particular interest here are the songs "Cybergod," "Body of Christ," and "Godless." In "Cybergod," for example, lyricists "Al" and "Amy" spew out the following lyrics over a grinding guitar and driving drum beat:

> *His omnipresent power is felt in every home . . .*
> *You know without his guidance you surely would be lost . . .*
> *Praise the Cybergod for the fools you put in power . . .*
> *Praise the Cybergod for a world of misery*

The message is clear: televangelists serve hegemonic interests by equating happiness with "money and fast cars" and by defining religiosity as unquestioning obedience to the self-appointed representatives of God. In short, like other critics, punk rock and otherwise, Nausea takes aim at the exploitative and destructive nature of mindless anti-intellectual fundamentalist Christianity. In "Godless," Nausea offers not just a critique of right-wing Christian fundamentalism but also a personal rejection of its attempt to control all of social life. Again, Al and Amy unleash the following lyrical assault:

> *Take your religious chains*
> *You don't own my soul*

You've . . . blessed us with this living hell
Your pious solve their problems with their guns

A chorus that warns mainstream religious leaders to "beware" of their "Godhood" because "they will rebel" accompanies these straightforward verses and, in the process, places Nausea, if only for a fleeting moment, as a counterhegemonic Christian punk rock band. Nausea's uncompromising, in-your-face attitude and unmistakable agency are not uncommon characteristics within the do it yourself (DIY) punk movement. Providing one of the most interesting responses to "the faith of the slavemaster," the self-identified fundamentalist Christian punk rockers, the Knights of the New Crusade, who are signed with Alternative Tentacles, represent a wildly complex and contradictory manifestation of Christotainment. Unlike Nausea, who merely flirt with the practice of using Christianity to critique current uses of Christianity, The Knights fully embrace this perspective in their songs and within their whole identity. The Knights, therefore, first and foremost, are an example of a band whose identity cannot be understood outside the context of Christotainment.

As a result of their emergence in Christotainment, their songs cover a wide rang of topics, each written from the philosophical perspective of the band's interpretations of Christian religious texts, which alternately challenge and accommodate mainstream forms of Christianity. For example, The Knights sing about kicking big-money fundamentalists out of the church for using the good word to get rich. Their two releases, *My God Is Alive! Sorry about Yours* (2005) and *A Challenge to the Cowards of Christendom* (2006), together offer over twenty tracks of the most comprehensive critique of Christian hypocrisy in musical form to date. However, their subject matter, in other ways, is little different from contemporary Christian fundamentalism and Christian rock in particular. For example, "Ain't No Monkey's in My Family Tree," on their 2005 release, offers a challenge to the science of evolution not dissimilar to current fundamentalist doctrine. The song, situated in the white supremacist context of the dominant society, can too easily be interpreted as transmitting antiblack, racist messages. For example, in the opening verse, vocalist Leaky sings, "There's monkeys in the jungle, there's monkeys in the zoo, you'll even find monkeys in some of our schools."

Another example of their lyrics from *A Challenge to the Cowards of Christendom* (2006) include, "Some of the people who get on our case for being Knights are under the influence of the same war-mongering demons as the politicians who ignore the commandments that Jesus affirmed." The Knights' lyrics, like these, are sung over a garage punk sound that is about as raw as it comes. Their look? They appear to be Knights Templar taken right out of a movie about the Middle Ages.

The Knights seemed to have left most of their reviewers, reviewers who typically review Alternative Tentacles releases, utterly confused. Are they for real, or are they a joke gone too far? No one seems to know for sure, but the consensus seems to be that they may actually mean what they say and say what they mean, while simultaneously making fun of the idea of the Christian fundamentalist crusader. They have stated that their own personal mission is to "take Christianity back from the powerful hypocrites who have hijacked it and to make Christian rock that actually rocks." While their critiques of right-wing Christian fundamentalism are not uncommon within the cultural spaces of left-wing/counterhegemonic punk rock, their positionality as white Christian fundamentalists against greed and war, as far as I know, is 100 percent original. Again, the band's employing the sounds of 1960s U.S. garage band rock 'n' roll and 1980s skatepunk rock, together with its use of the image of the European Dark Age Christian crusader fused with leftist political moments seen through the eyes of a contemporary Christian fanatic, has sparked a whole debate centered on the question, is this real or a parody?

In one of the premier punk rock journals/magazines, *Razorcake*, in a "staff" written review of The Knights' *My God Is Alive, Sorry about Yours* (2005), the editors argue that "if this is, in fact, a joke," then it should be counted as some of "the best" work of "pointed parody," but if it is not a joke, "then Jesus' army is in sorry shape" (*Razorcake* 2007). The authors point to The Knights' appearance, which includes crusader helmets, that is, "buckets on their heads," as evidence for why they are not taken seriously. While their attire makes for an interesting visual experience, in my judgment, it is the extreme complexity and deep contradictions within their lyrics that leave listeners confused because they simultaneously resemble both liberation-theology radicals and conservative, self-righteous fundamentalists; therefore, it is not clear whether they are real or a joke. For example, The Knights attack warmongering and pro-death-penalty Christians for ignoring the commandments of Jesus, while, at the same time they attack science for propagating the theory of evolution.

Debates surrounding these issues on sites such as *punknews.org* are not uncommon. For example, a review of The Knights 2006 release, *A Challenge to the Cowards of Christendom*, by FuckYouOiOiOi reflects on the contradictions embedded within the album, then notes that the Knights are so over the top that one must wonder if they are being serious. FuckYouOiOiOi's reflections sparked a lengthy debate, drawing the attention of punk rock bloggers. The discussion started with people just assuming "there is no way this is not a joke." However, not all listeners are convinced that the band is a parody, and they note that the band members themselves state their mission basically to be to expose mainstream Christians as frauds. Another poster theorizes that The Knights are a joke but will never admit as much because then they would cease to be funny to their audience, that is, to those who think they have comedic value. Attempting to end the discussion, situating the issue of authenticity in the context of the band's label, Alternative Tentacles (AT), another discussant rants, "Its on AT!!! Anyone who sees that and still thinks it's serious knows nothing." The Knights themselves have been quoted as saying that their band is *both* real *and* a joke. Others joined the discussion, it seems, to just express that they like the band. One blogger wrote, "I don't care if it is joke or not, I love these guys." Another similar observer notes, "I love this band, they're so nuts and they actually play some really good rock 'n' roll."

As if the lyrics weren't enough, one need only examine a few of The Knights' live performances on YouTube to begin to understand why they would be described as "nuts." While all the members wear crusader metal mesh and the traditional cotton shirt over their old-school skate shorts and vans, only the singer, Leaky, waves a four-foot battle sword around the stage as he sings. However, through any given performance, Leaky can be observed waving around not a sword but a bottle of beer, stumbling with intoxication, reassuring the audience that "beer is not evil, it is proof that God loves us and wants us to be happy." Another aspect of the band's theater is an informal holy communion, during which Leaky and an assistant pass small paper cups to a few audience members in the front and distribute wine and crackers, while the band moans on in the background. The audience, "every freak, faggot and bull dyke" as Leaky addresses them, is continuously reminded that no matter what they have done in their lives, God will always love and forgive them, but on judgment day, when the trumpets sound in the sky, they will have to move, that is, change. This rant leads into the bluesy punk rock 'n' roll song "You Gotta Move." The drunk, stumbling punk rock Leaky, who moves in and out of sarcasm and genuine critique, while simultaneously blurring the line between reality and imagination, does come across as genuinely "nuts."

However, even though the conceptual ground from which punk rock has been built is tension and paradox, the contradiction between the band's identification with the crusading Christians of the Middle Ages who created Christopher Columbus and his lasting spirit of conquest and plunder and their simultaneous call for peace and democracy might be a bit unsettling for those on the Left not fluent in punk rock, regardless of The Knights' original intentions. Again, I cannot overstress that The Knights of the New Crusade are an aberration in the punk scene. While it is common practice for punk rockers to call themselves what they are protesting—such as Riot Cop, the left-wing, activist punk band that sings about its members' own experiences battling riot police in the streets as part of the struggle against the capitalist system of dehumanization and exploitation—The Knights of the New Crusade argue that they are reappropriating Christianity from corruption. In other words, while Riot Cop resists what they call themselves, The Knights also resist what they call themselves at the same time that they embrace what they call themselves through a process of reappropriation and sarcasm. It is much easier to "get" Riot Cop because they do not dress up like riot cops; they dress like the punk rock, anarchist, riot cop street fighters they portray themselves as being.

However, as previously stated, while The Knights maintain the appearance of the old soldiers of Christian imperialism with more than a trace of sarcasm and comedy, they nevertheless seem to be serious. Because of the magnitude of what their image represents—a long legacy of genocidal greed and intolerance predating Columbus by centuries—the punk rock community does not seem to be ready to fully embrace The Knights as Biafra possibly has, as is indicated by his signing them to his label. One more twist: as an avid proponent of democratic practice and embracing the Zapatista idea of *a world where many worlds fit*, I feel more enlightened and aware of the concrete context of ideas and interventions as a result of having been exposed to The Knights. That is, my understanding of punk rock, Christianity, and social protest as part of the complex and contradictory nature of social production and reproduction (change) has been enhanced.

CONCLUSION

This analysis demonstrates that the hegemonic struggle to maintain a hierarchy of power and privilege in the material world, the concrete context, at its heart, is cultural, as the late Italian Communist Party member Antonio Gramsci argued after he was imprisoned for his beliefs during World War I. Situating this struggle for the hearts and minds of men and women, and therefore for the relationships that define our existence, in the context of philosophy, Jonathan Israel notes,

> Only philosophy can cause a true "revolution." . . . A revolutionary shift is a shift in understanding, something which, though intimately driven by the long-term processes of social change, economic development, and institutional adaptation, is in itself a product of "philosophy" since only philosophy can transform our mental picture of the world and its basic categories. . . . Most modern readers [however] resist attempts to envisage "philosophy" as what defines the human condition. (2006, 13)

Philosophy, from this perspective, is the lens through which we view the world and that ultimately informs our daily interventions and interactions in the world. Every conscious, functioning person has a particular way of thinking about and making sense of the world, which we can call a philosophy—everyone therefore has one. It follows that every song is written from one or more philosophical perspectives. Popular music, in complex and contradictory ways, both accommodates and resists dominant society. The cultural terrain of Christotainment, as we have seen through the example of The Knights, is incredibly complex as it is informed by a wide range of competing philosophical paradigms.

If we do not realize or believe that we are all informed by a philosophy, it is because we have not yet become conscious of our own consciousness (Freire 2006). That is, we have not yet begun reflecting on the values, ideas, and beliefs about the world and everything in it that we have internalized as a result of living in a particular context. In other words, it means that we have not yet realized that the differences between our own thoughts and that of those who live on the other side of the world, for example, are simultaneously philosophical *and* material. Our philosophy, the way we see and make sense of the world, determines what we value and the choices we make, but it is always situated in a concrete context; the individual is part of that context, and the mind is the individual's primary mediator between the physicalness of his or her own body and the physicalness of the surrounding material, animate and inanimate. For example, do we passively accept the determinism of Christian fundamentalism, or are we informed by an ontology of hope that refuses to submit to a determinism? Without the development of a critical consciousness, we do not need an external censor to turn off the radio; we will censor ourselves. This ontological imposition manifests itself through a process of homogenization—toward a system of knowledge production with but one channel, that is, a radio that transmits just one Christian fundamentalist message, betraying the spirit of democratic, heterogeneous wholeness that The Knights contribute to, that is, a form of counterhegemonic Christotainment.

References

Abu-Jamal, M. 1997. *Death blossoms: Reflections from a prisoner of conscience.* Farmington, PA: Plough Publishing House.

Ackerman, F. 1982. *Reaganomics: Rhetoric vs. reality.* New York: South End Press.

Albelda, R., E. McCrate, E. Melendez, J. Lapidus, and the Center for Popular Economics. 1988. *Mink coats don't trickle down: The economic attack on women and people of color.* New York: South End Press.

Banyacya, T. 1994. Thomas Banyacya: Hopi elder (North America). In *Voice of indigenous peoples: A plea to the world,* ed. Alexander Ewen, 112–118. Santa Fe, NM: Clear Light Publishers.

Barber-Kersovan, A. 2004. Music as a parallel power structure. In *Shoot the singer: Music censorship today,* ed. Marie Korpe, 6–10. New York: Zed Books.

Biafra, J. 1987. *No more cocoons.* Spoken Word Album #1. Alternative Tentacles, Virus 59.

_______. 1989. *High priest of harmful matter: Tales from the Trial.* Spoken Word Album #2. Alternative Tentacles, Virus 59.

_______. 1991. *I blow minds for a living.* Spoken Word Album #3. Alternative Tentacles, Virus 94.

_______. 1998. *If evolution is outlawed, then only outlaws will evolve.* Spoken Word Album #5. Alternative Tentacles, Virus 201.

_______. 2000. *Become the media.* Alternative Tentacles, Virus 260.

Biafra, J., with Nomeansno. 1991. *The sky is falling and I want my mommy.* Alternative Tentacles, Virus 85.

Cloonan, M. 2004. What is music censorship? Towards a better understanding of the term. In *Shoot the singer: Music censorship today,* ed. Marie Korpe, 3–5. New York: Zed Books.

Cole-Malott, D., and C. Malott. 2008. Jamaica. In *The destructive path of neoliberalism: An international examination of education,* ed. Brad Porfilio and Curry Malott, 157–172. New York: Sense.

Deloria, V. 1994. *God is red: A native view of religion.* Golden, CO: Fulcrum.

Diop, C.A. 1987. *Precolonial black Africa: A comparative study of the political and social systems of Europe and black Africa, from antiquity to the formation of modern states.* New York: Lawrence Hill Books.

Ewen, A., ed. 1994. *Voices of indigenous people: Native people address the United Nations.* Santa Fe, NM: Clear Light Publishers.

Fischer, P. 2003. Challenging music as expression in the United States. In *Policing Pop*, ed. Martin Cloonan and Reebee Garofalo, 221–238. Philadelphia: Temple University Press.

Freire, P. 1992. *Pedagogy of hope: Reliving* Pedagogy of the Oppressed. New York: Continuum.

_______. 1999. *Pedagogy of the oppressed.* New York: Continuum.

_______. 2006. *Teachers as cultural workers: Letters to those who dare teach.* Boulder, CO: Westview.

FuckYouOiOiOi. A Review of The Knights of the New Crusade's *A Challenge to the Cowards of Christendom.* PunkNews.org, www.punknews.org/review/5454 (accessed May 4, 2008).

Gore, T. 1987. *Raising PG kids in an X-rated society.* Nashville, TN: Abingdon Press.

Grinde, D. A. 1992. Iroquois political theory and the roots of American democracy. In *Exiled in the land of the free: Democracy, Indian nations, and the U.S. Constitution*, ed. Chief Oren Lyons and John Mohawk, 227–280. Santa Fe, NM: Clear Light Publishers.

Israel, J. 2006. *Enlightenment contested.* London: Oxford University Press.

Jones, C., and J. Jefferies. 1998. "Don't believe the hype": Debunking the Panther mythology. In *The Black Panther Party reconsidered*, ed. Charles E. Jones, 25–56. Baltimore: Black Classic Press.

Kincheloe, J. 2005. *Critical constructivism primer.* New York: Peter Lang.

_______. 2008. Critical pedagogy in the twenty-first century: Evolution for survival. In *Critical pedagogy: Where are we now?* Ed. Peter McLaren and Joe Kincheloe, 9–42. New York: Peter Lang.

Lusane, C. 1998. To fight for the people: The Black Panther Party and black politics in the 1990s. In *The Black Panther Party reconsidered*, ed. Charles E. Jones, 443–468. Baltimore: Black Classic Press.

Lyons, O. 2005. Preamble to *Basic call to consciousness*, ed. Akwesasne Notes, 13–25. Summertown, TN: Native Voices.

Lyons, O., and J. Mohawk. 1992. *Exiled in the land of the free: Democracy, Indian nations, and the U.S. Constitution.* Santa Fe, NM: Clear Light Publishers.

Malott, C. 2008. *A call to action: An introduction to education, philosophy and Native North America.* New York: Peter Lang.

Malott, C., and M. Peña. 2004. *Punk rockers' revolution: A pedagogy of race, class, and gender.* New York: Peter Lang.

Marsden, G. 1991. *Understanding fundamentalism and evangelicalism.* Grand Rapids, MI: Eerdmans.

______. 2006. *Fundamentalism and American culture.* 2nd ed. New York: Oxford University Press.

McGuire, M. 1992. *Religion: The social context.* Belmont, CA: Wadsworth.

Nausea. 2006. *The punk terrorist anthology, Vol. 1.* Alternative Tentacles, Virus 348.

NOFX. 2006. *Wolves in wolves' clothing.* Fat Wreck Chords.

Nuzum, E. 2004. Crash into me, baby: America's implicit music censorship since 11 September. In *Shoot the singer: Music censorship today,* ed. Marie Korpe, 149–159. New York: Zed Books.

Razorcake. 2007. From "Andy Griffith's Front Porch"-core to Finnish thrash: Record reviews that didn't fit in issue 21. *Razorcake,* www.razorcake.org/site/modules.php?name=News&file=article&sid=402 (accessed May 4, 2008).

Smith, P. 1984. *The rise of industrial America: A people's history of the post-Reconstruction era.* Vol. 6. New York: Penguin Books.

Subhumans. 2006. *New dark age parade.* Alternative Tentacles, Virus 366.

Vale, V. 2001. *Real conversations no. 1: Rollins, Childish, Biafra, Ferlinghetti.* San Francisco, CA: RE/Search Publications.

Willis, P. 1977. *Learning to labor: How working class kids get working class jobs.* New York: Columbia University Press.

AFTERWORD

End Times in America

Religious Fundamentalism and the Crisis of Democracy

HENRY A. GIROUX

With George W. Bush's presidency ended, religious fundamentalism seems once again to be in overdrive in its effort to define politics through a reductive and somewhat fanatical moralism, this time centered on its support for Sarah Palin, the newest light in the evangelical quest to make religion the ultimate measure of one's politics. This kind of religious zealotry has a long tradition in American history extending from the arrival of Puritanism in the seventeenth century to the current spread of Pentecostalism. This often ignored history, imbued with theocratic certainty and absolute moralism, has been quite powerful in providing religious justification to the likes of the Ku Klux Klan, the parlance of the Robber Barons, the patriarchy-imbued discourse of "family values," and the recent gold standard of religious fanaticism and spectacularized violence on full display in Mel Gibson's film, *The Passion of The Christ.* A glimpse of this history was evident when George W. Bush kicked off his first presidential campaign by speaking at Bob Jones University and soon afterwards appointed Ralph Reed, former head of the Christian Coalition, as one of his top advisers. A more recent indication of the mixing of power, religion, and politics occurred when Republican presidential candidate John McCain, in 2008, fully embraced the support of right-wing religious television personality John Hagee, who has argued among other things that all Muslims have a "mandate to kill Christian and Jews."[1] McCain also courted the support of Rod Parsley and the late Jerry Falwell, right-wing religious extremists whom McCain had once labeled as "agents of religious intolerance."[2]

The historical lesson here is not only that absolute moralism, when mixed with politics, produces zealots who believe they have a monopoly on the truth and a legitimate rationale for refusing to engage ambiguities, but that it also fuels an intolerance toward others who do not follow the scripted, righteous path of officially sanctioned beliefs and behavior. "Family values" is now joined with an emotionally charged rhetorical appeal to "faith" as the new code words for cultural conservatism. As Lewis Lapham has noted, "merchants of salvation" such as the former Jerry Falwell, Sun Myung Moon, and James Dobson united in the early 1990s in endorsing Christian evangelist Pat Robertson's claim that feminists "leave their husbands, kill their children, practice witchcraft, destroy capitalism, and become lesbians."[3] Giddy with power and a newfound legitimacy in American politics, these moral apparatchiks now believed that Satan's influence shaped everything from the liberal media to "how Barbra Streisand was taught how to sing."[4] As right-wing religion conjoins with conservative political ideology and political power, it not only legitimates intolerance and antidemocratic forms of religious correctness but also lays the groundwork for a growing authoritarianism that easily derides appeals to reason, dissent, dialogue, and secular humanism. This trend has been most evident under the former presidency of George W. Bush, whose policies nourished and strengthened a number of antidemocratic forces, including the Republican Party's war on science, an elaborate system of wiretapping, extreme interrogation techniques, an imperial presidency, the rise and influence of right-wing Christian extremists, and a government draped in secrecy and an all-too-casual willingness to suspend civil liberties.[5] In the tawdry mix of politics and religious extremism that has marked the beginning of the new millennium, we have witnessed an alliance of conservative politicians and right-wing conservative Christians who "seek to influence policies on abortion, stem cells, sexual conduct and the teaching of evolution."[6] How else to explain the growing number of Christian conservative educators who want to impose the teaching of creationism in the schools, ban sex education from the curricula, and subordinate scientific facts to religious dogma?

For the last eight years under the Bush administration, religious correctness exercised a powerful influence on American society. The morality police were everywhere, denouncing everything from Janet Jackson's out-of-wardrobe display to the wanton satanic influence of the television show *Desperate House-*

wives. But the morality police did more than censor and impose their theocratic moralism on everyone else's behavior; they also elected politicians whose religious fanaticism and democratic bad faith did not augur well for the future of democracy in the United States. The rise of the religious zealot as politician is readily apparent in the rise to the highest levels of government by religious hucksters, such as former attorney general John Ashcroft and born-again Christian conservatives, like former president Bush, as well as in the emergence of a new breed of faith-bearing politicians who cut across party lines. For instance, David Kirkpatrick, writing about religion and politics, argues that if theological conservatives on the right were losing ground in 2008, it was only because the then "democratic presidential front-runners—Senator Hillary Rodham Clinton, Senator Barack Obama and former Senator John Edwards—sound like a bunch of tent-revival Bible thumpers compared with Republicans."[7] Conservative Christian moralism in the last decade traveled straight to the highest levels of power, as was most obvious in the 2004 election to the U.S. Senate of a new crop of what *New York Times* writer Frank Rich called "opportunistic ayatollahs on the right."[8] For instance, the then elected senator from Oklahoma, Tom Coburn, not only publicly argued for the death penalty for doctors who perform abortions but also insisted that lesbianism is so rampant in the schools in Oklahoma that school officials let only one girl at a time go to the bathroom. Jim DeMint, then a senator from South Carolina, stated that he would not want to see "a single woman who was pregnant and living with her boyfriend teaching in the public schools."[9] DeMint has also declared that he wanted to ban gays from teaching in public schools, as well. Jon Thune, the then newly elected senator from South Dakota, supported a constitutional amendment banning flag burning, not to mention another amendment making permanent Bush's tax cuts for the rich. Four years later, vice-presidential candidate Sarah Palin argued that women should be denied an abortion even if they conceive a child as a result of rape or incest. Her reactionary Bible-thumping ideology and scorn for the environment, science, and women's rights were on full display in her classic right-wing fundamentalist opposition to abortion, same-sex marriage, and stem cell research coupled with her support for teaching Creationism in public schools.

Widely recognized as creating the first faith-based presidency, George W. Bush did more during his two terms in office to advance the agenda of right-wing evangelicals than any other president in recent history, and it is conceivable given the current need for affirming one's faith in politics that his successor will not challenge those faith-based policies. Bush's legacy is disturbing in a multitude of ways, but what is most unsettling is not simply that many of his religious supporters believed that Bush was their leader but that they also embraced him as a "messenger from God"[10] whose job it was to implement God's will. For example, Bob Jones III, the president of the fundamentalist university of the same name, argued in a written letter to President Bush: "Christ has allowed you to be his servant" in order to "leave an imprint for righteousness. . . . In your re-election, God has graciously granted America—though she doesn't deserve it—a reprieve from the agenda of paganism. You have been given a mandate. We the people expect your voice to be like the clear and certain sound of a trumpet. . . . Don't equivocate. Put your agenda on the front burner and let it boil. You owe the liberals nothing. They despise you because they despise your Christ."[11] Jones went on to claim that since "Christ has allowed you [Bush] to be His servant in this nation . . . you will have the opportunity to appoint many conservative judges and exercise forceful leadership with the congress in passing legislation that is defined by biblical norm regarding the family, sexuality, sanctity of life, religious freedom, freedom of speech, and limited government."[12] Appearing on the NBC News program *Meet the Press*, Jerry Falwell, founder of the Moral Majority, stated, "My prayer, my hope [is] that he will appoint men or women to the court who will overturn *Roe v. Wade*."[13] This was the same "man of God" who claimed that the tragic events of 9/11 had been caused by "the pagans, and the abortionists, and the feminists, and the gays and lesbians [and] all of them who have tried to secularize America."[14] What is perhaps most disturbing is that many right-wing Christian movements and politicians continue to play strategies designed "to strip the federal judges of their right to hear cases involving the separation of church and state."[15] For instance, Republican representative John Hostettler of Indiana introduced a bill in Congress "that would deny federal courts the right to hear cases challenging the Defense of Marriage Act, which bans same-sex marriage."[16]

According to Hostettler, "When the courts make unconstitutional decisions, we should not enforce them. Federal courts have no army or navy. . . . The court can opine, decide, talk about, sing, whatever it wants to do. We're not saying they can't do that. At the end of the day, we're saying the court can't enforce its opinions."[17] Although this bill failed, it points to the ongoing determination of Christian social conservatives and "power puritans," as Maureen Dowd calls them, to appoint conservative judges, prevent homosexuals from securing jobs as teachers, dismantle the power of the federal judiciary, and approve legislation that would stop stem cell research and eliminate the reproductive rights of women. It is also exemplifies the "bloodthirsty feelings of revenge" that have motivated many of Bush's religious boosters.[18]

The ideological fervor, if not the desire for vengeance, that drives many of Bush's Christian fundamentalist supporters is also evident in the words of former Bush supporter Hardy Billington: "To me, I just believe God controls everything, and God uses the president to keep evil down, to see the darkness and protect this nation. Other people will not protect us. God gives people choices to make. God gave us this president to be the man to protect the nation at this time."[19] Bush, of course, throughout his tenure, harbored the same arrogant illusion, out of which emerged a government that pushed aside self-criticism, uncertainty, and doubt in favor of a faith-based certainty and moral righteousness bereft of critical reflection. In fact, fear, slander, and God formed the cornerstone of the Bush 2004 presidential campaign. First, Cheney argued that if Kerry were elected, it would mean the country would be subjected to terrorist attacks, a message that amounted to "Vote Bush or Die." Second, the Swift Boat campaign successfully led the American people to believe that Kerry was a coward rather than a war hero, in spite of the five medals he won in Vietnam. And finally, God became the ultimate referent to mobilize millions of additional votes from Christian fundamentalists. Matthew Rothschild, the editor of *The Progressive*, points out that the Republicans sent out pieces of literature in Arkansas and West Virginia "claiming the Democrats were going to take everyone's Bibles away. . . . On the front of one such envelope, sent from the Republican National Committee, was a picture of a Bible with the word 'BANNED' slapped across it. 'This will be Arkansas . . . if you don't vote,' it said."[20] The high-pitched righteousness proclaimed by Bush's evangelical army of supporters apparently took a vacation in order to play dirty politics during the Bush/Kerry campaign. The same religious fanaticism and dirty tricks can be seen in the attacks on Barack Obama's 2008 presidential bid. Ads have appeared claiming Obama mocks the Bible, is really a Muslim, wants to teach sex education to preschoolers, and has affiliated with terrorists.[21]

Ron Suskind, the widely regarded author and journalist, has argued that the one key feature of Bush's faith-based presidency is that it scorned "open dialogue, based on facts, [which] is not seen as something of inherent value."[22] Jim Wallis, a progressive evangelical pastor whom Bush called upon to bring together a range of clergy to talk about faith and poverty, discovered rather quickly that Bush was not open to inconvenient facts or ideas at odds with what he often refers to as "his instincts." Wallis claims that, over time, as he worked with Bush in the White House, what he "started to see at this point was that man that would emerge over the next year—a messianic American Calvinist. He doesn't want to hear from anyone who doubts him."[23] Bush became widely recognized as a president who exhibited dislike, if not disdain, for contemplation, examination of facts, and friendly queries from others about the reasons for his decisions. More recently, Bob Woodward, among the more famous chroniclers of the Bush presidency, argued in *The War Within* that one of the most disturbing qualities about Bush is that even as he was about to leave office, he exhibited the same impatience, bravado, certainty, and impatience that characterized most of his presidency.

Rampant anti-intellectualism coupled with a rigid moralism now boldly translates into everyday cultural practices as right-wing evangelicals live out their messianic view of the world. For instance, more and more conservative pharmacists are refusing to fill prescriptions for religious reasons. Mixing medicine, politics, and religion means that some women are being denied birth control pills and other products designed to prevent conception. It gets worse. Bush's much exalted religious fundamentalism has done more than promote a disdain for critical thought and reinforce retrograde forms of homophobia and patriarchy; it has also inspired an aggressive militarism, wrapped up in the language of holy war. One telling example can be found in a story announced by *Agence France Presse*. It reported that a group of evangelical marines prepared to "battle barbarians" before their assault on Fallujah in Iraq by listening to heavy metal–flavored lyrics in praise of Christ while a "female voice cried out on the loudspeakers 'You are the sovereign, Your name is holy. You are the pure spotless lamb.'" Just before the battle, a chaplain had the soldiers line up in order to dab their heads with oil, while he told them "God's people would be anointed with oil."[24] It now appears that Bush's war for "democracy" was largely defined by many of his followers as a holy war against infidels. Although the Bush administration is an important marker of the destruction of the separation of religion and politics in American life, it would be a mistake to assume that this tendency in American politics ended with the emergence of a new administration in 2009. The mixing of religion and politics, while not synonymous with bigotry, reveals a dark side whenever it is largely shaped by fanatics and extremists. If religious faith is to be a force for liberation, compassion, spirituality, and justice, it cannot be allowed to undermine the democratic imperative of keeping organized religion out of politics.

The turn to religion as a central element of politics suggests important considerations that need to be addressed by those of us who believe in a democracy that maintains the legitimate separation of church and state as fundamental to religious freedom and the flourishing of diverse public spheres. First, we need to address the search for community through social formations, values, and movements that bring people together through the discourse of public morality, civic engagement, and the ethical imperatives of democracy. This is not just a matter of discovering America's secular roots but also of creating a cultural politics in which the language of community, shared values, solidarity, and the common good play an important pedagogical and political role in the struggle for an inclusive and substantive democratic society. This means developing a language of critique in which the rabid individualism and atomism of neoliberal market ideology can be unmasked for its antidemocratic and utterly privatizing tendencies. It means rooting out all those fundamentalisms so prevalent in American society, including the market, political, religious, and militaristic fundamentalisms that now exercise a powerful influence over all aspects of U.S. society. Fundamentalism in itself cannot simply be dismissed as antidemocratic or evil. As the welfare state declines, many right-leaning Christian churches offer not only eternal salvation but also material assistance in the form of day care, low-priced dinners for poor families, psychological help for the abused, and a ministry for inner-city at-risk youth. As social services are privatized, churches constitute one of the few public spheres left where people can form a semblance of community, network, find soup kitchens, and become part of a support group.[25] Fundamentalism performs a certain kind of work that taps into real individual and collective needs. Unfortunately, right-wing faith-based groups provide people not only with a sense of identity in a time of crisis but also with a sense of public efficacy; that is, they furnish the promise of social agency by which individuals can exercise solidarity through a sense of meaning and action in their lives. Yet such groups often trade on what Ernst Bloch once called the "swindle of fulfillment," promising moral values even while it also supported the party that produced the horror of Abu Ghraib and a government that practiced torture, abductions, and the suspension of basic civil liberties.

If democratic politics and secular humanism are worth investing in, defending, and fighting for, then cultural studies theorists, educators, and other progressives need more than a language of critique; they also need a language of possibility. Such a discourse should both challenge the antidemocratic values claimed by the right and offer a notion of moral values in which "care and responsibility, fairness and equality, freedom and courage, fulfillment in life, opportunity and community, cooperation and trust, honesty and openness" are wedded to the principles of justice, equality, and freedom.[26] Barbara Ehrenreich is right on target in arguing that progressives need to

> articulate poverty and war as the urgent moral issues they are. Jesus is on our side here, and secular liberals should not be afraid to invoke him. Policies of pre-emptive war and the upward redistribution of wealth are inversions of the Judeo-Christian ethic. . . . At the very least, we need a firm commitment to public forms of childcare, healthcare, housing and education—for people of all faiths and no faith at all . . . progressives should perhaps rethink their own disdain for service-based outreach programs. Once it was the left that provided "alternative services" in the form of free clinics, women's health centers, food co-ops and inner-city multi-service storefronts. Enterprises like these are not substitutes for an adequate public welfare state, but they can become the springboards from which to demand one.[27]

Second, as many of the articles in this book argue, identity must be experienced beyond the atomizing call of market forces. For identity to be meaningful in a democratic society, it must be nourished through connections to others, a respect for social justice, and a recognition of the need to work with others to experience both a sense of collective joy and a measure of social responsibility. Hence, educators, artists, parents, activists, and others need not only to defend existing democratic public spheres but also to develop alternative ones where the language and practice of democratic community, public values, civic engagement, and social justice can be taught, learned, and experienced. Educators and cultural studies theorists must fight against the manufactured culture of cynicism based on the culture of fear and insecurity that is now so rampant in the United States. This means resurrecting hope as both a condition for individual and social agency and a basis for opposing an immobilizing politics of fatalism. Education must be seen as a moral and political practice that, as Paulo Freire, the late internationally renowned critical educator, points out, calls us beyond ourselves and creates the possibilities for social transformation.[28] Our capacity for agency is based on the ability to invest in the future, ask disturbing questions, make authority accountable, and recognize that hope is an essential component of politics. Moreover, as this book demonstrates, religion has now become both a big business and a powerful educational force in the world of the new and old media. It is crucial that educators and others make visible, critically engage, and challenge the sites, knowledge, and ideological circuits of power that religious extremists use to spread their bigotry and violence. This suggests a need to address with great urgency the way popular culture has become a force for what Shirley Steinberg and Joe Kincheloe call Christotainment. At stake here is a struggle not only against the attack on the separation of church and state but also against the ongoing attempt to incorporate young people and others into the armed and ever ready army of right-wing Christian fanatics and demagogic populists.

Part of the struggle against religious extremism involves acknowledging how the directive nature of pedagogy operates through a radical notion of hope whereby students learn how to be critical as well as socially responsible—that is, learn to both read the world critically and act on the world to foster social, racial, economic, and cultural justice. A pedagogy without hope is an educational practice that forecloses any chance of challenging those forms of cynicism and despair that cripple our willingness to act as engaged citizens in a world in which democracy is more than a promise. The dominant visions currently available to us demand our loyalty only as passive citizens and eager consumers. Educated hope, on the other hand, unsettles the present and opens up horizons of comparison; it provides what Zygmunt Bauman calls an "activating presence" that offers a vision that "brings us back in touch with our deep democratic energies and sense of possibility."[29] Hope is thus articulated as both a project and a pedagogical condition for providing a sense of opposition and engaged struggle. As a project, Andrew Benjamin insists, hope must be viewed as "a structural condition of the present rather than as the promise of a future, the continual promise of a future that will always have to have been better."[30] As part of a pedagogical struggle, hope is seen not merely as an individual proclivity but as part of a broader politics that acknowledges those social, economic, spiritual, and cultural conditions in the present that make certain kinds of agency and democratic politics possible. At its best, hope pluralizes politics and dissent while enticing us to pay attention to those democratic public spheres in which a language of critique, possibility, and vision can be nurtured by evoking not just different histories but different futures.

But different futures, if they are to be imagined, need public spaces where the language of critique and hope is spoken. All too often, progressives pay too little attention to the inextricable linkage between the struggle over politics and democracy, and the need to create, sustain, and defend those vital public spheres where individuals can be engaged as political agents equipped with the skills, capacities, and knowledge they need to perform as autonomous political agents and to believe that such agency is worth taking up. What is becoming increasingly clear is that public and higher education may be two of the few sites left in which public values can be learned and experienced, and both should be defended vigorously by broadening the terms of learning to define a new democratic mission for the university. When approached as democratic public spheres, public and higher education not only can encourage dialogue and the expansion of the intellect but also can prepare students as critical agents capable of intervening in the world to create and sustain a substantive and inclusive democracy. At the same time, democracy needs to be supported and nourished across a wide range of overlapping sites—from film and television to talk radio and the Internet—that engage in diverse forms of public pedagogy, or organized practices that mainly produce ideas, values, and knowledge.

Cultural politics is alive and well in the United States; regrettably, it is a politics controlled by the right and largely ignored by progressives of various ideological stripes. While it may be true, as *New York Times* columnist Frank Rich points out, that the morality police actually have much less support among the American people than Ralph Reed, John Agee, Pat Robinson, and the dominant media would have us believe, the problem that Rich seems to overlook is that this minority has exercised an enormous influence in shaping government policy and that this is where the danger lies—not in their numbers but in their influence.[31] And such influence would not likely end with the election of a new administration. Authoritarianism takes many forms. Its most recent expression appears to be gaining ground through the relentless force of a moral values crusade at home and abroad. Although cultural politics is thriving in the United States today, it has to be reinvented so as to *serve* democracy rather than shut it down. In spite of what many religious fundamentalists claim, bigotry rather than religious tolerance is the enemy of democracy. Chris Hedges is right in arguing that "the Right is a sworn and potent enemy of the open society [and] its ideology bears within it the tenets of a Christian fascism."[32] Within the last twenty years, public rationality, if not politics itself, has been undermined in part by the promise of personal transformation, a promise that is increasingly nurtured by the collective fervor and popular fantasies of a dramatic evangelism offering a bad-faith claim of moral certainties and a vow to miraculously cleanse the world of the evils of secularism, the pitfalls of critical thinking, and those modes of democratic agency essential to any viable democracy. Religious fundamentalism is antipolitics because it denounces critical thought and undermines judgment and judicious discrimination, qualities essential to any viable notion of politics. Religious fundamentalism not only contains the seeds of intolerance and anti-intellectualism, it also reminds us of the "dark times" ahead if the American public does not take seriously the recognition that each generation must fight to expand and deepen the promise of democracy. At stake in this struggle is not only the viability of politics but democracy itself.

Notes

1. John Wendland, "John McCain Embraces Endorsement by Religious Bigot," PoliticalAffairs.net, March 3, 2008, http://www.politicalaffairs.net/article/articleview/6557/ (accessed October 2, 2008).

2. McCain cited in CNN Transcript, "Sen. John McCain Attacks Pat Robertson, Jerry Falwell, Republican Establishment as Harming GOP Ideals," CNN *Tonight* (aired February 28, 2000, 9:59 A.M. ET), http://transcripts.cnn.com/TRANSCRIPTS/0002/28/se.01.html (accessed October 2, 2008).

3. Lewis Lapham, "Tentacles of Rage: The Republican Propaganda Mill, A Brief History," *Harper's*, September 2004, 37.

4. Ibid., 39.

5. Chris Hedges, *American Fascists: The Christian Right and the War on America* (New York: Free Press, 2007).

6. John Horgan, "Political Science," *New York Times*, December 18, 2005, http://www.nytimes.com/2005/12/18/books/review/18horgan.html?scp=4&sq=John%20Horgan&st=cse (accessed October 2, 2008).

7. David Kirkpatrick, "The Evangelical Crackup," *New York Times*, October 28, 2007, http://www.nytimes.com/2007/10/28/magazine/28Evangelicals-t.html?pagewanted=print (accessed October 2, 2008).

8. The phrase, "opportunistic ayatollahs on the right" comes from Frank Rich, "The Great Indecency Hoax," *New York Times*, November 28, 2004, http://www.nytimes.com/2004/11/28/arts/28rich.html?8hpib=&oref=login&pagewanted=print&position= (accessed October 2, 2008).

9. Maureen Dowd, "The Red Zone," *New York Times*, November 4, 2004, A27.

10. Esther Kaplan, *With God on Their Side: How Christian Fundamentalists Trampled Science, Policy, and Democracy in George W. Bush's White House* (New York: The New Press, 2004).

11. Bob Jones, III, "Congratulatory Letter to President George W. Bush from Dr. Bob Jones III," http://www.bju.edu/letter.

12. Ibid.

13. Transcript for November 28, 2004, *Meet the Press*, www.msnbc.msn.com/id/6601018 (accessed October 2, 2008).

14. A transcript of Falwell's comments from Pat Robertson's 700 Club telecast can be found on "Jerry Falwell and Pat Robertson say immorality and anti-Christian groups should share in the blame for the Terrorist Attacks on America—Truth!" Truth or Fiction, http://www.truthorfiction.com/rumors/f/falwell-robertson-wtc.htm (accessed October 2, 2008).

15. George McEvoy, "Courts First to Go in Right-Wing Revolution," *Palm Beach Post*, November 27, 2004, http://www.palmbeachpost.com/opinion/content/opinion/epaper/2004/11/27/m11a_mcevoy_1127.html (accessed October 2, 2008).

16. Ibid.

17. Cited in ibid.

18. Both the quote and the comments are from Maureen Dowd, "Slapping the Other Cheek," *New York Times*, November 14, 2004, http://www.nytimes.com/2004/11/14/opinion/14dowd.html?oref=login&hp (accessed October 2, 2008).

19. Ron Suskind, "Without a Doubt," *New York Times Magazine*, October 17, 2004, 44–51, 64, 102.

20. Matthew Rothschild, "Fear, Smear, and God," *The Progressive*, November 2004, 4.

21. Endless examples of these ads accompanied by critical commentaries that debunk them can be found at Fight the Smears, http://fightthesmears.com/articles/14/sermononthemount.

22. Suskind, "Without a Doubt," 47.

23. Ibid., 50.

24. Editorial, "Holy War: Evangelical Marines Prepare to Battle Barbarians," Agence France Presse News Line, November 7, 2004, http://www.commondreams.org/headlines04/1107-02.htm (accessed October 2, 2008).

25. All of these examples are taken from Barbara Ehrenreich, "The Faith Factor," *The Nation,* November 29, 2004, 6.

26. George Lakoff, "Our Moral Values," *The Nation,* December 6, 2004, 6.

27. Ehrenreich, "The Faith Factor" *The Nation,* 7.

28. Paulo Freire, *Pedagogy of Freedom* (Lanham, Md.: Rowman and Littlefield, 1999).

29. Peter Beilharz, *Zygmunt Bauman: Dialect of Modernity* (London: Sage, 2000), 59; Cornel West, "Finding Hope in Dark Times," *Tikkun* 19:4 (2004): 18.

30. Andrew Benjamin, *Present Hope: Philosophy, Architecture, Judaism* (New York: Routledge, 1997), 1.

31. Frank Rich, "The Great Indecency Hoax," *New York Times,* November 28, 2004, AR1, AR17.

32. Chris Hedges, *American Fascists: the Christian right and the War on America* (New York: Free Press, 2006), 207.

ABOUT THE EDITORS

Shirley R. Steinberg is an associate professor at the McGill University Faculty of Education. She is the director of the Paulo and Nita Freire International Project for Critical Pedagogy. She is the author and editor of numerous books and articles and co-edits several book series. She is the founding editor of *Taboo: The Journal of Culture and Education.* Steinberg's most recent books are: *Diversity and Multiculturalism: A Reader; Encyclopedia of Boyhood Culture;* and *Media Literacy: A Reader* (edited with Donaldo Macedo). Steinberg has also recently finished editing *Teen Life in Europe,* and with Priya Parmar and Birgit Richard, *The Encyclopedia of Contemporary Youth Culture* (Library Reference Award Winner). She is the editor of *Multi/Intercultural Conversations: A Reader.* With Joe Kincheloe she has edited *Kinderculture: The Corporate Construction of Childhood* and *The Miseducation of the West: How Schools and the Media Distort Our Understanding of the Islamic World.* She is co-author of *Changing Multiculturalism: New Times, New Curriculum,* and *Contextualizing Teaching* (with Joe Kincheloe). Her areas of expertise and research are in critical media literacy, social drama, and youth studies.

The late **Joe L. Kincheloe** was the Canada Research Chair of Critical Pedagogy at the McGill University Faculty of Education. He was the founder of the Paulo and Nita Freire International Project for Critical Pedagogy. He was the author of numerous books and articles about pedagogy, education and social justice, racism, class bias, and sexism, issues of cognition and cultural context, and educational reform. His books include: *The Sign of the Burger: McDonald's and the Culture of Power; City Kids: Understanding Them, Appreciating Them, and Teaching Them; Changing Multiculturalism* (with Shirley Steinberg); *Teachers as Researchers; Classroom Teaching: An Introduction;* and *Getting Beyond the Facts: Teaching Social Studies/Social Sciences in the Twenty-first Century.* His co-edited works include *White Reign: Deploying Whiteness in America* (with Shirley Steinberg, et al.) and the Gustavus Myers Human Rights award winner *Measured Lies: The Bell Curve Examined* (with Shirley Steinberg). Along with his partner, Shirley Steinberg, Kincheloe was an international speaker and lead singer/keyboard player of *Tony and the Hegemones.*

ABOUT THE CONTRIBUTORS

Philip M. Anderson is Professor of Secondary Education at Queens College and Professor of Urban Education at the Graduate Center of the City University of New York. Professor Anderson has written extensively on culture and humanities pedagogy in schools. Recent publications include chapters on general education in college, class, and curriculum; pedagogical theory; and evaluation policy. He is an editor of *Urban Education: A Comprehensive Guide for Educators, Parents, and Teachers* (Kincheloe, et al., Rowman & Littlefield, 2007).

Silvia Giagnoni, a writer, documentarian, and researcher, received her Masters in Communications from "La Sapienza" University in Rome. She came to the United States to study and spent three years investigating Christian rock and Evangelical culture and ended up producing and directing a documentary with Eleonora Orlandi and writing her dissertation on that phenomenon, titled *Christian Rock goes Mainstream: Youth Culture, Politics and Popular Music in the U.S.* Silvia is working on a creative nonfiction book about the farm worker community of Immokalee, Florida, and on a documentary about immigration. She is an assistant professor in the Department of Communication and Dramatic Arts at Auburn University Montgomery, Alabama.

Michael D. Giardina is a visiting professor of advertising and cultural studies at the University of Illinois, Urbana-Champaign. He is the author of *Sporting Pedagogies: Performing Culture & Identity in the Global Arena* (Peter Lang, 2005), which received the 2006 "Most Outstanding Book" award from the North American Society for the Sociology of Sport. His work on globalization, cultural studies, qualitative inquiry, and the racial logics of late capitalism has also appeared in journals such as *Harvard Educational Review, Cultural*

Studies <> Critical Methodologies, Journal of Sport and Social Issues, and *Qualitative Inquiry.*

Henry A. Giroux holds the Global TV Network Chair in English and Cultural Studies at McMaster University in Canada. His most recent books include: *America on the Edge* (2006), *Beyond the Spectacle of Terrorism* (2006), *Stormy Weather: Katrina and the Politics of Disposability* (2006), *The University in Chains: Confronting the Military-Industrial-Academic Complex* (2007), and *Against the Terror of Neoliberalism: Politics Beyond the Age of Greed* (2008).

Rhonda Hammer is a research scholar at the UCLA Center for the Study of Women and is a lecturer in education and women's studies at UCLA. Her publications include a number of articles and chapters in the areas of critical media literacy, cultural studies, and feminist theory and practice. She is the author of *Antifeminism and Family Terrorism: A Critical Feminist Perspective,* co-author of *Rethinking Media Literacy: A Critical Pedagogy of Representation* (with Peter McLaren, David Sholle, and Susan Reilly). Her most recent book, co-edited with Douglas Kellner, is *Media/Cultural Studies: Critical Approaches.*

Michael Hoechsmann is an assistant professor in the Department of Integrated Studies in Education. His research interests are in the areas of media, new media, literacy, new literacies, youth, cultural studies, and education. He is the author, with Bronwen E. Low, of *Reading Youth Writing: "New" Literacies, Cultural Studies and Education* (Peter Lang, 2008). For four years, he was the Director of Education of Young People's Press, a non profit news service for youth 14–24 (www.ypp.net).

Douglas Kellner is the George Kneller Chair in the Philosophy of Education at UCLA, and the author of many books on social theory, politics, history, and culture, including *Media/Cultural Studies: Critical Approaches* (edited with Rhonda Hammer); *Media Culture and Media Spectacle; Media Culture: Cultural Studies, Identity and Politics, Between the Modern and the Postmodern;* a trilogy of books on the Bush administration, including: *Grand Theft 2000; Media Spectacle and the Crisis of Democracy, Herbert Marcuse and the Crisis of Marxism.* He is also the author (with Stephen Best) of a trilogy of books on postmodern theory. Kellner is editing collected papers of Herbert Marcuse.

Curry Stephenson Malott works and lives in Buffalo, New York, where he is an assistant professor of education at D'Youville College. He has published in the areas of cultural studies, critical pedagogy, social studies, Marxism, teacher education, urban education, neoliberalism, and Latin American education. He is the author of *A Call to Action: An Introduction to Education, Philosophy and Native North America* (Peter Lang, 2008), and *Punk Rockers' Revolution: A Pedagogy of Race, Class, and Gender* with Milagros Peña (Peter Lang, 2005).

Ruthann Mayes-Elma received her Doctorate from Miami University of Ohio. A researcher, scholar, and teacher, her interest areas are children's literature, feminism, and issues of social justice and education. She is the author of *Females and Harry Potter: Not all that Empowering* and *Harry Potter: Feminist Friend or Foe?*

Joshua I. Newman holds a Doctor of Philosophy degree from the University of Maryland's Physical Cultural Studies program. Dr. Newman is currently an assistant professor in the Department of Kinesiology and affiliate member the Cultural Studies Program at Towson University. Through a number of research manuscripts published in scholarly outlets including *Cultural Studies <> Critical Methodologies, International Review for the Sociology of Sport, Sociology of Sport Journal,* and the *Journal of Sport and Social Issues,* his current research project interrogates the intersection of Bush-era neoconservativism and a Milton Friedman–inspired neoliberal hegemony on the sport and body cultures of the American South.

Christine M. Quail is an assistant professor in the Department of Communications Studies and Multimedia at McMaster University in Hamilton, Ontario. Her most recent book is *Vulture Culture: The Politics and Pedagogy of Daytime Television Talk Shows* (with K. Razzano and L. Skalli). She has just guest-edited a special issue of *Taboo: The Journal of Culture and Education* on Canadian Media and has two forthcoming books on reality television and media literacy. Her areas of research include political economy and communications, hip hop and youth, documentary films, and the cultural studies of television.

Lisa Trimble is a feminist teacher, writer, activist, and doctoral student at McGill University in Montreal. Her research focuses on youth education in both formal and nonformal contexts, particularly in regard to sexualities education and community pedagogical partnerships with schools. She has published on girlhood culture, youth sex education, purity markers, and the ways knowledge is constructed, experienced, and lived through both things and ideas.

INDEX